Boeing 737

Other titles in the Crowood Aviation Series

Aichi D3A1/2 Val	Peter C. Smith
Airco – The Aircraft Manufacturing Company	Mick Davis
Avro Lancaster	Ken Delve
BAC One-Eleven	Malcolm L. Hill
Bell P-39 Airacobra	Robert F. Dorr with Jerry C. Scutts
Boeing 747	Martin W. Bowman
Boeing 757 and 767	Thomas Becher
Boeing B-17 Flying Fortress	Martin W. Bowman
Consolidated B-24 Liberator	Martin W. Bowman
De Havilland Mosquito	Martin W. Bowman
Douglas AD Skyraider	Peter C. Smith
English Electric Canberra	Barry Jones
English Electric Lightning	Martin W. Bowman
Fairchild Republic A-10 Thunderbolt II	Peter C. Smith
Fokker Aircraft of World War One	Paul Leaman
Hawker Hunter	Barry Jones
Hawker Hurricane	Peter Jacobs
Junkers Ju 87 Stuka	Peter C. Smith
Junkers Ju 88	Ron Mackay
Lockheed C-130 Hercules	Martin W. Bowman
Lockheed F-104 Starfighter	Martin W. Bowman
Luftwaffe – A Pictorial History	Eric Mombeek
McDonnell Douglas A-4 Skyhawk	Brad Elward
McDonnell Douglas F-15 Eagle	Peter E. Davies and Tony Thornborough
Messerschmitt Bf 110	Ron Mackay
Messerschmitt Me 262	David Baker
Nieuport Aircraft of World War One	Ray Sanger
Night Airwar	Theo Boiten
North American B-25 Mitchell	Jerry Scutts
North American F-86 Sabre	Duncan Curtis
North American T-6	Peter C. Smith
Panavia Tornado	Andy Evans
Short Sunderland	Ken Delve
V-Bombers	Barry Jones
Vickers VC10	Lance Cole

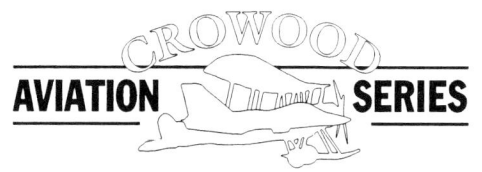

Boeing 737

Malcolm L. Hill

The Crowood Press

First published in 2002 by
The Crowood Press Ltd
Ramsbury, Marlborough
Wiltshire SN8 2HR

© Malcolm L. Hill 2002

All rights reserved. No part of this publication may be reproduced or transmitted in any form or by any means, electronic or mechanical, including photocopy, recording, or any information storage and retrieval system, without permission in writing from the publishers.

British Library Cataloguing-in-Publication Data
A catalogue record for this book is available from the British Library.

ISBN 1 86126 404 6

Typefaces used: Goudy (*text*), Cheltenham (*headings*).

Typeset and designed by
D & N Publishing
Baydon, Marlborough, Wiltshire.

Printed and bound in Great Britain by Bookcraft, Midsomer Norton.

Contents

Acknowledgements		6
1	TO MESSRS BOEING, A BOUNCING BABY	7
2	FIRST STEPS	23
3	NEW CUSTOMERS, NEW APPLICATIONS	37
4	INTO SERVICE	51
5	IMPROVING THE BREED	65
6	WORLDWIDE INFLUENCES	83
7	THE BABY GROWS	101
8	A NEW LEASE OF LIFE	117
9	THE LAST OF THE OLD GENERATION	135
10	THE NEXT GENERATION	153
11	THE BBJ AND BEYOND	171
Appendix I	Early 737s – Comparisons with their Contemporaries	184
Appendix II	The 737, 100–900	188
Index		191

Acknowledgements

Grateful thanks are extended to all the following persons and organizations, whose co-operation, time and invaluable funds of information and memories made this book possible:

Thomas Becher, Steve Bunting, Ron Carter, Sibylle Dietrich, Martyn East, Phillip Eastwood, Thierry Gatouillat, Jenny Gradidge, Joe Grant, Ivar Hakonsen, Chris Harrison, Richard Howell, Tim Kincaid, Jeff Luysterborghs, William F. Mellberg, Larry Pettit, Brian Pickering, Jon Proctor, Dennis Regan, Mel Roberts, Frankie Scott, Becky and Buddy Scott-Ward, Robert Walz and Tony Ward; and also to Aeroflot Russian Airlines, Air France, American Airlines C.R. Smith Museum, Aviation Hobby Shop, Boeing Business Systems, Braathens, Deutsche BA, Lufthansa and Military Aircraft Photographs.

Whilst every effort has been made to identify the source of illustrations used in this publication, this has not been possible in all cases. All persons claiming accreditation should contact the author via the publisher.

American Airlines ordered a large fleet of modern 737-800s to replace older, less economic, narrow-body aircraft on their short- and medium-haul network. American Airlines C.R. Smith Museum

CHAPTER ONE

To Messrs Boeing, a Bouncing Baby

Overseas Pioneers

By the early 1960s it was certainly unusual for the Boeing Airplane Company not to be the trend-setter in producing a new commercial aircraft type. However, the Washington State-based company was definitely a latecomer when it came to offering a new product on the short-haul twin-jet airliner market. By the time their new model 737 was made available to the world's commercial operators, there were no fewer than six alternatives either already in service or in advanced stages of development, on offer to the world's airlines.

Boeing's official announcement launching their 737 project into production came on 22 February 1965. This was only three days before the first flight of their arch rival, Douglas Aircraft's DC-9, and only six weeks before the British contender, the BAC One-Eleven, actually entered scheduled airline service. The very first twin-jet airliner design, also Russia's first jet airliner, the Tupolev Tu-104, although intended more for medium/long-haul services than short-haul work had been on the scene since 1956. The first twin-jet designed specifically for short-haul routes, France's Sud-Est Caravelle had been in worldwide service since April 1959.

The Soviet Union had later developed the Tu-104 into a smaller version, more suited to short-haul networks. The resulting Tupolev Tu-124 had been in service since 1962 with its much redesigned successor, the Tu-134 first flying in 1963. The Tu-134 had followed the design philosophy of the Caravelle, One-Eleven and DC-9 by adopting the increasingly popular rear engine, T-tail configuration.

Of course, the launch of the 737 was no overnight whim thought up by the

(*Above*) Soon casting off its 'latecomer' image, the Boeing 737 went on to populate most of the world's busiest airports. Tim Kincaid Collection

(*Below*) The first twin-jet airliner actually hailed from the Soviet Union. The Tupolev Tu-104 was designed for medium/long-range service, although it was also operated on shorter inter-city services on busier routes in the USSR and Eastern Europe. Via author

company merely to keep up with airliner design fashion trends. Boeing had been studying their short-haul jet airliner options for several years and were only prepared to offer a definitive design once they felt that they had got it right. Since the entry into service of Boeing's first jet airliner design, the medium/long-range Boeing 707 in 1958, the company had been working towards offering a 'family' of designs. Each different member of the 'family' was to be able to serve the airline's needs in different operational markets, but with enough of a degree of commonality in design so as to reduce production costs to the maker and significantly decrease operating costs to the customer.

In the Beginning

Boeing had actually not been a major supplier of civil airliners until the advent of the 707 in the 1950s. Military orders had been the backbone of Boeing's production lines for many years, with the few civilian designs produced usually being 'spin-offs' from US military contracts. Initially, even the Boeing 707 was just such a 'spin-off' from a design study to develop an in-flight refuelling tanker for high-speed jet fighters and bombers that had emerged as the KC-135. The suitability of the new type for redesign as a jet airliner was recognized very early in the design process and the company made the historical decision that changed its commercial direction.

The Boeing Airplane Company had been founded by William E. Boeing, a successful Seattle businessman involved in the local timber industry, and a friend, Cdr G. Conrad Westervelt of the US Navy. Both had been fascinated by the new flying craze and had founded the Aero Club of Seattle in 1915. The club's first aircraft, a Glenn L. Martin Seaplane, was damaged in an accident and Boeing and Westervelt elected to build an improved version of the aircraft, rather than simply replace it from the original source. Thus, in June 1916, William Boeing piloted the new aircraft, the B&W Model 1, a single-engined, twin-pontoon biplane from Lake Union, near Seattle.

Westervelt was posted to the East Coast and Boeing continued to develop the design with an increasing team of engineers and designers that he was able to attract. A second design, the improved model 2, the first real all-Boeing project, took to the air in 1917, by which time Boeing had incorporated his aviation interests into the new Pacific Aero Products Company.

The even more improved Model 3 soon appeared, with a landplane version, the Model 4, of which only two were supplied to the US Army as primary trainers. The US Navy eventually placed an order for fifty Model 5s, as the company changed its name to the Boeing Airplane Company. The Navy order was to be the first sizable contract to the US military, which was to remain Boeing's primary customer for many years.

Postwar Slump

Throughout the immediate post-First World War years Boeing enjoyed mixed fortunes. There were simply too many surplus aircraft around for the military to be interested in sponsoring expensive new projects. The small number of non-military sales did little to dispel the gloom as the valuable military market had vanished overnight with the arrival of the armistice. The first two B&W aircraft were sold to the New Zealand government for postal work, Boeing's first international sales and a small number of B-1s, a flying boat design, were also sold for use by airmail contractors.

At one point the company was obliged to start building furniture in order to keep its skilled woodworking force together. Contracts were also gained from the US military for conversion and modification of British-designed DH-4 'Liberty Planes' that helped the company survive the leaner times.

By the mid-1920s, however, Boeing was gaining production orders for its own new designs again, as a series of fighter and attack aircraft were supplied to the US military. More civil projects were making an appearance too, with the Boeing Model 40A, designed to carry two passengers as well as 1,200lbs (544kg) of mail beginning operations over the San Francisco–Chicago route in 1927.

New Owners, New Direction

Boeing had set up its own airline, Boeing Air Transport, to operate the route, and acquired another West Coast-based carrier, Pacific Air Transport, to expand their operation. Boeing itself was purchased shortly afterwards and became part of the new United Aircraft and Transport Corporation that had its headquarters at Hartford, Connecticut. As well as Boeing and its airline subsidiaries, United soon also controlled the Chance Vought Corporation, Pratt & Whitney, the aero engine manufacturer, and the Hamilton Aero Manufacturing Company that made propellers.

The airline side also expanded, with pioneer carriers Stout Airlines, National Air Transport and Varney Airlines all being taken into the UATC family. The large combined airline network became so unwieldy that a new management company

The Boeing B&W Model 1, the company's first aircraft, being manhandled at the original waterside factory. Boeing

was formed, called United Air Lines, to co-ordinate their operation, although each carrier retained its identity for the time being.

A major improvement in comfort for passengers on Boeing's scheduled service from Chicago to California arrived with the introduction of a new airliner design, the Boeing Model 80, and slightly larger Model 80A, in 1929. The 12 to 18-passenger biplanes were positively spacious compared to the claustrophobic Model 40A and saw the introduction of a new crew member, the Stewardess. A number of American carriers had already employed male stewards or 'Couriers' on larger aircraft and European airlines had used stewards to serve their passengers for many years, but Boeing Air Transport was the first carrier in the world to employ female flight attendants.

While Boeing Air Transport and its United Air Lines partners were introducing modern styles of air travel to their passengers, the Boeing Airplane Company was increasing its portfolio with a number of successful military designs.

The Arrival of the Modern Airliner

The sleeker lines of Boeing's new high-speed military types were soon being applied to commercial designs. Research and development of one military design, the B-9, had provided a great deal of useful data and solutions to problems that were arising with the design of larger aircraft. Although the B-9 failed to attract an order this new technology was channelled into a new civil airliner type, the Boeing 247.

(*Top*) By the late 1920s, the Boeing factory was once again busy with aircraft under construction, rather than producing furniture as a 'stop-gap'. Boeing

(*Above*) The Boeing Model 40B gave sterling service to the company's airline subsidiary. NC178E is seen wearing joint Boeing/Pacific Air Transport and United Air Lines titles. Boeing

(*Above*) The Boeing 247 finally brought modern lines to airliner design in 1933. The first aircraft, X-13301, was a production model. There was no designated prototype and this aircraft was later delivered to the Boeing division of United Air Lines. Boeing

The Douglas DC-1 was designed at the instigation of TWA and soon overtook the Boeing 247 in its developed production version, the DC-2. Via author

The United Air Lines group had been struggling against competition from Transcontinental & Western Air and American Airways, both flying more modern Ford Trimotors or Fokker models that outclassed the Boeing 80s. Although United's airline partners were trying their best to compete, they were soon looking to their Boeing partner to provide a new type to push them ahead of their rivals.

Although United had wanted an aircraft as large as the 18-passenger Boeing 80s, the Boeing 247 emerged with capacity for only ten passengers. Boeing's allegiance to their United Aircraft and Transport partners meant that it was unable to consider the Wright 1820 engine, then under development, that would have been suitable for a larger aircraft. Boeing was obliged to go to Pratt & Whitney for an engine to power their aircraft, but they only had their well-tried, but less powerful, Wasp to hand. Another factor in deciding to develop the smaller design option was the rather voluble opinion of United's pilots. They were of the view that a larger aircraft would be unstable and difficult to control.

United decided, albeit reluctantly, that they were willing to overlook the lower capacity, in view of the new type's speed advantage. At over 70mph faster than its nearest rival, the 247 was a definite trendsetter, the first US transport to sport a low-wing monoplane and twin-engined configuration. The type first flew in 1932, with the first delivery to UATC's airlines being made on 30 March 1933.

The 247's Nemesis

The decision to produce the smaller capacity aircraft was to turn out to be only one mistake made by United Aircraft and Transport in selecting its new airliner. A large order, for sixty aircraft, was placed, to be delivered to its airline divisions. It was assumed that the exclusive use of the 247 by UATC's airlines would give them an unprecedented advantage on America's airways. It was naïve in the extreme for UATC to think that the other airlines were going to take this lying down and the rival carriers soon approached Boeing to place their own orders. However, the United contract totally monopolized the production capacity for nearly a year. Rather than have to wait until the initial order for sixty was delivered, the disappointed airlines approached other aircraft manufacturers to produce an alternative aircraft.

Transcontinental & Western Air contacted the Douglas Aircraft Company,

All Change for the Air Mail Act

As well as effectively having shot itself in the foot by forcing the non-UATC airlines to look elsewhere for new equipment, United Aircraft was thrown into turmoil by the 1934 Air Mail Act.

Introduced to put an end to growing monopolies within the transport industries, a Senate Special Committee investigated both ocean steamship and airline mail contracts, following questions being raised on the subject of subsidy and the fairness of certain contract awards. This led to the disclosure of some dubious practices and decisions in the way a number of airmail contracts had been awarded by the Postmaster General, Walter Brown.

All airmail contracts were cancelled with effect from 9 February 1934. Another consequence of the Act was to forbid the close tie-up of aircraft manufacturers and airlines. As a result, Boeing became a separate company again. William Boeing actually resigned over the issue from the company he had founded, accusing the Roosevelt administration of unfairness.

Although innocent parties suffered as much as the guilty, the airlines soon emerged from the legislative gunsmoke relatively unscathed. The airmail service was initially handed over to the military, but chaos ensued. Following a number of accidents and a general public outcry, the airlines were invited to tender for the contracts again. Certain airlines and their managements were forbidden, by their past involvement in irregular practices, from applying, and a flurry of name-changing and corporate manoeuvres followed.

UATC had already combined its four major airlines subsidiaries, Boeing Air Transport, Pacific Air Transport, National Air Transport and Varney Air Lines, into one unit in May 1934, now officially named United Air Lines. A new company, TWA Inc, applied for Transcontinental & Western Air's old contracts, and promptly 'took over' the old company assets once the contracts were awarded, swiftly reinstating the original name. Similarly, American Airways became American Airlines, Eastern Air Transport became Eastern Air Lines, and so on.

---

among others, inviting tenders to produce a trimotor, all-metal monoplane. Douglas came up with the 12-passenger, twin-engine design, the DC-1. This was enlarged to a 14-passenger capacity in its production version, the DC-2. As well as having a much more spacious cabin, the DC-2 was actually faster than the 247, wiping out all the 247's initial advantages overnight. TWA placed the new aircraft into scheduled service in August 1934 and both US and foreign carriers were soon beating a path to Douglas' door to place orders for the type.

When the DC-2 was enlarged again into the 21-passenger DC-3, in 1936, any hopes Boeing had for the continued production of the 247 vanished. The DC-3 went on to become one of the most successful airliner designs of all time, with many examples flying on into the twenty-first century, over sixty years after the type entered service. Even United had to admit the Douglas aircraft's superiority. From 1936, the airline began to replace the 247's on major routes with their own fleet of DC-3s.

Bigger Boeings

Struggling to remain in the airliner business after the debacle of the 247 sales, Boeing looked to bigger, even more revolutionary designs. A series of military aircraft had been more successful than the civil projects and provided the company with vitally needed work. With its wings, engines and undercarriage taken from the B-17 bomber, the Model 307, Stratoliner, was unique in its day for having a large pressurized fuselage. Able to operate at high altitude, above the worst weather, it promised unprecedented smooth flights for its passengers. Another Boeing bomber project also provided the wing design for another civil type, the giant 314 flying boat that saw Boeing returning briefly to its marine roots.

The Stratoliner saw only limited airline service, with a handful being operated by TWA, on domestic routes, and Pan American on services to the Caribbean and South America. The millionaire flyer, Howard Hughes also acquired a Stratoliner as his personal 'Flying Penthouse'. The giant 314 flying boat saw long-range passenger service with Pan American, on both Pacific and Atlantic scheduled flights. A small number were also diverted, before their intended delivery to Pan American, to serve Great Britain's BOAC on wartime transport services.

Although they failed to sell to airlines in very large numbers, mainly due to the intervention of the Second World War, the 307 and 314 models kept Boeing in the forefront of airliner design. Once the war was over, Boeing continued to be preoccupied with military contracts, fuelled by the Korean conflict and ongoing 'Cold War' with Communist Europe.

Boeing's 307 Stratoliner pioneered the use of a pressurized cabin in passenger service. TWA introduced their fleet on transcontinental scheduled flights in July 1940. Via author

A gigantic aircraft for its day, the Boeing 314 flying boat operated luxurious pre-war transoceanic air services over both the Atlantic and Pacific. Via author

Postwar Airliner Developments

Until the arrival of the 707, Boeing's sole contribution to the postwar airliner market to reach the production stage was the model 377 Stratocruiser. This itself had been a civil version of the C-97/KC-97 military transport and in-flight refueller, derived from the B29 bomber design. Despite large numbers of C-97s and KC-97s being ordered by the US military, civilian versions had only enjoyed limited success with the airlines. Although its luxurious, spacious cabin and legendary lower-deck cocktail bar were immensely popular with passengers, it was a horrendously expensive aircraft to operate and maintain on a commercial basis.

When jet-powered airliners first came on to the scene it was all about reducing flying times over long-ranging flights. Only five years before putting the world's first jetliner, the De Havilland Comet 1, into revenue service, advertising for the British Overseas Airways Corporation 'boasted' of UK–Hong Kong journeys taking 'only five days'! This leisurely scheduled service was flown by Shorts Sandringham Flying Boat, with night-stops being made en route. Although the first commercially operated jets were usually obliged to make a number of refuelling stops, they were assigned to long-distance flights, still managing to cut piston engine-powered, propeller airliner schedules in half.

The Turbo-Prop Era

The future for shorter-ranging flights, in particular those involving any degree of 'mass travel', was perceived to lie in the direction of turbo-prop, or prop-jet, power. In the turbo-prop the jet engine's thrust is diverted to driving a propeller, instead of directly powering the aircraft through the air. This is much more economical in terms of fuel consumption, although giving nearly the same speed advantages of pure-jet power. The Vickers Viscount, contemporary with the Comet 1, introduced turbo-prop travel to a very enthusiastic travelling public in the early 1950s.

Sadly, the Comet turned out to suffer from chronic metal fatigue problems. A trio of mysterious crashes, all involving the loss of all passengers and crew on board the unfortunate aircraft, brought the problem to light. Only an extensive investigation, on a scale not previously seen in civil aviation, finally identified the metallurgical problem that had lain hidden until the accidents brought it to the industry's attention. Although the turbo-props were still successfully making their mark around the world, the pure-jet airliner was temporarily grounded.

Soon, larger versions of the Viscount, as well as much larger turbo-prop aircraft, such as the Vickers Vanguard and Lockheed Electra, were on the horizon and it was surmised that the turbo-prop would rule over the shorter ranges, leaving the jets to concentrate on longer flights. Long-range, large-capacity turbo-props, such as the Bristol Britannia, were also on the drawing board to operate economical services on far-flung flights, the plan then being to leave the expensive pure-jets to first-class travellers willing to pay a premium fare. This rather cosy plan of action, however, was soon turned on its head.

If the Comet had achieved one thing, it was to prove the underlying market for jet travel. The all-First-Class passenger load factors on the early Comets briefly operated for BOAC, as well as two French airlines,

(*Above*) The De Havilland Comet 1 series blazed a trail for jet airline travel in the early 1950s. Unfortunately their demise, due to unforeseen metal fatigue, was swift and only three airlines and the Royal Canadian Air Force took delivery from a once impressive order book. Via author

(*Below*) Contemporary with the flawed early Comets, the Vickers Viscount was a much more successful venture. Aer Lingus was an early customer, eventually operating the type for over fifteen years. Jenny Gradidge

Air France and UAT, had been well beyond expectations. Tourist-Class travel was introduced on a handful of the busier routes in the earl1950s and its success surprised even the most optimistic supporters of 'mass travel'. As the Comet was being redesigned into the larger, more robust, Comet 4 series and Boeing were looking at producing an airliner version of their KC-135 jet tanker design, France's Sud-Aviation was putting the finishing touches to their short-haul jet airliner design, the SE-210 Caravelle. From the start, the Caravelle, and the jetliners that followed it, were designed with both first- and tourist-class travellers in mind. Only rarely would there be any talk of 'First-Class Only' jet travel, at least until the arrival of the ultra-expensive supersonic transports.

Short-Haul Jet Revolution

When the elegantly designed, rear-engined Caravelle started European service in 1959, it soon had passengers voting with their feet. It did not matter to the paying public that the turbo-props were more economic over shorter distances or that the time-savings over close inter-city pairs

(*Above*) The Sud-Aviation Caravelle was designed from the outset for short-haul inter-city services. It soon outpaced the large turboprops originally seen as the answer to economic short-range service. Via author

(*Below*) The original purpose of the KC-135 design was as an in-flight refueller for high-speed bombers like the Boeing B-52. Its potential as a commercial jet transport was soon recognized and the design was modified to produce the 707 airliner. Boeing

Pan American introduced the 707-100 into scheduled service in 1958. The airline later took delivery of the larger, more powerful -320 series, as seen here. MAP

were minimal or even non-existent. Propellers were old-fashioned. The passengers wanted jets and they wanted them now.

If it had a propeller on it, the public did not want to know and soon sought out the airlines with jet-powered alternatives. Caught unawares, the British European Airways Corporation, which had placed all its eggs firmly in the turbo-prop basket by ordering large fleets of economical Viscounts and Vanguards, were forced to commission a 'stop-gap' short-haul version of the Comet, the 4B.

The BEA Comet 4Bs were initially assigned to the longer routes on their network, especially to the eastern Mediterranean, but were soon also pressed into service on shorter trunk routes where rival European operators such as Air France, Alitalia, Finnair, Iberia, Sabena, SAS and Swissair were flying their new Caravelles. Although much less suitable for the shorter runs, the Comets were required to win back passengers until BEA could place a more economically viable inter-city jet into service.

Boeing's Jetliner Success

Europe's only long-range challenge to the 707, at least in its early years, was confined to the De Havilland Comet 4. Even the 'new' Comet 4 was technically inferior to the 707. However, the Comet 4 still achieved the distinction of becoming the first commercially operated jet over the Atlantic when Britain's BOAC placed it in service on the London–New York route in October 1958. This was only a matter of weeks before Pan American World Airways

Swissair was one of the few customers for the Convair CV-990A, operating them on long-haul services to South America and Asia, as well as busier European routes. Via author

United's Postwar Growth

Once established as a strong, independent airline in its own right, United Air Lines enjoyed a period of unprecedented growth. When the USA entered the Second World War the airline, along with most of the nation's commercial air carriers, made most of its carrying capacity available for military use. United operated a trans-Pacific air service for the US Navy, as well as flying numerous domestic contracts for the US war machine.

After the return of peace, United turned its attention to modernizing and expanding its domestic network. Unlike many of its rivals, it did not use its wartime long-range experience to press for international service authority. Instead, United satisfied itself with extending its coast-to-coast network to the Hawaiian Islands in 1947.

The airline remained a major force in US airliner design, being heavily involved in the development of the Douglas DC-4, DC-6, DC-7 series and Convair CV-340 piston-engined aircraft. A small fleet of Boeing Stratocruisers was also operated briefly on the Hawaiian network, although these were disposed of as uneconomic compared to the DC-6s and DC-7s that replaced them. With the arrival of the jet era, United greatly influenced the design of the DC-8 and the Boeing 720 and 727, as well as the 737.

United's acquisition of financially ailing Capital Airlines in 1961, saw the creation of the largest airline in the Western world. When the 737 programme was announced in 1965, United was operating thirty-eight Douglas DC-8s, three DC-8Fs, twenty-nine Boeing 720s, twenty-eight Boeing 727-100s, with eighty-two more 727-100s and -200s on order and twenty Sud Caravelle 6Rs in its jet fleet. In addition, United still operated twenty-three DC-7s, six DC-7Fs, thirty DC-6s, seven DC-6As, forty DC-6Bs, seventeen Convair CV-340s and forty-five Viscount 700s in their propeller-driven, piston and prop-jet-engined fleet. Most of the surviving propeller aircraft were planned to be phased out and replaced by the remaining 727s on order, as well as the new order for 737-200s.

(*Above*) The Boeing Stratocruiser served briefly on United's new prestige Hawaiian schedules in the early 1950s. MAP

(*Below*) The DC-8 had benefited from a great deal of input into the design from United. The type was to serve the airline for nearly thirty years. Via author

introduced their first imported Boeing 707 jets.

Booming worldwide sales of the 707 had soon pushed Boeing into the forefront of civil airliner design, overtaking Douglas and Lockheed in a few short years. Sales of the 707's main US rival, the similar Douglas DC-8, had suffered from being later into service than the 707, although respectable sales figures were later achieved and developed versions of the aircraft kept the type in production for many years. Lockheed had elected to ignore the long-haul jet airliner market, and concentrated on developing its L-88 Electra turbo-prop for inter-city airline work. The rise of the short-haul jet was to restrict the Electra market considerably and Lockheed did not attempt to return to full-scale airliner production for many years.

and CV-990 jet airliner models specifically with these markets in mind.

Initially, Boeing had concentrated on improving the long-range and load-carrying capabilities of the 707. Larger, more powerful versions were offered that eliminated the need for refuelling stops on many flights. However, encouraging early sales figures for the medium-range Convair jets alerted Boeing to a threat to their customer base, several members of which were already in preliminary negotiations with Convair. Not surprisingly, an intermediate-range version of the 707 was also soon on offer.

Lighter, shorter and more powerful, with a redesigned wing and flap layout that improved take-off and cruising performance, the Boeing 720 first flew on 23 November 1959. Boeing took particular satisfaction in obtaining early orders for the 720 from Douglas DC-8 operators

The improved take-off and landing performance of the Boeing 720/720B also allowed jet service to a number of airports not previously able to accommodate the heavier 707s and DC-8s.

From Four Engines to Three

Boeing's first offering on the short-range jet airliner market came about as a result of direct discussions with airlines. Eastern wanted a small twin-jet. United, with a major operations centre at Denver in the Rocky Mountains, wanted the security and power reserves of four engines and were pushing for a yet smaller version of the 720B. Boeing's engineers managed to persuade the Eastern and United managements that a three-engined, T-tail design was a workable compromise. On 5 December 1960, the company announced that

United's Boeing 727s were among the first to roll off what was to become a long and successful production run. MAP

Boeing and the Short-Haul Market

The operationally and commercially successful use of early model 707s and DC-8s on domestic routes within the USA had shown a market for jet services on busy inter-city sectors. Douglas had been selling versions of the DC-8 tailored for domestic US service and another aircraft manufacturing company, General Dynamics, producing aircraft under the Convair name in San Diego, had offered their new CV-880

United Air Lines and Eastern Air Lines, that had both been seriously considering the Convair options. Established US-based 707 customers, such as American Airlines, Braniff Airways and Continental Airlines also ordered the 720, and the later turbo-fanned engined version, the 720B, in some numbers.

Away from the home market, several foreign scheduled carriers also placed 720s and 720Bs in service on longer-ranging flights where passenger loads were lighter and did not justify the use of larger 707s.

they would be putting the Boeing 727 into production.

Wing high-lift devices were incorporated into the design for an even more improved take-off performance. As well as being useful in the thin mountain air of Denver, the high-lift devices would also allow the 727 operators to introduce jet service to important East-Coast US airports such a New York's La Guardia and Washington's National that had restricted runway lengths. Also, from the cabin floor upwards, the fuselage cross-section was identical to

The 1940s–50s vintage, piston-powered DC-6 series still featured heavily in United's fleet in the mid-1960s.
Aviation Hobby Shop

the Boeing 707 series and the idea of family 'commonality' was finally up and running.

Both airlines placed their first orders, for forty aircraft each, and the Boeing 727-100 flew for the first time on 9 February 1963. Several other carriers, including the first European customer for the 727, West Germany's Lufthansa, followed United and Eastern's example. The worldwide sales figures for the tri-jet were soon rivalling those of the already successful 707 and 720 series.

Surviving Props

With the 727 making its development flights, Boeing's attention turned more to the market for smaller, more regionally focused jetliners, preferably with even better short-field performance. That such a market existed was being demonstrated by Douglas, Sud and BAC, with the increasing sales of their T-tail configured twin jets. That a major domestic customer for Boeing aircraft, American Airlines, had ordered no less than thirty-one BAC One-Elevens from Great Britain, to supplement their much larger 727s on short-haul routes, gave the design team even more incentive to come up with a Boeing-built contender.

The 1960s still saw a large number of routes served by ageing propeller fleets even in the largest airline networks. Although the Boeing 727, and other short/medium-haul jets had begun to make inroads into the denser markets, 1940s and 50s vintage, piston-engined, DC-6s, DC-7s and Constellations, shunted from longer, prime routes by the early jets, still flew thousands of passengers on busy inter-city services every day.

United Air Lines also flew a sizable fleet of Vickers Viscount turbo-props inherited when they took over Capital Airlines in 1961. With the Capital network, United had also taken on a number of multi-stop routes linking both large and small cities. It was these routes that saw the greatest concentration of operations for United's remaining turbo-prop and piston-engined aircraft fleets. Passenger loads were not enough to support the Boeing 727 and many of the airports were unable to accept the smaller Caravelle, of which United did operate a small fleet on East Coast and Mid-West routes.

Design Decisions

The first generations of short-haul jets had already shown that they could operate as cheaply, if not more so, and also attract more passengers with their modern jet-age image. Although initial acquisition costs were large, the jets were soon earning their keep, carrying more passengers on more daily sectors and beating any piston or turbo-prop competition into the ground. If Boeing could produce a more flexible jet, capable of carrying economic loads over shorter routes and into smaller airfields, as well as the larger cities, the company would have a valuable, profitable, new addition to its jet 'family'.

In November 1964, Boeing finally gave the go-ahead for their designers to investigate the options for the new jet airliner design. It was specifically aimed at recapturing markets being lost to the BAC One-Eleven and DC-9, where the Boeing 727 was regarded as too large. A reliable workhorse aircraft, capable of operating several sectors a day carrying economic loads at low cost, was required. The Boeing sales and marketing departments envisaged a sales potential of more than 600 units of the new design.

With their 'family' concept in mind, the newly formed Boeing project team, under the leadership of John E. Steiner, elected to make the fuselage of the new type the same width as the 707/720 and 727. This gave a definite advantage in terms of passenger comfort. The BAC One-Eleven, Caravelle and DC-9 all had narrower cabins, with the economy-class passengers in all the aircraft being seated in a five-abreast, 2–3 configuration. The Boeing aircraft would be able to offer an exceptionally comfortable five-abreast layout or, as turned out to be the case in most airlines' service, a more economical 3–3, six-abreast configuration.

T-Tail or Pylon?

Two groups of Boeing engineers looked independently at either the T-tail or under-wing engine design options. The T-tail, with the engines placed on the rear fuselage, had been a popular design with the earlier types, especially from the point of view of reducing noise in the passenger cabin. A potentially dangerous 'deep-stall' problem, with T-tail configured aircraft, where the aircraft entered an unrecoverable stall under certain aerodynamic conditions, had eventually been solved. Unfortunately this was not until after the tragic loss of the prototype One-Eleven and its test crew as a result of just such a stall.

Eventually Boeing opted for the under-wing location for its engines, two Pratt & Whitney JT8-Ds, with a conventional tail layout. Apart from the deep-stall considerations, the wider cross-section of the Boeing made the fitting of the engines on the rear fuselage an aerodynamic nightmare.

Wing-mounted engines also meant that more of the fuselage was available for fare-paying passengers, with less 'dead-areas' involved in mounting engines on the rear fuselage. The wing-mounted configurations also led to less problems in achieving a satisfactory centre of gravity in most load distribution scenarios.

The engines could not be hung on pylons, as on the 707/720, due to the closer proximity of the smaller aircraft's wing to the ground. Instead, the engine nacelles

(*Above*) The BAC One-Eleven had to cure a 'deep-stall' problem with its T-tail design, which led to the loss of the original prototype on a test flight. The eventual solution benefited all such designs that followed. Aviation Hobby Shop

(*Below*) The Boeing 727's impressive flap system, seen to effect on this taxying American Airlines aircraft, was adapted for the 737. MAP

were of a revised 'string-tube' type, and attached more directly to the wings. The wings themselves were designed from the outset with excellent airfield performance in mind, using lessons learnt from the 727. The increased dihedral outboard of the wings not only contributed to this performance, but also added to fuel capacity. Features such as the onboard auxiliary power unit and optional airstairs further added to the 737's attractiveness, as it would be able to operate from many smaller airports with limited facilities.

By the time Boeing announced the definitive design, as the Boeing 737, in February 1965, the aircraft had already grown from a 60-seater to a 75–103-passenger airliner. The 'family' concept had survived, with 60 per cent commonality with the Boeing 727 design being retained. The 727's dual hydraulic-powered ailerons, elevator and rudder, the leading edge slats and Krueger flaps were adapted for the 737, as was the 707's dual electric motor-driven variable-incidence tailplane trim system, with a manual backup. The company was also able to announce its first order for the 737 on the day the final design was revealed.

First 737 Sales

Surprisingly, this order was not from one of the major US domestic carriers, despite United having been a major target and contributing a great deal of input into the design. At the time that the design studies on the Boeing 737 were being initiated, United and Eastern Air Lines had been the only major US carriers uncommitted in the second-generation, short-haul twin-jet market.

Although an enthusiastic operator of the 727, Eastern eventually opted for ordering a large fleet of DC-9s, that could be delivered quicker than the 737 that was still on the Seattle drawing boards. United, however, continued to co-operate with Boeing on their project. United was more interested in the slightly larger development of the Boeing design, later to emerge as the Series 200, 6ft 4in (1.4m) longer than the Series 100. As a result, West Germany's Lufthansa had been the first to place an order for twenty-two of the initial 737-100 series, thus becoming the first Boeing airliner to be launched by a non-US customer.

Lufthansa had been looking for a jet replacement for its remaining fleets of piston-powered Convair 440 Metropolitans, as well as their turbo-prop Vickers Viscounts, then operated on West German domestic and busy short-haul European routes. Also earmarked for replacement were a handful of piston-powered Lockheed Super Constellations, long since deposed from the long-haul services, but still used on Lufthansa's higher-capacity domestic and European schedules and some inclusive-tour charter services.

Lufthansa was already operating Boeing 707s and 720Bs on long-range flights, as well as 727s on both short and medium-length routes. Originally approached by both BAC and Douglas as a possible customer for their own short-haul jet options, Lufthansa had been less impressed with the smaller capacity and shorter range of the designs initially on offer. With the addition of the 737, after disposing of its last propeller-powered airliners, Lufthansa would be able to offer Boeing jet service standards to all its customers, throughout its network.

Eastern opted for the DC-9 as its short-haul jet, rather than wait for the 737, still in its early design stages.
Via author

Postwar Lufthansa

The original company was formed in 1926, when two of Germany's pioneering air transport companies, Deutscher Aero Lloyd and Junkers Luftverkehr, merged on 24 January, resulting in Deutsche Luft Hansa. D.L.H. went on to develop into one of Europe's largest pre-war airlines, both in terms of fleet size and network mileage.

The Second World War saw D.L.H., like most airlines operating within the protagonist nations, working increasingly for the military. A limited civil network was maintained throughout the war years though, and continued until the advance of the Allies made the operation impossible. At the end of hostilities, the once mighty airline was down to six serviceable aircraft, a Focke-Wulf Fw 200 Condor, a DC-2, a DC-3, two JU-52/3ms and a Junkers JU-88.

In the immediate postwar period, with the old German nation divided into two separate countries, neither the newly formed Federal Republic of Germany, nor the People's Democratic Republic of Germany were initially permitted to operate their own airlines. An East German carrier, initially also called Lufthansa, later named Interflug, was established by the Communist authorities. However, airlines of the occupying allies continued to operate domestic flights in West Germany and international routes were flown solely by visiting airlines of foreign nations.

Eventually, as the Federal Republic recovered economically, permission was granted for the formation of a new West German airline and a provisional stock company, Luftag, was established in January 1953.

Reviving the old name of Lufthansa on 6 August 1954, the airline opened a scheduled domestic network on 1 April 1955. Orders had been placed for four 44-passenger Convair CV-340s for regional services and Lockheed delivered an equal number of long-range L-1049G Super Constellations. International European flights opened in May 1955 and the Super Constellations inaugurated trans-Atlantic flights in June.

Over the following years Lufthansa steadily expanded throughout Europe and opened more long-range flights to South America and the Far East. Viscount prop-jets joined the Convairs, the CV-340s being supplemented with improved CV-440s, in 1958 and the Super Constellations were also augmented by even longer-range L-1649A Starliners.

The airline's success mirrored the financial recovery of the Federal Republic and Lufthansa's first jet, the first of a fleet of Boeing 707s, arrived in March 1960, barely five years after operations had started. Boeing 727s, dubbed 'Europa Jets' by Lufthansa, began appearing on European services in April 1964.

The Boeing 737 order was placed with a view to replacing the remaining propeller airliners, then consisting of the Convairs, Viscounts and the surviving passenger Constellations. The standardization on the 727 and 737 on the short-haul network was designed to offer cost savings by reducing the number of types in use, as well as giving the airline the public relations accolade of an all-jet fleet.

(*Above*) **Lufthansa inaugurated postwar scheduled services with Convair CV-340s in 1955.** Jenny Gradidge

The Vickers Viscount was to be operated by Lufthansa on European and domestic routes. Lufthansa

(*Below*) **Lufthansa introduced the first 727s to Europe, naming them 'Europa jets'. They were operated to North Africa and the Middle East as well as on busier short-range flights.** Via author

Lufthansa's Influence

Lufthansa had actually been responsible for persuading Boeing to stretch the original 737 design. In particular, Lufthansa's Chief Executive, Technical Services, Gerhard Holtje, pressured Boeing into proceeding with the design to match the airline's needs more closely. As first offered by Boeing's designers, the 737 would have been a 55–60-passenger airliner. Holtje, however, insisted on an aircraft capable of carrying up to eighty-two passengers, the capacity of their Super Constellations, each with 20kg (44lb) of baggage, as well as up to 450kg (990lb) of cargo and mail over a 500mi (804km) sector with fuel reserves. In the end, even the smaller 737-100 was to exceed these performance criteria, with the larger, higher-capacity Series 200, initially with less range, offering even more revenue-earning potential.

Lufthansa signed their order for twenty-two Series 100s on 19 February 1965, three days before Boeing officially announced the launch of the 737 project into production. United eventually placed their order, for forty Series 200s, on 15 April 1965.

Pulling It All Together

At first, the final assembly of the 737 was centred on a new 218,000sq ft (20,252sq m) plant at Boeing Field, the company's main plant, at Seattle. The wings and main body of the aircraft were built at the existing Plant 2. The tail was constructed at the Boeing facility in Wichita, originally established for Boeing by the US government during the war to build the B-29 bomber. The B-47 jet bomber was also later produced at Wichita. Much of the 737's other components, such as the building of the landing gear and much of the airliner's interior work, were contracted out to third parties.

In 1967, Wichita was given responsibility for the construction of fuselages for all 737s, which were then transported to the assembly line by train, a practice that continues to the present day. After the 271st 737 was completed, in 1970, following a major reorganization within the company due to financial problems, all final assembly for the aircraft was moved south to the nearby Boeing factory at Renton.

Located 15 miles southeast of Seattle, the Renton facility was already responsible for much of the company's commercial airliner production and the 737 production line initially ran alongside that of the 727. The move of the final assembly work to Renton was greatly facilitated by the 737's production jigs for the wings having been made portable from the beginning. Originally this had been to enable the entire assembly process to be moved to Wichita, if required, at a later date.

With the placing of production orders by Lufthansa and United, and other sales in advanced states of negotiation, the 737 had finally been firmed up from an ever-changeable 'paper' proposition to a definitive design. The serious task of transforming the paper design into a flying, commercially viable, working airliner was now underway.

Boeing 737s finally started rolling down the production line in 1966/67. Lufthansa

CHAPTER TWO

First Steps

New Sales

Despite the difficulties, by the time the first aircraft was assembled and 'christened' in a much-publicized ceremony at Seattle, on 17 January 1967, no less than seventeen carriers had been wooed by Boeing's ever-efficient sales department into placing orders for the 737. As well as the launch orders from Lufthansa and United, the order book now included aircraft for Avianca (two), Braathens (three), Britannia Airways (three), Aer Lingus-Irish International (two), Lake Central Airlines (three), Mexicana (two), Nordair (three), Northern Consolidated Airlines (one), Pacific Air Lines (six), Pacific Southwest Airlines (six), Pacific Western Airlines (two), Piedmont Airlines (six), South African Airways (two), Western Air Lines (twenty) and Wien Alaska Airlines (one).

Apart from the Avianca and Mexicana orders, all were for the larger series 200. The Lake Central, Nordair and Northern Consolidated orders were for versatile, convertible, passenger-cargo aircraft.

It is interesting to note that, apart from major US carrier Western Air Lines, all the above orders were for comparatively small numbers. Many carriers were still unconvinced of the prospective economies of short-haul jet services. Two of the 'Big Four' US domestic airlines, Eastern and TWA had already ordered DC-9s over the 737, due to their earlier availability. American Airlines had long committed itself to operating a mixed fleet of One-Elevens and 727s on their medium and short-haul network. This left United as the only 'Big Four' carrier still interested in the 737. The medium-sized and specialist airlines, although eager to upgrade their services with jets, only had a requirement for small fleets to serve their networks.

The Third Pilot Issue

The 737 also had a political disadvantage in that pilots' unions and organizations in the United States were insisting that the aircraft be operated either with three pilots, or two pilots and a flight engineer. This arrangement, as well as being expensive for the airlines, was also rather impractical as the 737 flight deck had been designed from the start as a two-pilot environment, with only a small 'jumpseat' available for any supernumerary personnel that may need to be carried from time to time.

The third pilot issue had originally been raised shortly before the Lockheed L-188 Electra turbo-prop entered service in the late 1950s. Although never intended to be operated by just two pilots, the Air Line Pilots' Association (ALPA), wanted the third crew member to be a pilot, not a flight engineer, as had been the case on most previous three-cockpit-crew aircraft. ALPA wanted all jet-powered equipment to carry the third pilot. As well as ALPA's stand on safety and workload issues, the demand for a pilot in place of a flight engineer was seen as a political move in an attempt to seriously weaken the rival Flight Engineer's International Association (FEIA).

Two of the Electra's earliest operators were targeted by the pilots' union as test cases during contract negotiations, with a view to persuading them to take ALPA's view and establish a precedent. Miami-based National Airlines managed to reach a compromise that deferred the issue until it was put to arbitration when the Electra's had been delivered. Western Air Lines' management were less flexible and a bitter strike followed a failure in negotiations. From 21 February to 10 June 1958, Western was grounded, with both sides refusing to budge. Finally, after the airline threatened to hire new pilots to replace

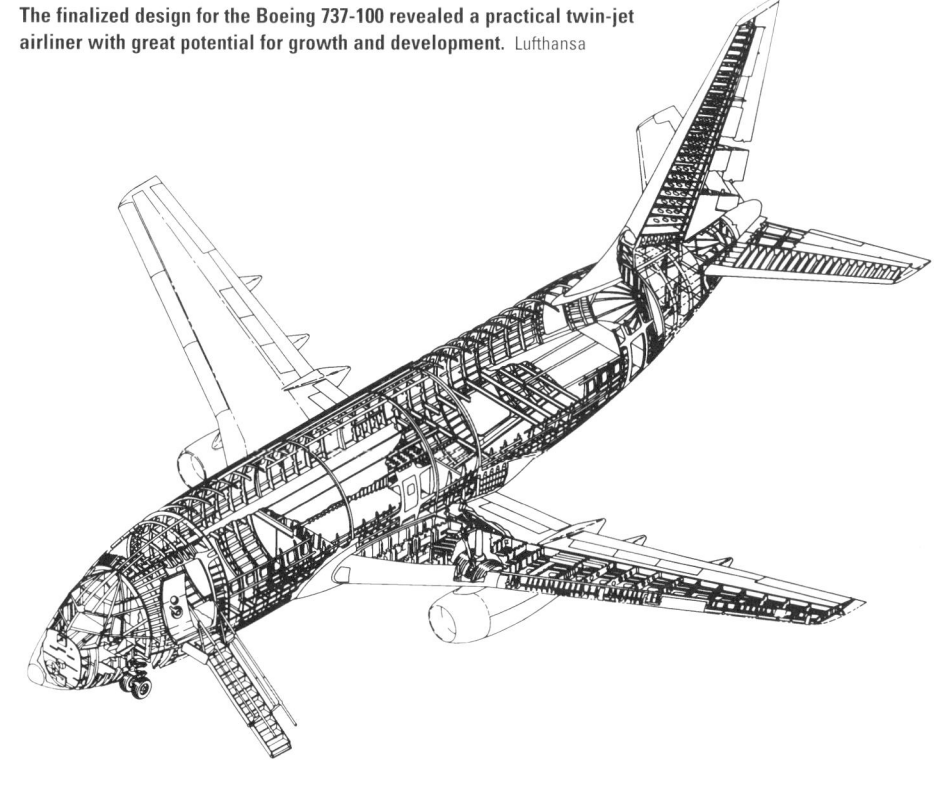

The finalized design for the Boeing 737-100 revealed a practical twin-jet airliner with great potential for growth and development. Lufthansa

the strikers, a new contract was signed and once again the third pilot issue was deferred.

Two or Three on the 737?

ALPA and FAA representatives were shown a mock-up of the 737 flight deck design in the autumn of 1965. Although the FAA was unable to make any determination as to likely certification based on the mock-up, which was very basic with no working features, United's pilots were quick to make it known that they disapproved of the two-crew concept based on this mock-up. Twelve months later, an animated mock-up was used to test crew workloads on the aircraft, Once again, the United pilots' group concluded that a three-pilot crew would be required.

November 1966 saw the meeting of ALPA's directors adopting a resolution requiring three pilots on Boeing 737s at all times. A month earlier, annual contract negotiations had opened with United and the question of crewing on the 737 soon became a major issue. However, at the same time, the FAA notified Boeing in writing that it tentatively accepted that the 737 could be operated with only two pilots, barring any changes or new information that may result from the flight test programme.

The negotiations had failed to solve the issue by April 1967 and a mediation board was appointed in an attempt to find a compromise between ALPA and United. However, the board was recessed on 25 July with no agreement reached. ALPA took a strike vote at United and 92 per cent of their pilots were shown to favour striking if the 737 was not operated by the three-pilot crew.

During the Summer, ALPA proposed to FAA's Western Region and the FAA Administrator that three-man crews operate on the Boeing 737 *and* the One-Eleven and DC-9. According to ALPA:

The FAA, by establishing a requirement for a three-man crew for airline jet transport operations, could ensure that no carrier would have economic incentive to provide service with less than the highest possible degree of safety in the public interest.

Following instructions from its membership, ALPA later dropped the request for three-pilot crews on the One-Eleven and DC-9. Nonetheless, the union stated that if the Boeing 737 was to be legally required to operate with three crew, ALPA would reopen the issue on the other two types as well. However, in September 1967, The Air Transport Association of America and the Aerospace Industries Association filed a report with the FAA, supporting the two-crew position. ALPA responded by rebutting the ATA–AIA arguments, point by point.

Until the dispute was settled, the possibility of having to operate the 737 under these conditions was to deter a number of possible US domestic customers. This especially aided Douglas in selling both their standard and stretched DC-9s to several smaller American regional airlines.

The dispute rumbled on, with Boeing, the airline managements, the FAA and ALPA, as well as several other bodies, all making their views as well known and as volubly as possible.

Lost Custom

In addition to the three-pilot issue deterring some potential customers, not all the seventeen carriers represented at the christening ceremony were to take delivery of their ordered aircraft.

Northern Consolidated and Wien Alaska Airlines combined their operations in February 1968 and the 737s were delivered to the resulting new carrier, Wien Consolidated Airlines. Mexicana later cancelled their order, leaving Lufthansa and Avianca as the only initial customers for the Series 100. However, Malaysia-Singapore Airlines did eventually order five Series 100s, followed later by a further order for Series 200s.

A bitter dispute between the pilots' union, ALPA, and Western Air Lines' management centred around who should occupy the Lockheed Electra's third flight-deck seat, pilot or flight engineer. Aviation Hobby Shop

FIRST STEPS

US operators of the DC-9 and BAC One-Eleven twin-jets were not directly affected by the ALPA campaign for a third pilot on the 737. Pictures courtesy of Aviation Hobby Shop

The Loss of the Lake Central Orders

After struggling with equipment problems and a precarious financial position for many years, Lake Central Airlines, of Indianapolis, was to vanish before they could take delivery of their 737s, after begin bought out by Allegheny Airlines. The Lake Central network stretched from east to west from Chicago to Washington DC and north to south from Buffalo and Grand Rapids to Cincinnati in the south. Although serving a prosperous, largely industrialized region, the airline was hampered by being obliged to serve numerous short inter-city routes in between these points. Some limited non-stop authority had been granted between larger cities on the network, but it was not enough to turn red ink into black. Re-equipment was a top priority and the 737s, as well as two 727-100s also on order, would have been the first step in replacing a fleet of Convair 580 and Nord 262 turbo-props, of which a dozen of each were operated.

The airline had placed a lot of faith in the small, 27-passenger Nord. Replacement of Lake Central's long-serving DC-3s had begun in 1960 with the arrival of several ex-United Convair 340s. The sturdy, but increasingly unfashionable, DC-3s had been in service since the airline's founding, as Turner Airlines, in 1949. In 1965, the Nords arrived to bring jet-prop service to Lake Central's less busy routes, where the Convair was too large and the remaining DC-3s were in desperate need of a more modern replacement. In common with many other regional carriers at the time, Lake Central started converting their second-hand Convairs to propeller

25

Lake Central Airlines had relied on their faithful DC-3s (*above*) for many years before introducing larger Convair CV-340s (*left*) that were later re-engined as CV-580s with turbo-prop power plants. Pictures via author

(*Below*) The French-built Nord 262 was a great disappointment to Lake Central, although the modified aircraft went on to serve Allegheny and its associates for many years after the merger. MAP

turbine power, with Allison 501 prop-jets replacing their original piston engines.

Unfortunately, serious engine problems led to grounding of the Nord fleet in August 1966. Although not leading to the loss of any of the aircraft, on no less than four occasions turbine wheels had failed in the French-built aircraft's Turbomeca Bastan engines. In one incident, on 7 July 1966, an engine actually exploded in flight. The crew managed to regain control and land safely, but passengers had been badly injured when parts from the disintegrating engine had punctured the cabin.

Following another engine failure a month later, the Nords were grounded and the old DC-3s taken out of storage, where they had been awaiting sale, and swiftly placed back into service. The Nords did done Lake Central any favours and the tragic loss of the three crew and all thirty-seven passengers on one of the Convairs a month later, caused by a propeller shaft failure, saw more passengers avoiding travelling with the airline.

A new management team took over and began promoting the carrier as the 'Airline with a Heart', painting large white hearts on a bright red tail. This was also derived from Lake Central's earlier advertising claim to be 'Serving the Heart of the Nation'. New route extensions saw the carrier reaching St Louis in the west and Louisville in the south, with Convair 580 flights from Indianapolis. But it was too late to save the airline. Many of the new management team had originally come from Allegheny Airlines and it came as no quite neatly and the merger was the first step in a substantial period of growth for the airline. Through later merger acquisitions and a vigorous policy of route expansion, Allegheny grew from a purely local service carrier into one of the largest airline operators in the USA. But, at the time of the Lake Central takeover, the Boeing 727 and 737 formed no part of the airline's plans and the orders were cancelled.

Pacific's Problems

Yet another of the numerous post-Second World War local service carriers, established to take advantage of the increased interest in air transport, Pacific Air Lines was originally known as Southwest Airways.

Pacific Air Lines' choice of DC-3 replacement was a mixed fleet of Martin 202s and 404s. N40408 previously served with TWA. Via author

not return to service until February 1967 when problems with water methanol and mineral corrosion that had caused the turbine failures, had been sorted out. At this time, negotiations began with Boeing to acquire a small 737 fleet, intended for service between the larger cities on the network. However, the bad publicity had not great surprise when merger negotiations began between the two companies. These culminated in a vote to merge by both airlines' stockholders on 14 March 1967, with Lake Central's absorption into Allegheny taking effect on 1 July.

The Lake Central network dove-tailed into Allegheny's more easterly system The airline pioneered a number of highly original passenger handling methods, such as integral airstairs on their DC-3s, keeping an engine running on tight turnarounds and employing travelling in-flight pursers to issue tickets. Although it worked, the new system was not further exploited by Southwest. More conventional handling methods were utilized when larger aircraft, in the shape of Martin 202s and 404s, replaced the DC-3s. Ironically, it was left to one of the larger major US carriers to refine Southwest's novel ticketing methods into the highly successful Eastern Air Lines 'Shuttle' between East Coast cities.

Expansion had led to the company name being changed to Pacific Air Lines in March 1958. Despite operating a modern fleet of Boeing 727 jets and Fairchild F-27 jet-props that had replaced the Martin 202s and 404s, by the mid-1960s, Pacific Air Lines was beginning to suffer from severe local competition from both low-cost and mainline carriers in its California-based network. Although it operated between several important West Coast cities and boasted an extensive network that stretched from southern California to Oregon and across the Nevada border to Las Vegas, Pacific Air Lines was held back by unprofitable local service routes. Most of these were left over from Southwest's original network, designed to feed traffic from suburban Californian points into San Francisco and Los Angeles area airports. Legally obliged by its route licences to serve the uneconomic smaller communities that it would dearly have liked to have dropped from its network, Pacific relied heavily on revenue from service between the larger cities such as Los Angeles, Sacramento and its home base at San Francisco.

The 100-passenger Boeing 727-100s had entered Pacific service on 20 July 1966. A giant leap from the 48-passenger Fairchilds, the new jets were necessary to compete against the major operators in the region such as United and Western. As well as already operating 727s of their own, United were also utilizing their larger four-jet, medium-range Douglas DC-8s and Boeing 720s in the area. Western also flew later model Boeing 720Bs throughout the region.

Pacific's attempts to compete by placing the 727s into service on non-stop flights between the few major cities on their network were hampered further by increasing competition from local low fare rival, Pacific Southwest Airlines. Effectively suffering competition from both mainline and low-fare sectors of industry, costing it large amounts of revenue, Pacific was finding its situation increasingly untenable A fleet of 737-sized airliners was seen as being necessary to compete more economically.

Nonetheless, events overtook Pacific Air Lines' fleet planning and, in April 1968, the airline was to merge with similarly disadvantaged West Coast Airlines and Bonanza Airlines to form Air West. The hope was that the combined operation, with a new network extending further into the Pacific northwest and east as far as Arizona and Utah, would form the basis of a commercially much stronger carrier.

Air West favoured the DC-9 as their preferred smaller, short-haul, jet. Both Bonanza and West Coast had operating the type since 1966, and Pacific Air Lines' 737 orders were cancelled. Pacific's 727s continued in Air West service for a while, and larger 727-200s were later operated before the company lost its identity in yet another merger, in June 1979.

Airborne!

After the January roll-out and christening ceremonies, the development Boeing aircraft, registered N73700, was prepared for its first flight and the ensuing flight test and certification programme. Taxi tests took place on 8 April 1967, a year after the order book for the aircraft reached the 100 mark. In the year, sales had increased to 141 aircraft.

The next day, at 13.15, local time, N73700 took to air for the first time. It was commanded by Brien Wygle, Boeing's assistant director of flight operations, with S.L. 'Lew' Wallick Jnr, the company's senior experimental test pilot, as co-pilot. The first flight lasted two and a half hours. Although it departed from Boeing field, N73700 was to make its first landing at Paine Field, Everett, also in Washington State. This airport had been designated as the base for the first ten flying hours, for preliminary assessment of the 737's handling characteristics and aircraft systems.

Pacific's Boeing 727s were taken over in the Air West merger, but were later disposed of in favour of more DC-9s. Aviation Hobby Shop

The Boeing 737 prototype, N73700, took to the air for the first time, from Boeing Field on 17 April 1967.
Boeing

On finally landing at Paine Field, Wygle reported: 'I hate to quit. The airplane is a delight to fly.'

Clocking up the Hours

With the programme already well behind schedule, the company needed to get the test and certification work underway as soon as possible. In its first month, N73700 managed to achieve a total flying time of 47 hours, 37 minutes. This was 30 per cent more than the 727 prototype had put in over the same period, and over three times that of the Dash 80, prototype of the 707, Boeing's first jet transport, over ten years earlier.

The first of United's Series 200s flew on 8 August 1967 and was one of the five early production aircraft that joined the test and certification programme as soon as they could be released from the production line. Together with N73700, they accomplished more than 1,300 hours of flight testing that included, for the first time in a certification programme, approaches under CAT II bad weather conditions. Ship number 3 sacrificed most for the project. Never intended to fly, the aircraft was subjected to vibration tests, stretched and overloaded to destruction to prove the strength of the design, and show that Boeing's engineers had got their sums right.

The FAA Two-Crew Decision

During the 1967 Thanksgiving holiday week, the FAA undertook a series of flights with the 737 in the busy Boston– Washington corridor, using a two-pilot crew. One pilot was from the FAA, the other from Boeing.

Two round-trips were made on each of six days that week. Forty hours of flight time were amassed, including day and night flights. Both IFR and VFR weather conditions, below minimum landing conditions and diversions to alternative airports, were examined. In addition, simulated instrument failures and crew incapacitation were included.

Primarily as a result of the Thanksgiving week flying, the FAA issued a statement in December 1967 regarding the two-crew issue.

The far-reaching evaluation of the Boeing 737 was started in September 1965, with the evaluation of the cockpit mock-up. Continuous evaluations over the past two years included regular

(*Top*) The first of the slightly larger 737-200s joined the flight test programme on 8 August 1967, wearing full United colours. Boeing

(*Above*) Lufthansa's first 737-100, D-ABEA, participated in the new type's certification programme before being handed over to the airline for initial crew training. Lufthansa

operations of the aircraft in a high-density air traffic environment to determine workload, complexity, and safety of operations in a fail-safe concept. These flights were part of a very extensive flight-testing programme accomplished by the FAA and Boeing personnel. The technical findings coming out of these evaluations are that the aircraft can be safely flown with a minimum of two pilots.

Even once the issue had been settled as far as the federal regulators were concerned, a number of American Pilots' organizations insisted on three flight-deck crew for the 737 as part of bargaining negotiations with the airline employers. Both United and Western found themselves obliged by their agreements with ALPA to operate the aircraft with three crew members on the flight deck. However, they were the only carriers to be so encumbered, other US operators and foreign carriers were under no obligation to consider adding the extra crew member. Most of the operated the aircraft with a two-pilot crew, as originally designed from the beginning.

Certification Awarded

In December 1967, both the series 100 and 200 Boeing 737 received simultaneous certification for airline operations. The early production aircraft that had participated in the test programme were finally handed over to their new owners for the first airline crews to be trained and converted to the aircraft. Once the first crews, and other operational and maintenance personnel, were trained, they returned to train their own colleagues and prepare for full-scale commercial operations.

The value of the test programme was apparent by the number of changes that were made as a direct result of the data gathered. In particular, the 737 was originally fitted with 'clam-shell'-style thrust reversers, as previously used on the 727. These proved to be ineffective on the 737 configuration and a new deflector was designed and tested on the 737 prototype. It was retrofitted on early production aircraft and later became standard equipment. Also, inflatable seals, originally designed to replace conventional doors over the main landing gear, were tested on the prototype and soon discarded.

A more serious problem that was brought to light by the flight test programme was the increased drag, particularly during the cruise, over the predicted amount. In fact, drag was over 5 per cent more, resulting in loss in speed of 30kt. Fortunately, more lift than predicted and the availability of more powerful, flat-rated JT8D-9 engines, allowed an increase in operating weights. This permitted the basic mission guarantees to be met. For the long term, an intensive wind-tunnel testing programme was embarked upon to cure the problem. Ten months later the resulting aerodynamic modifications were introduced onto production aircraft, and upgrade kits were made available for adding retroactively to aircraft already in service.

As the first production aircraft were delivered, the prototype, N73700, switched its attention to developing modifications to allow the 737 to operate from unpaved runways. Changes included new high-lift

N73700 visited remote rough airfields to demonstrate its versatility and rugged nature. Via author

The 737's New Home

Boeing's decision to move 737 final assembly to its Renton facility came at a time of increasing hardship for the company. Commercial aircraft sales had dipped severely, resulting in massive lay-offs in 1969. Production delays and the three-pilot controversy had slowed down sales of the 737 since the initial spurt of interest. The 707 was nearing the end of its production life, with the 747 wide-bodied airliner project barely underway and suffering its own teething and delayed production problems, particularly affected by late engine deliveries. The 727 production figures that had experienced steady growth, dipped sharply in response to worldwide financial problems and overcapacity within the airlines. As part of its cost-cutting measures, Boeing decided to consolidate the 707/727 and 737 production lines at Renton, the first Renton-assembled 737, a Series 200 for Indian Airlines, being flown in December 1970.

The company's association with the site dated back to its earliest days, with a Boeing B-1 flying boat having been based at a makeshift seaplane facility on the shore of Lake Washington in 1922. The flying boat was operated by Edward Hubbard (who also flew part-time as a test-pilot for Boeing), as a mail service to Victoria, over the Canadian border in British Columbia. A new, unpaved, landing strip was built on the same site, at Bryn Mawr, later that year. Hubbard sold his mail flight operation in 1928, on his becoming a vice-president of Boeing Air Transport.

In October 1928, the airfield was renamed Renton Airport. Over the next few years, although overshadowed by the development of Seattle's Boeing Field as the northwest's main aerial gateway for commercial airline operations, Bryn Mawr remained in use as a busy general aviation field, serving the city of Renton.

World war was responsible for Renton's sudden transformation from backwater airfield to major aircraft assembly plant. July 1941 saw the US Navy and Boeing announcing the immediate erection of a new aircraft construction plant on the shores of Lake Washington, on a plot of land to the east of Renton Airport. Originally, it was intended that Boeing would build large flying boat patrol bombers on the 1.6 million sq ft site.

Opened in April 1942, the plant had an immediate effect on the local economy, with Renton's population rising from 4,000 to 16,000 during the war years. Although few flying boats were finally built at Renton, 1,119 Boeing B-29 heavy bombers rolled off four Renton production lines instead. However, Boeing ceased production at the end of hostilities and only utilized a small part of the once busy facility for storage.

The immediate postwar period saw little activity at Renton, although the War Assets Administration turned the deeds over to the City of Renton and it became Renton Municipal Airport. However, in 1949 Boeing reopened the factory to build the C-97A Stratofreighter, the military tanker/transport version of the Stratocruiser airliner.

The 875 Stratofreighters built at Renton were followed, in 1954, by the single Model 367-80, forever afterwards known as the 'Dash 80'. The Dash 80 was a totally private venture project by Boeing to develop a tanker aircraft to refuel the B-47 and B-52 jet bombers in flight. As well as being ordered in large numbers by the US military, as the KC-135A, the design was further adapted as the Boeing 707, American's first jet airliner. The phenomenal success of the 707 led to a great deal of expansion at Renton and production of the 727 tri-jet began on the site in 1963.

(*Above*) The Boeing facility at Renton, known locally as 'Jet City'. Boeing

(*Below*) The Boeing Model 367-80, the precursor of the KC135 and Boeing 707 models, first flew from Renton in 1954. Boeing

devices and braking improvements and low-pressure tyres, as well as new deflectors fitted to protect the lower fuselage and engine intakes from scuffed-up stones and debris on rough runways. FAA certification for gravel runway operations was forthcoming in February 1969. In April and may, N73700 demonstrated its new rough-field capabilities to airline and government agency representatives.

Particularly interested in these modifications were operators such as Wien Consolidated, Nordair and Pacific Western. These carriers were already planning to fly their 737s into smaller, isolated communities on their networks in Alaska and northern Canada, served by only basic airport facilities and unpaved runways. The Boeing 737's ability to provide jet airliner service to remote areas with dispersed populations was set to become one of its major selling points.

Western's Short-Haul Plans

Although from one of Boeing's more archetypal 737 customers, the Western Air Lines' order had been an important boost for Boeing's corporate ego, and not only as it was for a sizeable number of aircraft. Western had seriously considered the 737's main rivals, the BAC One-Eleven and the DC-9. Initial models of both aircraft had finally been dismissed as too small. The only larger version of the DC-9 then available, the series 30, was also thought not to be big enough and the five-abreast passenger seating was seen as inferior to the 737's six-abreast layout.

Western, that claimed to be the United States' oldest surviving carrier, was then operating a network that, although covering much of the western half of the USA, mostly comprised short inter-city services. A fleet of Boeing 720B jets already operated on longer non-stop routes, linking the more distant parts of Western's system, such as Los Angeles–Minneapolis, as well

The first 737-200 was also used for numerous test programmes. Seen here on water ingestion tests, examining the characteristics of the 737's then unique engine installation. Via author

Just as Western was poised to take delivery of the then ultra-modern 737, it became the proud owner of a fleet of vintage ex-Pacific Northern Airlines piston-powered Lockheed Constellations, following its purchase of the latter airline. MAP

as services to Mexico and to busier, commercially important California–Pacific Northwest regional flights.

However, cities served between the terminal points were usually only about an hour's flying time, or even less, apart. These routes were earmarked for jet service by Western's new 737s. A large fleet of Lockheed Electra turbo-props and a handful of surviving piston-engined DC-6Bs were operated on these US West Coast, western regional and multi-stop California–Southwest–Minnesota–Canada routes. A small number of piston-powered Lockheed Constellations and early model, non-fan engined, Boeing 720 jets, operating an Alaskan network, were also to be inherited when Western took over Pacific Northern Airlines in 1967.

The much publicized 'commonality' with other Boeing types also worked heavily in favour of Western ordering the 737, with some parts, such as tyres, being interchangeable with the Boeing 720B fleet. Larger Boeing 727-200s were also ordered by Western to supplement the 737s and, eventually, replace the 720Bs.

Northern Frontier Customers

Although the one-plane orders of Northern Consolidated and Wien Alaska Airlines were destined to become a 'fleet' following the merger of the two carriers, it was still a small order by Boeing standards. However, for the airlines concerned it was a major leap forward in equipment policy.

Fairbanks-based Wien was the senior airline of the two, tracing its origins back to pioneer 'bush' carriers in Alaska operating as early as 1924. Northern Consolidated Airlines had begun operations in 1945, from Anchorage. Both had benefited from a postwar boom in the Alaskan economy, as well as a redistribution of a number of local trunk routes previously operated by Alaska Airlines and Pan American's Alaskan subsidiary.

Routes were served by a variety of small types, such as Cessna and Pilatus single- and twin-engined aircraft, well suited to the geographically challenging Alaskan terrain. Wien also flew a handful of larger aircraft, such as DC-3s, C-46s, a Fairchild Packet, as well as single examples of the much larger DC-4 and a Lockheed L-749 Constellation on busier services. Both airlines had also been early operators of the Fairchild F-27B turbo-prop. Their F-27Bs had large forward cargo doors and were convertible to a variety of passenger/cargo configurations. This flexibility was important for the rugged, ever-changing, Alaskan commercial air transport scene.

The merger of the two carriers was approved by the Civil Aeronautics Board in February 1968. This created a much stronger carrier, better able to compete with an increasingly strong Alaska Airlines and the powerful new entrant into Alaska, Western Air Lines, following the latter's take-over of Pacific Northern. The Wien Consolidated Airlines' 737s, especially those fitted with cargo doors and convertible cabins, were to provide new jet service to more remote arctic points, as well as linking the major Alaskan cities.

Foreign Interest

Any disappointment within Boeing over the initially slow domestic sales of the 737 were offset by growing interest from export customers. Avianca's choice of the higher performance Series 100 was dictated by conditions on routes into operationally difficult airports, many at high altitude with basic facilities and restricted runways. The Avianca aircraft were intended for the busier domestic and regional route network, based on the Columbian capital, Bogota. Even Bogota's own airport was at 8,355ft (2,547m) above sea-level, with notoriously difficult, mountainous approaches.

By the mid-1960s Avianca was operating its longer-ranging services to the USA, the Caribbean and Europe using Boeing 720Bs. New Boeing 727 jets also flew major regional and domestic flights, alongside Lockheed Constellations, deposed from international routes by the 720Bs. A large fleet of piston-engined, Douglas DC-3s and DC-4s operated on the domestic network. Many of these were fitted with uprated engines, and even rockets, to assist take-offs from short runways at high elevations.

The addition of the 737 to the Avianca fleet would allow the retirement of more of the ageing piston aircraft and see the introduction of jet service to more regional cities. The type's promised high performance from smaller airfields was especially attractive to Avianca, and others, operating routes into airports located among difficult terrain.

Both Wien and Northern Consolidated made good use of the DC-3 on their Alaskan services for many years. Via author

Ship One

Once the initial certification and test flights were completed, the first 737, development aircraft N73700, was effectively redundant. Apart from the rough-field operations research that continued into early 1969, work assignments for the pioneering aircraft were rapidly declining. Later production-model aircraft tended to undertake any development research, any modifications being able to be made during that particular aircraft's manufacture. As such, several 737s took on N73700's Boeing livery, with similar generic test registrations. However, the actual prototype was parked up, engineless, at Renton, having completed 978 hours of test flying.

Having been much modified during the test programme, conversion for resale and certification for commercial operation of N73700 was out of the question. It would have required an expensive rebuild, even assuming a customer for a single Series 100 could be found.

After four years in storage, N73700 finally found a saviour in the shape of the National Aeronautics and Space Administration. NASA had originally been formed to promote and organize the US space programme, in response to Russian success in the 'Space Race'. As space-oriented work declined, NASA became more involved in research into fixed-wing aircraft operations and technology. Much of this involved work on civilian projects and an aircraft was needed for a new project at NASA's Langley Research Center in Virginia. Established to investigate advanced technology for conventionally configured aircraft, the Terminal Configured Vehicle Program eventually selected the redundant N73700 as an ideal airborne test-bed.

A New Life

Re-registered N515NA, the aircraft was delivered to Langley on 17 May 1974, after considerable work was completed for NASA by Boeing. The most striking modification was the addition of a second cockpit in the forward cabin. This cockpit could be equipped with experimental layouts and could be used to control the aircraft, with the conventional cockpit still manned and capable of taking over at any time.

For over twenty years, N515NA participated in the development of many advanced technologies. The 'glass cockpit' flight display, microwave landing systems, GPS performance evaluation, windshear sensor and wake-turbulence testing were only a few of over twenty aerial research projects assigned to the aircraft over the years.

Following its replacement at Langley by a Boeing 757, retirement finally came on 19 September 1997, with all due ceremony. That evening it was flown back to its birthplace at Boeing Field, to its new owners at the Museum of Flight. Initially stored at Moses Lake, Washington and still with a modest 3,000 hours flying time, the aircraft will eventually join a Boeing 247, 727, the prototype 747 and a De Havilland Comet 4C in the museum's new airliner extension at Boeing Field.

N73700 was initially placed in storage at the end of its 737 development work, before being rescued by NASA. Boeing

FIRST STEPS

Eastern Market Entry

The choice of the 737 by Malaysia-Singapore Airlines, the type's first Far Eastern customer, had less to do with operations into difficult airports, although the high take-off performance would certainly prove useful under some tropical conditions. MSA, which began operations as Malayan Airways in 1947, opened jet services in December 1962, with a leased BOAC Comet 4. This supplemented a fleet of DC-3s, a DC-4, Viscount 700s and a new fleet of Fokker F-27 Friendships. The Comet flew regional trunk scheduled services from Singapore to Hong Kong, Kuala Lumpur, Jakarta and Bangkok.

A change of name to Malaysian Airways followed the 1963 formation of the Federation of Malaysia. The next change, to Malaysia-Singapore Airlines in 1967, occurred after Singapore had seceded from the Federation in 1965. By then the leasing arrangement for the single Comet had been terminated when five second-hand Comet 4s were purchased from BOAC, the first having been delivered in late 1965. The new fleet enabled jet services to be extended to Manila, Taipei, Perth and Phnom Penh. Longer-ranging ambitions saw a pair of Boeing 707s being ordered for new routes to Europe, and the 737s were ordered to eventually replace the Comets on the regional jet flights.

(*Above*) Ex-BOAC De Havilland Comet 4s were the first jet equipment for the Singapore-based carrier. Aviation Hobby Shop

(*Below*) The first 737-100s displayed Lufthansa's then current tail livery, soon replaced by a new design before delivery. Boeing

CHAPTER THREE

New Customers, New Applications

New Markets

When the orders from various pontificating carriers did start to come in for the 737, it was not always from operators interested in utilizing the aircraft in the purely short-haul, inter-city, scheduled airline climate for which it had originally been conceived. Although a number of such customers were placing orders, the 737 was increasingly being seen as a candidate for charter service, regional international routes and even some longer-range operations.

US Regional Interest

Despite the Lake Central and Pacific Air Lines orders being cancelled after the carriers vanished in mergers, other orders from US regional carriers were symptomatic of the interest in the rapidly expanding sector of the US airline industry, providing profitable jet service on local routes. Two other regional US carriers represented at the 'christening' that were to take delivery of their ordered aircraft, Pacific Southwest Airlines and Piedmont Airlines, operated very different networks, serving very different customer bases. Nonetheless, both were anxious to take advantage of the 737's promised flexibility on their regional routes.

The neat, two-pilot, flight-deck of the initial Boeing 737-100. Lufthansa

Southern Regional Pioneer

Piedmont Airlines had followed a traditional evolution in US local air service. Formed in 1940 as a charter and general aviation company in North Carolina, Piedmont moved into scheduled services in 1948. As the new carrier expanded during the 1950s, a large fleet of DC-3s was built up linking numerous southern towns with larger cities, roughly bordered between Washington, Charleston, Atlanta and Louisville.

The airline had been a pioneer among the local service carriers in operating turbo-props, Fairchild F-27s, a version of the Dutch-designed Fokker F.27 Friendship built under licence in the USA, from 14 November 1958. However, Piedmont was not to totally abandon piston-engined operations, placing the first of a large fleet of second-hand Martin 404s in service in 1962. Larger Fairchild FH-227s began replacing the earlier F-27s from early 1967. A surprise order, for ten Japanese-produced Nihon YS-11A, 60-passenger, turbo-prop airliners was placed later that year.

Turbo-Prop to Jet

Expansion of Piedmont's network, with a number of non-stop route authorities being granted, led to the airline actively looking for jet equipment. The acquisition of jets by regional carriers was initially resisted by the Civil Aeronautics Board,

(*Above*) The piston-powered Martin 404 was introduced into Piedmont Airlines' service after the carrier had already acquired turbo-prop F-27s. Aviation Hobby Shop

(*Below*) The Japanese-designed NAMC YS-11A turbo-prop also served on Piedmont's regional and local services. Via author

which was responsible for allocating mail subsidy payments, a vital lifeline for most of the local service carriers. However, their awarding of routes encroaching on the major trunk airlines left the CAB with little choice but to approve the upgrading of equipment in order for the smaller carriers to be able to compete with the 'majors' on their new routes.

Intervention by the CAB had led to the cancellation of a number of early orders for the British BAC One-Eleven from US carriers. However, such action was resisted by Mohawk Airlines, who persisted in their wish to acquire a jet fleet for their local routes. Mohawk eventually convinced the CAB that they would not require any extra subsidy to operate the jets. Within four years, every one of the local service carriers, as designated by the CAB, had ordered jets. For the most part, their orders were for the Douglas twin-jet, the DC-9, but the larger 737 was also attracting some interest.

Piedmont's Jet Debut

Piedmont actually began jet operations on 15 March 1967, when a Boeing 727-100 was leased from the manufacturer. As well as providing a competitive edge on new direct flights to New York and Washington, the use of this aircraft was to provide Piedmont with valuable jet experience before taking delivery of the 737s. A second leased 727-100 arrived in April. However, tragedy struck on 19 July when the original aircraft was involved in a mid-air collision. Climbing out of Asheville/Hendersonville, during an Atlanta–Asheville/Hendersonville–Roanoke–New York/La Guardia service, the aircraft collided with a Cessna 310 light twin aircraft that was approaching the same airport. The seventy-nine occupants of the 727, and the three in the Cessna, all perished in the ensuing crashes. Piedmont Airline's initial 737 order was for six series 200s, earmarked for longer routes between larger cities on the network.

California's Jet Commuter

Like Piedmont Airlines, Pacific Southwest Airlines had already been a jet operator before ordering the 737. Their Boeing 727 fleet had entered service in 1965 and a fleet of the larger 727-200s were also on order to replace their initial Series 100s. The 737s were on order as more economic supplements to the 727s on services with lower average loads, in addition to replacing the last of a fleet of Lockheed Electra turbo-props.

PSA was seen by the trunk carriers as a 'maverick' carrier and its continued survival was a major headache for United and Western Air Lines, encroaching as it did on their traditional West Coast operations. Initially operating as a flying school at San Diego, in southern California, founded by Kenneth Friedkin in 1945, PSA inaugurated a scheduled service from San Diego to San Francisco on 6 May 1949.

A single DC-3 was operated and Pacific Southwest's early passengers were checked in through the lobby of the old flying school, using a set of bathroom scales to weigh baggage. Despite the primitive style of the early operations, 15,000 passengers were carried on the route in the first year. No doubt this was mostly due to the low PSA fare of $10, instead of the regular $25 charged by United and Western. PSA was able to undercut the other carriers as its scheduled services were wholly conducted within the borders of the state of California, and therefore the federal CAB had no jurisdiction over the company. As long as PSA satisfied the California Public Utilities Commission as to its fitness to survive, it could set its own fares with no outside influence other than market forces.

CCA's Failure

Although concerned at the loss of their traffic, the incumbent carriers fully expected PSA to be a passing phenomenon. Another low-fare carrier, California Central Airlines, was also operating under California PUC authority at the time. CCA also began operations with DC-3s, in January 1949, with scheduled flights from San Francisco (Oakland) to Los Angeles (Burbank). Larger DC-4s, Martin 202s and a single Lockheed Constellation were acquired to cope with the demand for seats sold at $9.99, one way. However, California Central had made the mistake of expanding far

California Central's colourful fleet of Martin 202s failed to make money, despite attracting high passenger loads on their low-fare services. MAP

(*Above*) The use of new Lockheed L-188 Electras made PSA's major airline rivals start to take the San Diego-based airline seriously. Aviation Hobby Shop

(*Below*) Pacific Air Line's F-27 turbo-prop services from San Jose were badly hit by the arrival of PSA jets on local routes from the area. Via author

too quickly and was struggling to cover the costs of day-to-day operations, let alone expensive re-equipment costs. CCA recorded a deficit of over $1,000,000 in 1953, notwithstanding the impressive total of 137,000 passengers carried. In February 1954, California Central Airlines went into voluntary bankruptcy.

United and Western sat and waited for PSA to follow CCA's fate, only introducing nominal fare reductions and schedule changes to combat PSA's intrusion into their 'territory'. However, they were to be disappointed. Four DC-3s were in service with PSA by 1952 and new routes were only steadily introduced, including a Los Angeles–San Francisco (Oakland) flight in 1955. The 31-seat DC-3s were replaced by 70-seat DC-4s, purchased in November 1955. The frequent, low-fare, services were popular with passengers from many different walks of Californian life. They were especially popular with personnel on leave from the many US Navy establishments up and down the California coast. As a result, PSA soon gained the nickname of 'Poor Sailor's Airline'.

A New Fleet

PSA made a very bold move in 1957, with the announcement of an order for three new Lockheed Electra turbo-props. Friedkin had actually announced his intention to order two French Sud Aviation Caravelle jets for PSA earlier that year, but the deal was never finalized. Instead, the 98-passenger Electras were acquired, entering service in December 1959 and quickly replacing the DC-4s.

With the arrival of the Electras, United and Western finally began to take PSA much more seriously and introduced low-fare jet services to compete. However, by now PSA was firmly established as a popular alternative to the trunk carriers and managed to fight off the big guns. Three additional Electras began arriving from 1961 as frequencies and loads built up throughout PSA's exclusively Californian network. Even with the arrival of the first 727s in 1965, the Electras continued to provide valuable, economical service to PSA.

As well as the trunk carriers, PSA's operations also had a major effect on local service carriers on whose routes it competed. When, in 1965, it opened services from San Jose to Los Angeles, it practically wiped out the long-standing operator on the route, Pacific Air Lines, overnight. PSA was able to charge $12, while CAB-controlled Pacific was legally obliged to charge $24. The adverse economic effect of PSA on Pacific's operation was one of the main factors in Pacific Air Lines' eventual dire need to merge into Air West.

Charter Airline's Choice

A new market that was to become very important to Boeing in the following years was the rapidly growing number of charter airlines, especially in Europe. The independent Norwegian airline, Braathens, had ordered the 737 for its scheduled domestic network, but also operated an extensive programme of charter flights. The bold placement of an order by all-charter operator Britannia Airways, based at Luton in the United Kingdom, for brand new 737s sent a message to their commercial rivals to modernize as well or soon risk losing business.

The postwar explosive growth of commercial charter flights, especially in the European inclusive-tour holiday market, had been an extraordinary phenomenon. Beginning with a handful of enterprising operators in the late 1940s and early 1950s, the inclusive-tour industry had mushroomed, until by the mid-1960s it started to rival scheduled services for the carriage of the majority of air travellers within Europe. The road had not been an easy one, with many early operators running foul of regulatory authorities, or succumbing to commercial pressures.

Braathens' Shipping Origins

A subsidiary of a long-established shipping concern, Braathens had begun operations as a long-haul scheduled operator, flying services from Norway to the Far East and South America. Norway's involvement in the formation of SAS (Scandinavian Airlines System), the joining together of the Danish Airline DDL, the Swedish carrier ABA and Norway's DNL, meant that the Norwegian authorities were unable to renew Braathen's authority for international scheduled services when it came up for renewal in 1954. The agreement between the three Scandinavian countries meant that SAS was to be given the monopoly on such routes.

Braathens survived as a scheduled domestic carrier within Norway and continued to

The Douglas DC-6Bs served Braathens on worldwide charters as well as seeing service on the busier routes on its Norwegian domestic network. MAP

fly internationally on charter services throughout the world. Defiantly continuing to operate as Braathens–South American and Far East Airtransport A/S, which was conveniently contracted to 'Braathens S.A.F.E.' in the aircraft livery, the airline enthusiastically entered the IT market as it grew in Europe.

Norwegians enjoy a cheap holiday as much as any other Europeans and soon Braathens was flying clients for several Scandinavian tour operators. The charter network rapidly expanded to reach as far as southern Europe and Africa. On a daily basis, Braathens' fleet of Fokker F.27 turbo-props and piston-engined DC-6Bs were just as likely to be carrying sunseekers to a Mediterranean island resort, as carrying Oslo businessmen to appointments in cities near the Arctic Circle. The extra capacity and jet speeds of the 737s on order was to be welcomed by Braathens in both markets.

Britain's Holiday Specialists

It was the order from Britannia Airways that drew other non-scheduled operators' attention to the potential of the Boeing 737 as a charter aircraft. Still a comparatively young airline, Britannia Airways had started operations in 1962, formed as a subsidiary of Universal Sky Tours, one of the UK's leading inclusive-tour operators. UST had previously chartered from several different companies to carry their clients. However, the summer of 1961 saw a number of abrupt bankruptcies among Britains' independent airlines, including several contracted to UST.

The most significant of these was the cessation of operations by Overseas Aviation, which operated a large fleet of Canadair Fours and Vickers Vikings from Gatwick. UST was just one of their customers left with clients stranded all over Europe. The tour company was determined never to be left in that position again and to take more direct control over the air transport section of the holidays they sold.

Euravia Takes to the Skies

Euravia (London) Ltd, as the new airline was initially named, established offices and hangerage at Luton Airport, north of London, in early 1961. Three second-hand Lockheed Constellations were acquired and the first UST clients were carried from Manchester to Palma in May 1962.

With the financial security of UST behind them, Euravia's management were able to offer a standard of professional service rarely seen in the independent sector before. After only one summer season, Euravia bought out another Constellation operator, Skyways Ltd and, with the addition of the Skyways fleet and more second-hand Constellations, the airline had a 160 per cent increase in passenger capacity on offer for 1963. As well as using the extra capacity to increase UST's operations, much of it was snapped up by other inclusive-tour companies and Euravia's reputation within the industry grew apace.

The eight Constellations in use in 1963 were soon averaging 1,300 hours of revenue flying a month. However, the trusty Lockheeds were rapidly reaching the end of their useful life and Euravia began to look at their options for a replacement.

The Expanding IT Market

Euravia eventually chose to re-equip with a fleet of ex-BOAC Bristol Britannia 102s, then in storage at Cambridge Airport. Configured for 117 passengers, the Britannias entered service with a Luton–Tenerife charter in December 1964. Their arrival also saw a change of company name, to Britannia Airways. Although the Constellations continued in use until late 1965, they did not take on the new name.

As well as offering a more modern, comfortable, quieter ride than the Constellations, the Britannias also enabled Britannia Airways to offer one of the first hot-meal catering services by a British all-charter carrier. Their reliability became legendary in a sector of the UK's airline operations far too used to operating ageing airliners with dubious maintenance schedules. As Britannia, and the other IT operators, switched over to more modern types, the industry finally began to gain a reputation for a much higher quality of product and attract even more of the mass travel market.

The sudden demise of once-busy Overseas Aviation left travel companies like UST with angry and inconvenienced clients throughout Europe. Via author

Euravia's Constellation, G-AHEN, had originally been delivered to BOAC. It had later been California Central's sole Constellation, wearing California Hawaiian titles, before being sold on to Los Angeles Air Service and El Al, finally joining Euravia at Luton. Jenny Gradidge

The arrival of second-hand Bristol Britannia turbo-props prompted Euravia to change its name to Britannia Airways. Jenny Gradidge

BEA used much of their fleet's spare capacity on 'night tourist' schedules, improving utilization for their Comet 4Bs and other types. A large proportion of the available seats were sold to travel companies for use on IT holidays. Via author

The Competition's Jet Services

The use of jets on UK IT services was very limited in the early 1960s. The Comet 4B fleet of the state-owned British European Airways operated a number of night-time IT charters and cheaper, scheduled, night-rate tourist flights when not flying their European schedules in the daylight hours. The imminent arrival of BEA's fleet of Trident jets would see the Corporation making even more use of spare capacity for IT charters and tourist-class flights.

The independent British airlines did not offer jet services on any appreciable scale until the introduction of British United Airway's BAC One-Eleven and VC-10 fleets in 1964/65. British Eagle International Airlines followed with their One-Elevens in 1966. Both BUA and British Eagle sold much of their jet capacity to IT operators from the beginning of their One-Eleven operations, supplementing their use on scheduled services. More One-Elevens were on order for operators such as Channel Airways and Laker Airways, which were already major players in the IT market. Dan-Air Services took delivery of the first of what was to become a sizeable fleet of second-hand Comet jets, with ex-BOAC Comet 4s entering IT charter service from Gatwick in 1966.

Eager to remain competitive, Britannia Airways also looked at the BAC One-Eleven, but soon dismissed it as a viable Britannia replacement. The early One-Eleven models lacked the Britannia's capacity and although the stretched Series 500, still on the drawing board at the time, would match it, Britannia wanted to increase their passenger-carrying capacity. The only other home-produced passenger jet of suitable size, the three-engined Hawker Siddeley Trident, was deemed too expensive operationally on charter services. The airline's preference soon settled on the twin-engined Boeing 737, in particular the larger Series 200. However, the major obstacle of import duty had to be resolved before Britannia Airways could take delivery of any aircraft.

Britannia's Case

Although still liable for a 14 per cent import duty, Britannia Airways went ahead with their 737 plans and finally announced their order for three Series 200s in June 1966. Reacting to sensational newspaper headlines of the 'Britannia Orders American!' variety, the airline's then managing director, J.E.D. Williams, was swift to justify their choice of the foreign option:

> Britannia Airways has obtained government permission to import three Boeing 737-200 aircraft for delivery in spring 1968. The new twin engined jet will be operated on package holidays with 117 seats in addition to the existing fleet of eight Britannia's with identical seating capacity. Britannia Airways will be the first operator of the 200 Series in Europe, followed closely be Aer Lingus. The investment, including spares is about £4,250,000.
>
> Of course Britannia Airways would have preferred to buy British jets. However, our studies led inexorably to the conclusion that British jets offered to us could only be operated, in our particular set of circumstances, at a loss.
>
> At the request of the then Minister of Aviation we tried again last December with a leading British manufacturer to find some way out of our dilemma. This effort too failed. The Ministry of Aviation have never questioned our basic case presented to them months ago in an aide-memoire.
>
> Under the terms of the Import Duty Act of 1958, a British airline requiring aircraft of foreign manufacture in order to compete with foreign airlines on international routes may be allowed waiver of import duty. This waiver has not been allowed on the grounds that similar aircraft are procurable in the UK. Britannia Airways refutes this view and are asking for a reversal of this decision. To describe an aircraft which can only be operated against strong competition from foreign airlines at a loss 'similar' to one which can substantially assist the development of the British air transport industry is clearly preposterous.
>
> Unlike the government owned airlines, our traffic rights are not protected, nor is the charter rate we charge controlled in any way. If foreign airlines can offer better rates than we can there is nothing to stop them taking away our business.

One Rule for One?

British government permission to import such expensive items as airliners depended on there being no alternative item available on the home market. Otherwise, expensive customs duties would become due on their importation.

State-owned BOAC had managed to avoid paying inflated duties on their largely American-built fleets over the postwar years by consistently 'proving' that the UK-produced alternatives were 'inferior'. Even where BOAC had, reluctantly, accepted a UK-built fleet, such as with the Vickers VC-10 versus the Boeing 707, BOAC would demand some sort of subsidy to cover alleged extra costs of operating the British type.

Also state-owned, British European Airways had not been able to persuade the government to allow it to import aircraft from abroad. BEA operated its services with a fleet of British-built Tridents, Comets, Vanguards, Viscounts, Dart Heralds and Herons. The last foreign-built BEA fixed-wing aircraft in service had been DC-3s that had been with the airline since its formation in 1946 and that were disposed of in 1962. A small fleet of American-built Sikorsky helicopters were operated on scheduled and charter flights, in the absence of any viable European, let alone British-built, alternatives. Perhaps in an attempt to placate the UK industry over BOAC's apparent pro-US tendencies, BEA was repeatedly told to 'Buy British'.

BOAC imported a large fleet of Boeing 707s, claiming that the UK-built alternatives were less suitable for their operations. Via author

Past Loopholes

One independent carrier, Cunard Eagle Airways, had found itself with an alternative option in the early 1960s. Eager to replace its fleet of Bristol Britannia turbo-props with jets, Cunard Eagle ordered a pair of Boeing 707s. Despite being powered by British-built Rolls Royce Conway engines, just like BOAC's early 707s, Cunard Eagle was faced with an import tax bill. Originally intended for a London–New York service, the licence for which was revoked following BOAC's protests before operations could begin, the Cunard Eagle 707s were quickly reassigned to Caribbean routes.

Cunard Eagle, when still known as Eagle Airways, had established subsidiaries based in the Bahamas and Bermuda in the late 1950s. Operating Viscount-scheduled services to mainland USA, and later across the Atlantic to the UK with London-based Britannias, the subsidiaries were, effectively, local airlines outside the control of UK authorities. Thus, the first Cunard Eagle 707 was re-assigned to the Bermudan company, with a Bermudan registration and opened scheduled trans-Atlantic services from London to Bermuda and the Bahamas, in May 1962

BOAC was unlikely to let Cunard Eagle's actions go unchallenged and a legal appeal was expected. The original licence for the route had been granted on the basis of low-fare, low-frequency, 'coach class' services being offered. The upgrade to jets was seen as a serious threat by the independent to BOAC's own established services. BOAC also protested that the Bermudan subsidiary was little more than a 'paper' airline, with the bulk of its operations now undertaken by the UK-based parent company that was not licensed for the scheduled services under its own name.

However, the whole argument suddenly became immaterial only a few weeks later when the shipping line owners of Cunard Eagle sold the trans-Atlantic network, along with the 707s, to BOAC, in June 1962. All the Cunard Eagle Caribbean and Atlantic network had been absorbed into BOAC by September. The European network of Cunard Eagle, bought back by the airline's disgruntled founder, Harold Bamburg, was later rebranded as British Eagle International Airlines and expanded its UK-based networks.

Cunard Eagle Airways registered its Boeing 707 with its subsidiary, Cunard Eagle (Bermuda), for scheduled trans-Atlantic services. Aviation Hobby Shop

(*Below*) **Following the acquisition of Cunard Eagle's Atlantic network, a number of BOAC aircraft carried 'BOAC Cunard' titles.** Aviation Hobby Shop

Caledonian's Dilemma

London/Gatwick-based Caledonian Airways faced a similar duty problem to Cunard Eagle, a few years later, when it attempted to order some 707s to replace its Britannias on trans-Atlantic charter services. Faced with a crippling tax bill imposed for importing the Boeings, Caledonian was forced to lease out its first 707 to an American charter carrier, Flying Tiger Line, for a year before the dispute was finally settled 'amicably' with the UK Customs authorities. The airline still had to pay a sizable import duty.

Caledonian was very keen on ordering the 737-200 for use in its European IT services. The Boeing 'commonality' with Caledonian's 707s was a major factor in the airline's choice, as was the high performance promised and its increased capacity available over rival types. Caledonian came close to signing the 737 contract, but found the customs issue getting in the way again.

Face with another long debate with the authorities, the airline was also warned that it may be expected to pay increased duty on its already delivered 707s if the 737 order went ahead. Under increasing pressure from tour companies to replace its remaining Britannias with jets as soon as possible, Caledonian was forced to withdraw from negotiations with Boeing. Instead, a fleet of British-built BAC One-Eleven Series 500s was ordered and placed into service in 1969.

(*Top*) Delivery of Caledonian Airways' first Boeing 707 was delayed by the question of import duty. Via author

(*Above*) Eventually, Caledonian was forced to abandon plans to acquire Boeing 737s to complement its 707s. Instead, three 'stretched' BAC One-Eleven Series 500s were placed in service on European IT charters. Via author

Refusal to waive duty in such circumstances would weaken the British air transport industry without protecting the manufacturing industry to the slightest degree.

Britannia Airways advised the government six months ago that under no circumstances could their operation be viable with a British manufactured jet and supported this assertion with technical and economic data. We stated that, regardless of the government's decision, we *could* not buy British.

If our assertions are accepted there is no question of protecting the home industry and no case for the refusal of waiver. If our assertions are not accepted we should be told why. We have repeatedly offered to give the government any information they may desire. Nothing has been requested since our original aide-memoire.

Very detailed studies of the capabilities of jet aircraft currently offered by British and American manufacturers, in our particular circumstances, led us to these conclusions:-

1. A commercially acceptable return on investment could not be obtained in our particular business on any British jet.
2. If we bought a British jet we could be swamped by any of several foreign airlines if they bought Boeing 737-200s or DC-9-30s.
3. The procurement of a Boeing 737-200 fleet would enable us to offer cheaper than ever transport between the UK and the Mediterranean, giving the opportunity of a holiday in the sun to an even larger sector of the population.

Before commencing negotiations with Boeing, we placed our studies and our conclusions before the leading British aircraft manufacturers and begged them to knock holes in our arguments. We offered them access to most confidential data regarding our business so that they could check for themselves. They did not make the slightest dent in the inexorable logic of the case.

We gave British Aircraft Corporation from July 1965 until February 1, 1966, to come up with a proposal that could make sense. They were not able to do so.

The Foreign Threat

Britannia's worries about foreign carriers being able to obtain 737s on more favourable terms, and therefore be able to undercut them in contract negotiations with tour operators, were more than mere 'make-weights' in their argument against import duty. When the inclusive-tour industry first took off, the carriers used were almost exclusively from the passengers' originating countries. However, both nationally and independently owned carriers of the resort countries soon latched on to the lucrative financial possibilities of the growing IT industry.

Spain's Iberia was particularly busy in this market, via its subsidiary, Aviaco. Iberia leased or chartered out surplus members of its mainline fleets to supplement Aviaco's own charter operations. Iberia's Super Constellations were kept especially busy operating Aviaco charters once they had been displaced from scheduled services by jets. The 'sub-charter' arrangement allowed Iberia to undertake IT work at lower charter rates than it would have been allowed to under its own name by stringent IATA rules.

Alitalia had also set up its own 'non-IATA' subsidiary, Societa Aerea Mediterranea Spa (SAM), operating DC-6s of various marks, deposed from front-line scheduled services by jets. SAM was so heavily involved with the UK originating IT market that a busy seasonal base was eventually established at Gatwick, serving several Italian resort areas.

As well as the threat to their livelihood from these subsidiaries, Britannia, and the other independent UK charter carriers, were facing competition from an increasing number of foreign independents. The better financed, but still vulnerable, carriers such as Britannia and its charter colleagues from several other European nations were starting to look over their shoulders at their southern rivals. Spain's Spantax, TAE, and Trans Europa were just

The expanding operations of 'non-IATA' subsidiaries, like Alitalia's associate, SAM, soon started to provide a commercial threat to UK charter carriers. MAP

UK charter carriers accelerated their jet acquisition plans once continental charter operators such as Air Spain began modernizing with modern turbo-props, such as the Bristol Britannia. MAP

Pacific Western's varied operations included scheduled local flights by DC-3s, supplemented by Convairs, DC-6s and DC-7s on busier routes. The larger Douglases also operated a substantial international charter programme. Via author

as likely to be carrying British holidaymakers. Lower operating costs were often the key to their gaining contracts from northern European tour companies.

Several of the Mediterranean-based independent charter carriers had already expressed an interest in acquiring some of the handful of first-generation jets that were starting to come on to the second-hand market. The 'non-IATA' subsidiaries already had access to jet fleets, through their scheduled parents. The new jets were more than a fashionable whim, they were becoming increasingly vital for commercial survival.

Pacific Western

Another airline represented at the 'christening', Pacific Western Airlines, would use their 737s for a mixture of charter and scheduled flying. Initially operating as Central British Columbia Airways, in 1945, the name Pacific Western Airlines was adopted in 1953 as the network expanded, mostly by the merging or purchasing of smaller operators. By 1965 the company was ranked as Canada's third largest airline, operating forty-seven aircraft on a scheduled network throughout British Columbia, Alberta, Saskatchewan and the Northwest Territories.

A pair of DC-7s operated international charters, including trans-Atlantic services, while the schedules were operated by a fleet as diverse as DC-6s and DC-6BS, DC-4s and DC-3s, C-46s and several smaller types such as Beech 18s, DHC Beavers, Otters and even two Grumman Goose amphibians. Turbo-prop CV-640s entered scheduled service in February 1967. A giant Lockheed Hercules turbo-prop cargo aircraft was also on order to operate international and domestic all-cargo flights. The Pacific Western 737s were intended for both regional scheduled and longer-ranging charter flights, especially to the southern USA, the Caribbean and Mexico.

Aer Lingus Second Choice

The Irish national carrier, Aer Lingus, had been operating jets since late 1960. Its trans-Atlantic division, Aerlinte Eireann, had introduced Boeing 720s on the Dublin–Shannon–New York route, replacing leased Lockheed Super Constellations, on 14 December that year. On short-haul routes to the UK and Europe, Aer Lingus operated a fleet of DC-3s, Viscounts and Fokker F.27s. A small fleet of Aviation Traders' Carvairs, converted DC-4s, operated car ferry and cargo services. The propeller-driven fleet had initially encountered only limited jet competition on some European routes with rival carriers such as Air France and Belgium's Sabena-operated Caravelles.

Nonetheless, Aer Lingus was anxious to update their image and modernize the fleet by operating jets on the short/medium-haul network. Initial plans to order their own Caravelles were thwarted by the Irish government's refusal to finance the purchase. Eventually, however, the airline was able to refute the government's objections to a short-haul jet fleet and a quartet of BAC One-Elevens were introduced into service in June 1966.

Even before they entered service, Aer Lingus recognized that the 74-seater One-

Later versions of the Vickers Viscount continued to form the backbone of Aer Lingus's European services through the 1950s and 60s. Aer Lingus

Aer Lingus had been an early customer for the BAC One-Eleven, buying four Series 200s. The airline soon realized that the aircraft was too small and argued for a larger version to be produced. Via author

Elevens were too small for the projected markets. When Boeing 707s replaced the 720s on trans-Atlantic routes, the medium-range Boeings were transferred to some of the higher-density European and UK services, especially the Dublin–London route. The 115-passenger 720s had the capacity for the busy route, but operating a four-engined jet airliner on such a short sector was an uneconomic proposal. When the last two 720s were leased out by Aer Lingus, to US carrier Braniff International, Aer Lingus's even larger Boeing 707s supplemented the One-Elevens on the London Service.

Bigger is Better?

Aer Lingus was very keen for the One-Eleven's manufacturer, the British Aircraft Corporation, to build a larger version of their twin-jet. Several others among BAC's early One-Eleven customers were just as interested and Britain's BEA had actually refused to place an order for a long-awaited 'Viscount Replacement' until a bigger version was available. Unfortunately, BAC procrastinated over their decision and by the time the larger Series 500 One-Eleven was finally launched, many of the potential customers had lost interest and/or patience and had ordered rival Douglas DC-9s or Boeing 737s instead.

Aer Lingus' own patience had run out in 1966. On 9 March, a $6 million order was placed for two 117-passenger Boeing 737-200s. It had been announced that the 737s were intended for use principally on the Dublin–London route where traffic had continued to increase. In 1965 over 285,000 passengers and 4,700 tons of cargo were flown between the two capitals. However, extra orders were eventually placed for more 737s and it became clear that Aer Lingus had plans to operate their new jet on more far-reaching routes around Europe.

Poised for Launch

Far from restricting their customer base to the short-haul scheduled carriers originally envisaged, Boeing's sales team had found themselves talking to a very disparate cross-section of the airline industry. It was clear that the 737 was poised to make an impact on more than one market, with some carriers even making a stand against their governments for the right to operate the aircraft.

Orders were soon added from a number of other operators scattered around the world. Canadian Pacific Airlines and New Zealand National Airways, among others, had placed new orders and some earlier customers had ordered further 737s. All Nippon Airways, of Japan, was negotiating not only with Boeing to place an order, but also with their own government for permission to import the aircraft for their extensive domestic network.

Even before carrying a single fare-paying passenger, the 737 was promising a lot to the operators. Would they prove to be promises it could live up to?

CHAPTER FOUR

Into Service

Lufthansa Leads the Way

In keeping with their pioneering order for the 737, Lufthansa was able to take delivery of their first production Series 100 on 27 December 1967. Remaining in Seattle for a little over a month, the aircraft immediately began to be used to convert the first of Lufthansa's crews to operate the type. This was less than two weeks after the 737 had received its FAA type certification and only a little over eight months since the prototype's first flight in May of that year.

After receiving its West German registration D-ABED, the first Lufthansa 737 made the trans-Atlantic ferry flight from Seattle to the airline's maintenance base at Hamburg, in Northern Germany, arriving on 4 February 1968. Greeted by a large crowd of Lufthansa employees, media and well-wishers, D-ABED was soon whisked away, after due ceremony and much speechmaking. Work then began on fitting out the passenger cabin in preparation for scheduled service.

Within the week, after further busy days of training and route-proving flights, D-ABED joined Lufthansa's operating fleet as the first '737 City Jet' as the carrier had chosen to promote the aircraft. D-ABED was to receive the individual name of 'Flensburg'. Previously, the airline's Boeing 727s had been christened as '727 Europa Jets'. The distinction between 'Europa' and 'City' was prompted by Lufthansa's initial plan for operating the larger 727s on medium-haul flights around Europe and to the Middle East, while the 737s were intended for the ultra-short hauls within West Germany and to neighbouring states.

On 10 February D-ABED took on its first load of fare-paying passengers, for flight LH147, the 07.25 departure from Frankfurt to Munich. From there, it became LH016 to Hamburg, then returned to Frankfurt as LH709, arriving at 12.45. A little over an hour later, it departed for Cologne as LH731, the first of two return runs between Frankfurt and Cologne, before closing its engines down for the last time that day, back

D-ABED arrived at a very cold, very damp Hamburg on 4 February 1968. Lufthansa

Lufthansa's Chief Executive – Technical Services, Gerhard Holtje (centre), was on the delivery flight. Holtje had been a major influence on the 737's final design. Behind him is Capt Emil Kuhl, Lufthansa's Chief Pilot – 737 Fleet. Lufthansa

at Frankfurt, at 19.25. Typical of what was to become the daily utilization of a Lufthansa 737, D-ABED's first day on the line marked the beginning of a long and very successful association between the airline and aircraft.

As further 737s rolled off the Seattle production line, or were released from development or training work, the followed D-ABED over the Atlantic. Lufthansa was anxious to introduce the aircraft throughout their intended network, following the production and delivery delays. On arrival, they were quickly assigned to more and more of Lufthansa's domestic and regional flights. The remaining Super Constellations had already been retired in October 1967, in anticipation of the 737's arrival on the busy inter-city domestic routes. The Convairs began to be withdrawn as the 737s became established in service and the airline was soon close to its ambition to become an all-jet carrier. A handful of the turbo-prop Viscounts were to remain in use for another couple of years, but were soon to follow their piston-engined colleagues out of Lufthansa's fleet.

The Boeing 737-100s quickly became busy members of the Lufthansa European fleet.
Lufthansa

Into the Friendly Skies

While Lufthansa was busy introducing its new '737 City Jets' to the European travelling public, back in the USA, United was also busy, converting crews to the larger Series 200, in preparation for their own introduction. As well as the 737s, a larger version of the Boeing 727, the Series 200, was due to enter service, joining the original Series 100s that had been in use since 1964. The arrival of the two new jets would see the final stage of the phasing out of the airline's remaining propeller-driven aircraft. The first United 737 was delivered to the airline on 21 December 1967, only two weeks after Lufthansa's first Series 100 was handed over.

Chicago Debut

Promoted by the airline's public relations department as 'The Biggest Thing in Little Jets', the 737-200 entered commercial service on regional flights out of United's busiest base, Chicago's O'Hare Airport, on 29 April 1968. William F. Mellberg was a passenger on the first flight.

> That morning I boarded United Flight 648 at Chicago-O'Hare with my cousin, Dave Mellberg. We were 16-year-old high school students who shared a keen interest in airliners. So, when we heard that United was inaugurating a 737 service in the United States with a flight between Chicago and Grand Rapids, Michigan, we made sure we were on board! Taking off at 7.39am, our brand new 737, N9003U, 'City of Grand Rapids', touched down 30 minutes later. There were inaugural celebrations onboard the flight and a red carpet was rolled out for us at Grand Rapids. (Flight 648 was the first scheduled jetliner to land there.)

Lufthansa's passengers soon began to appreciate the 'big jet' feel of the 737's cabin.
Lufthansa

INTO SERVICE

(*Above*) **N9003U was allocated to United's first 737-200 revenue service on 28 April 1968 from Chicago O'Hare.** William F. Mellberg

William F. Mellberg (left) and his cousin Dave Mellberg enjoy United's legendary 'Friendly Skies' cabin service on the short inaugural 737-200 flight from Chicago to Grand Rapids. William F. Mellberg

As the delayed 737s were finally delivered, United swiftly distributed the new aircraft to other bases on their system. The stretched 727-200s soon followed the 737s and the increasing short and medium-haul jet fleets were rapidly dislodging the remaining DC-6s and DC-6Bs from even the quieter routes to which they had already been consigned.

By the beginning of 1969, the only propeller-powered passenger aircraft in regular service in United's fleet were the jet-prop Viscounts. However, the British-built Viscount's days were numbered, as were the airline's less economic Caravelle twin-jets. Both types were already earmarked for disposal within the next two years, as even more 727s and 737s arrived from Boeing and were placed into service for United.

The Trickle Becomes a Flood

As production aircraft began to be delivered, albeit a month or two late, to their patient customers, the 737 finally started to make an impression on the world's commercial airways. Western, Piedmont, PSA and Wien Consolidated were among the US domestic carriers that followed United into the US 737 family over the following months.

February 1968 had seen PSA placing a record repeat order for no less than nine Boeing 727-200s and six more Boeing 737-200s. The largest single aircraft order by PSA, it was worth $69 million to Boeing. PSA was hoping to expand their previously all-California services to Portland, Oregon and Seattle, Washington and the new aircraft would be needed to operate the flights, as well as speeding up the replacement of the airline's remaining 727-100s and Electras.

The 737s were beaten into service as PSA's first twin-jets by a pair of DC-9-30s, the first of which had been delivered in 1967. However, the Douglas jets were replaced by the 737s as the latter's numbers built up. One of the DC-9s was sold on to Ozark Airlines in 1969 and the other aircraft was used on PSA's extensive training

The Boeing 737-200 proved an ideal stablemate for PSA's larger 727s, operating on less busy flights on the intra-California services. Jenny Gradidge

and conversion programmes that it had operated for a number of airlines and corporate customers.

California Competition

Others started to look to emulate PSA's success in providing low-cost intra-state air service in California. In December 1965, a group of five Californian businessmen met in Corona del Mar, in Orange County, southeast of Los Angeles. William Myers, Alan H. Kenison, Mark T. Gates Jr, William L. Pereira Jr and Lud Renick met to discuss forming a new airline to operate a scheduled service from the under-used Orange County Airport, near Santa Ana, and the San Francisco Bay area. They had commissioned surveys that indicated a huge traffic potential from the area.

With a population of well over a million, Orange County was one of the fastest growing metropolitan areas in the USA at the time. A trip by scheduled airline from the Orange County area would have required a long car journey to Los Angeles

Western's Boeing 737-200s were used to link smaller cities on a network stretching from southern California to the Great Lakes and midwestern Canada. Jenny Gradidge

International or Burbank Airports. This journey, even by highway, could be a tiring one, especially in the Los Angeles rush hour. As well as saving the Orange County residents the trials of a drive across Los Angeles, the major tourist attraction of Disneyland was nearby and could be relied on to attract traffic to the new services.

The young businessmen were joined in January 1966 by a number of seasoned airline executives, including J. Kenneth Hull, formerly president of Lockheed Aircraft International, and Thomas Wolfe, ex-Vice President of Sales for Western Airlines. They became President and Chairman respectively, of the new carrier, by now formally named Air California. Incorporated on 12 April, Air California was granted its first route certificate by the California Public Utilities Commission. The certificate covered a minimum of five daily flights from Orange County to San Francisco.

Turbo-prop to Jet

Services began on 16 January 1967, with two ex-Qantas Lockheed Electra turbo-props painted up in an eye-catching yellow, black and red livery. Aiming its sales drives firmly at the residents of Orange County, one gimmick involved driving a flat-bed truck, complete with Air California stewardesses, to Los Angeles Airport. On the side of the truck was a banner reading, 'If you came here from Orange County... *You could have been in San Francisco by now!*', emphasizing the time-saving of using their local airport.

Early results were very encouraging and the first of a pair of short-body DC-9-14 jets entered service on the original route on 1 April. The introduction of jets had been achieved only after a number of objections, on the grounds of noise nuisance, had been overcome. Orange County–San Francisco flights now operated seven times a day. Services opened to San Jose and Oakland on 23 September and two more Electras joined the busy fleet. The number of passengers carried in Air California's first year – 293,604 – encouraged expansion and investment to the point that a new maintenance base was opened at San Francisco International Airport in early 1968.

Growing Pains

Air California's rapidly increasing passenger boardings showed no sign of slowing down. However, the still comparatively new airline's resources were insufficient to finance the badly-needed additions to the fleet. In mid-1968 Air California announced a $1 million loss on an earned revenue of $6,650,000. Finally, Air California found a solution to the twin problems of the need for larger aircraft and financial aid in the form of the GATX/Boothe Aircraft Corporation. Specializing in leasing out aircraft, GATX/Boothe had taken over a number of cancelled 737 delivery positions, including the Pacific Air Lines places. Built as Series 200s, the aircraft were intended for leasing out on both short and long-term contracts to airlines. Wien Consolidated had taken advantage of their aircraft's early availability by leasing in GATX/Boothe 737s to inaugurate their jet services in Alaska, in May/June 1968, whilst waiting for their own delayed aircraft deliveries.

At the end of the Wien contract, GATX/Boothe negotiated a new deal with Air California, buying the four Electras and two DC-9s and replacing them with the 737-200s on lease contracts. The 737s performance was regarded as highly compatible with the noise-sensitive operating requirements at Orange County Airport. The improved rate of climb greatly assisted noise abatement procedures.

The 115-passenger 737s premiered, in October 1968, on the Orange County–San Francisco route and also opened new

The DC-9 was Air California's first choice of pure-jet equipment, supplementing the Electras. Aviation Hobby Shop

services from Hollywood/Burbank and Ontario to the Bay Area. The airline carried a total of 650,000 passengers during 1968 and, early in 1969, celebrated carrying its millionth passenger on 27 February. Yet further expansion included Palm Springs–Bay Area flights and 1969 also saw Air California offering first-class 'Fiesta Service' on its 737s, the first regional carrier to operate a two-class service.

Canadian Debut

Further north, as Western's 737s made early appearances on their cross-border routes into Canada, the aircraft's Canadian customers were poised to join the club as well. Early orders had been placed by Nordair and Pacific Western, but the production delays meant that they would not take delivery until late 1968/early 1969. Canadian Pacific Airlines, that had ordered their first five 737s in 1966, took delivery of their first Series 200 in October 1968. The aircraft was the first to be delivered displaying the airline's new image as CP Air, in a bright orange, red and silver livery.

The CP Air 737s, like many of those of many new 737 operators, were being used to replace outdated equipment on regional and local services, in their case, mostly

(*Above*) The Boeing 737-200s introduced Canadian Pacific's bright new image as CP Air. Jenny Gradidge

(*Below*) GATX/Boothe supplied 737-200s to Air California in a leasing deal as part of a major re-equipment programme. Aviation Hobby Shop

within Canada. Canadian Pacific had grown steadily since its formation in 1942, from a collection of merged local carriers into a major domestic operator within Canada. Long-range expansion saw the company eventually operating intercontinental services to Asia, Australia, Europe and South America from its Vancouver base. Douglas DC-6Bs, originally operated on the long-haul routes, were still flying on regional services within western Canada after being displaced from international and trans-Continental services several years before, initially by Bristol Britannia turbo-props and, later, by DC-8 jets.

The 737 entered scheduled service with CP Air with a Vancouver BC–Whitehorse, Yukon Flight, on 20 November 1968. Further 737 services were soon opened, taking over from the DC-6Bs on flights to Whitehorse, Terrace and Prince Rupert. When the final two 737s of the initial order were delivered in March 1969, the last of the DC-6Bs were sold off. This left CP Air an all-jet airline, except for a single DC-3, operated on local and charter flights. The 737s operated their first trans-Continental domestic revenue flight for CP Air on 1 April 1969. Nordair had been the next Canadian airline to place the 737 in service, on an Arctic route, with a Montreal–Frobisher Bay service on 3 December 1968.

The 200 Series Finally Reaches Europe

Britannia Airways were eagerly awaiting their 737s and had hoped to have them in service in time for the peak of the 1968 summer tourist season. However, the troublesome production delays at Boeing had ruled this out. Already suffering a slight capacity shortage following the tragic loss of one of their Bristol Britannia turbo-props in a fatal crash at Ljubljana, Yugoslavia, the year before, Britannia relied on the scheduled arrival of the new aircraft to fulfil its 1968 contracts. Instead, a pair of additional Britannias had to be leased in from rival carriers for most of the 1968 season. Like those in their own fleet, these were ex-BOAC aircraft. One came from Laker Airways, one from BKS Air Transport.

The first Britannia Airways 737, and Europe's first Series 200, G-AVRL finally arrived at the airline's Luton Airport base on 8 July 1968. This was actually a few days early, according to the terms of a new renegotiated contract with Boeing that took account of the production delays. Undeterred, Britannia Airway's initial order for three aircraft had already been increased to five. Although the delays had disrupted plans for the 1968 season's jet operations, deliveries for the next year were expected to be on time.

A great deal of British equipment was incorporated on to the Britannia 737s, including Marconi ADF, a Cossor transponder, as well as the galley fittings and equipment. To facilitate cabin service on busy charter flights, the galley facilities were accommodated in the forward section of the cabin, with passenger washrooms concentrated at the rear. The initial passenger capacity of 117 on Britannia Airway's 737s exactly matched that of their Britannia 102s, which assisted in smoothing the transition from turbo-prop to jet operation. An increase in the 737-200's passenger capacity, up to 124 on high-density charter services, was planned for later introduction and the new seats and their layout had already received FAA approval.

Into Charter Service

The first five Britannia crews to be assigned to the 737 received their conversion training with Boeing in Seattle. The training was completed back in the UK by four Boeing pilots on loan to Britannia. The next six crews, required when the second aircraft entered service, were to be checked out by Seattle-trained instructors. After delivery, the second 737, G-AVRM, spent much of its time at Shannon on training duties.

G-AVRL was to be the first Boeing 737-200 to be operated in Europe, and the first 737 to be flown by an all-charter carrier. Via author

G-AVRL received its UK Certificate of Airworthiness on 10 July, two days after delivery. On 19 July a proving flight was operated by G-AVRL from Luton to Palma, Majorca, and on the 22nd it entered commercial service with an IT charter from Luton to the Yugoslav resort of Dubrovnik. G-AVRM carried its first revenue load of holidaymakers on 16 August with a Luton–Venice IT charter.

Although too late to make much of an impact on the 1968 summer season, Britannia were still well impressed with their new aircraft. All five of the initial 737 orders were in use in time for the 1969 season and plans were in hand to acquire more of the Boeing jets. The 737s operated on most of the growing IT network, not only from Luton, serving London, but also from regional points such as Manchester, Glasgow, Birmingham and Newcastle. The increase in ITs originating at regional points continued to grow to the point that a number of the more important cities gained year-round holiday charter service for the first time in the winter of 1968/69.

It was calculated that, even with the original 117-seat layout, each of the airline's 737s was as productive as 2½ Bristol Britannias. A part of the Britannia turboprops were taken out of service at the end of 1969, although the older type was to continue to contribute to Britannia Airways' charter operations, alongside the 737s, until the end of 1970.

Early Days with Lufthansa

While Britannia was introducing their Series 200s to the holidaymakers of Britain, Lufthansa continued to deploy their Series 100s on more and more routes on their domestic and European network. Even with their previous experience in operating bigger Boeing jets, Lufthansa was very impressed with the comparatively trouble-free introduction into service of the 737.

There had been no major engine problems. At the very beginning of 737 operations there had been a starter valve problem when sand from treated runways was ingested. A filter screen had simply not been up to its job and the problem was fixed using a new screen with a finer mesh, as suggested by Boeing. Unscheduled engine removals in the first nine months of operation amounted to only three examples, two caused by reports of vibration and one by high oil consumption. There had been no in-flight engine shutdowns and no fire warnings, even false ones.

The auxiliary power unit (APU) gave some trouble at first. Thermostat difficulties had led to crews having trouble getting some systems on line without the APU shutting down. New acceleration control thermostats were designed and did much better. A certain amount of nosewheel corrosion was noted and put down to problems with the alloy used and there were some problems with the ram air inlet system that was solved by re-rigging.

The self-contained airstairs gave Lufthansa the most trouble. Although the rear steps, mounted in the downward opening door, were the most complicated design of the two, these gave little trouble. It was the simpler, forward steps that folded into a small compartment under the passenger door, that caused some delays. The improvement in the electrical circuit reduced the problem. As stowage of the forward airstairs was one of the last systems operated prior to departure, it was more likely to cause a delay than any other problem that may be fixed before departure time. Thus the blame on the airstairs for most delays was made to look worse than it was in delay statistics.

The rear airstair arrangement was an option not taken up by many 737 customers. It allowed swift turnarounds at airports not equipped with jetties for embarking passengers and saved having to have expensive mobile step units hand. However, although used by some early operators, especially Lufthansa, Wien Consolidated and Piedmont, they were usually removed in later years and a conventional door fitted, as a weight-saving measure. A few aircraft retained their original configuration, especially the 'combi' aircraft that carried freight in the forward cabin and passengers in the rear section and could only load their passengers through the rear doors. The smaller, forward airstairs, however, were a useful option taken up, and retained, by most customers.

Britannia Airways had five 737-200s in service in 1969, with more on order. Jenny Gradidge

Early Jet Days at Piedmont

Being an early customer, Piedmont Airlines also played its part in ironing out the wrinkles as the 737 proved itself in daily service. Eventually retiring as a District Sales and Marketing Manager for US Airways, Joe Grant was originally a Utility Agent with Piedmont, hired in 1966, after his honourable discharge from the USAF, with whom he had been a mechanic in Japan and Vietnam.

Joe's first base was the airport for Staunton/Harrisonburg, a small station serving the Shenandoah Valley in Virginia that one customer described to him as reminding her 'of Africa'.

> A small station is tough to work as you must know everything about running it. For instance, the ticket counter and customer service, reservations (all done locally in those days, no central reservations office), weight and balance of aircraft, weather, teletype, ramp service, loading and unloading, air freight, air express, some maintenance and even some air traffic control. Like I said, a lot to learn.

As already mentioned, Piedmont had leased a pair of 727s to cover the late delivery of the 737s. Originally intended for United, they still had the larger airline's comfortable 3-2, five-abreast configuration. Despite losing the first aircraft in the Asheville mid-air collision, the 727s proved a success with Piedmont and boded well for the smaller, much more economic, 737 on their network.

In 1968 Joe Grant visited Renton.

> I boarded Piedmont's first 737, N734N, while it was still being built. It had a plywood floor and the cockpit was protected from dust by being enclosed in a huge plastic bag! Piedmont was one of the few airlines to have the rear boarding airstairs installed. Several years later they were removed because they were heavy to fly around, plus they were expensive to fix if broken and they also got in the way of 'new' modern day catering equipment. The first Piedmont 737s were also fitted with the 3-2 seating configuration. It felt like first class. Later the seating was changed to 3-3, all coach class.
>
> The original engines of the 737 had rather non-efficient thrust reversers. These were replaced by huge 'clam-shell' reversers that worked 'almost too good' compared to the old ones. Captains said, referring to the old style reversers, that trying to stop with them on a wet runway was as slippery as putting your feet in a pie! The aircraft always wanted to hydroplane in those conditions.

Ron Carter was a mechanic with Piedmont when both the 727s and 737s went into service:

> The arrival of the 727s required a lot of training for the pilots, mechanics and flight attendants. When the 727s were leased in we had Martin 404s, YS-11s and Fairchild FH227s. Boeing was very helpful in setting up our training needs. At this time Piedmont had a very well trained mechanic group but we were not used to such complex aircraft and lacked training in the electrical systems. Boeing held additional classes in aircraft electrical for us and it paid great dividends later. The 737 was less complex than the 727, so the transition was easy.
>
> Initial in-service problems with the 737 were thrust reversers and hydraulic line failure, as well as a buffeting problem. These were soon corrected, with Boeing installing a new type of thrust reverser and issuing numerous service bulletins to correct the hydraulic line failure. Vortex generators were installed to correct the buffeting. We also had to analyse the engine oil and change it at frequent intervals. After about a year this was changed so the oil was never changed except at overhaul.
>
> The P&W JT8D engine had initial problems but these were soon corrected. At this time, the engine smoked and it was desirable to have this eliminated. The burner can modification solved this problem – but started two others! One was off-idle stall of the engine and the other was that the fumes were more toxic than when the engine smoked. Both these problems were corrected in about two years. The auxiliary power unit was a constant source of troubles, but we had good technical support and eventually solved some of the problems. Our climate is very hot and humid in the summer, but the cooling system handled it with ease. The aircraft was very reliable, but needed a few years to correct a lot of problems. Piedmont could not have picked a better aircraft than the 737 to enter the jet age, or a better company to guide us than Boeing.

Piedmont's introduction of the 737 had benefited from the airline's earlier use of leased 727s, and the valuable operational support of Boeing. Jenny Gradidge

INTO SERVICE

The 'Quick Change' Artists

Lufthansa took delivery on 17 December 1968 of the first order for six 737-200QC 'Quick Change' aircraft. Options had also been taken out on two more. The airline's first long-fuselage 737s were equipped with large cargo doors in the upper forward fuselage and strengthened cabin floors, the convertible aircraft being intended for passenger use in the daytime and for conversion to freight services at night. The switch from passenger to cargo configuration was designed to take less than half an hour. Lufthansa was already operating a fleet of convertible 727s on similar services, alongside their all-passenger 727-100s and -200s.

The convertible 'combi-version' of the 737 was first placed into service in Alaska, by Wien Consolidated in November 1968.

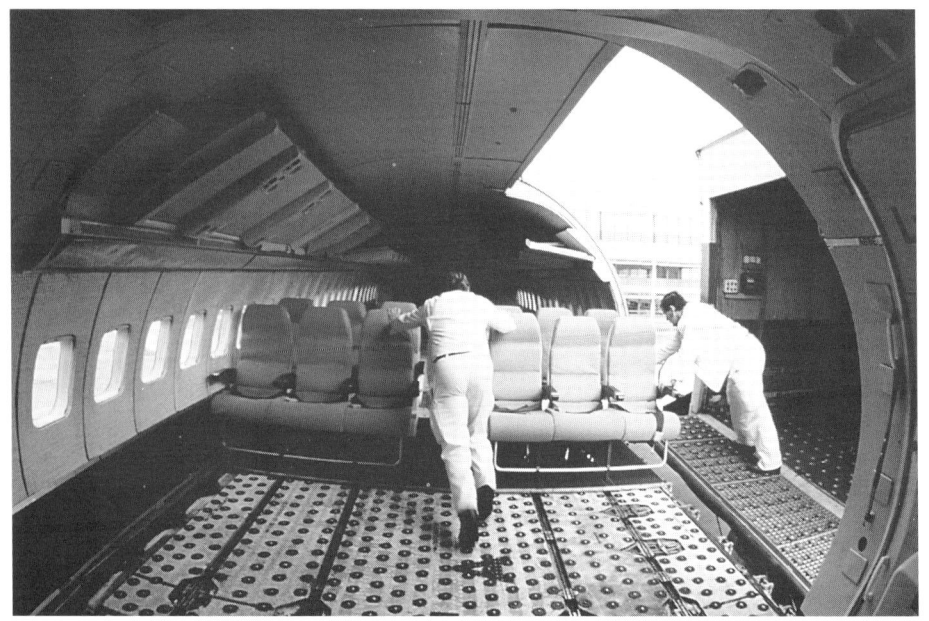

(*Above*) **The Boeing 737-200QC was able to operate both passenger and cargo schedules on Lufthansa's European network.** Lufthansa

Interior configuration on the 'QC' 737 could be swiftly modified by seat units on tracks, loaded through the large forward cargo door. Lufthansa

In all-cargo configuration, the 737 could carry up to seven standard pallets or containers. The units were loaded slightly off-centre, to the right, allowing a passageway to the left. With only six pallets, eleven passengers could be carried, and with only two pallets installed, up to eighty-one passengers could be accommodated in the rear section.

As well as serving the more populated points among the 170 scattered communities served by the airline in Alaska and the Canadian Yukon, the 737's joint passenger and cargo-carrying capabilities were put to good use on contract work for the Trans-Alaska Pipeline System, from Anchorage. Western's 737s were also soon reaching

Alaska and operating on busier local and regional routes taken over in the merger with Pacific Northern Airlines, of Fairbanks.

Similar rugged work was to be shortly undertaken by convertible 737s placed into service by Nordair, Pacific Western Airlines and Transair, all serving remote towns and outposts in northern Canada. The smaller Canadian operators' 737s, and those of Wien Consolidated, were also fitted for gravel runway operations. As well as low-pressure tyres, deflectors were attached to the undercarriage to shield the fuselage from stones being kicked up on landing. Vortex generators were also attached to the front of the engine nacelles, to blow debris away from the intakes and protect them from gravel damage. However, these aircraft were also just as likely to spend their weekends flying tourists from major Canadian cities, escaping from the northern winters to the sun of Florida, the Caribbean, or even Mexico.

Further South

The New Zealand National Airways Corporation (NZNAC), became the operator of three 737-200s on 14 October 1968. Ordered to replace Viscounts on trunk-scheduled services within New Zealand, the 737s would join a fleet of Fokker F.27s that had begun to replace DC-3s on local flights from 1960. The first of the trio had been delivered to Wellington, after a long island-hopping trek from Seattle, on 18 September and the introduction of the jet fleet within a month was a laudable achievement for the carrier.

NZNAC was the nationally owned domestic airline of New Zealand, international services to Australia and trans-Pacific flights being the preserve of Air New Zealand with their fleet of long-haul DC-8s and Electra turbo-props. Twenty-five destinations, served by 4,000 miles of routes, comprised NZNAC's network within and between the North and South Islands of the country.

New Zealand's link to Britain, via its membership of the Commonwealth, had led to high hopes in the UK of a possible order from NZNAC for the BAC One-Eleven jet. One of BAC's development aircraft had visited New Zealand during a world sales tour in 1966, operating demonstration flights for NZNAC between Dunedin, Wellington, Auckland and Whenupai before continuing the tour onwards to Australia. Unfortunately for BAC, it had been felt that inappropriate financial and political pressure had been applied to sway New Zealand towards ordering the One-Eleven and, as a result, the British aircraft was rejected as a candidate for NZNAC's Viscount replacement.

The One-Eleven fared little better in Australia, with only a pair of aircraft sold to Australia's air force for VIP transport work. Australia's largest domestic airlines, the privately owned Ansett-ANA and government-sponsored Trans Australia Airlines, both chose the Boeing 727 and Douglas DC-9 for their short-haul jet operations.

Nordair and Transair operated their 737s into more remote regions, as well as busy inter-city services and vacation flights to sunnier climes.
Via author/Aviation Hobby Shop

New Northern Highlights

The 737 seemed to be getting a reputation as a cold weather native, especially when, on the European side of the Arctic Circle, Braathens took delivery of their first two 737s in December 1968 and January 1969. Within a matter of weeks, Braathens had also taken delivery of their first Fokker F.28 twin jet, intended for use on routes where the 737 was considered too large. The F.28 also possessed exceptional short- and rough-field capabilities, making it a worthy successor to the F.27 turbo-prop that it was intended to replace.

The arrival of the 737 did not see the immediate demise of the seven Braathens DC-6Bs that it was intended to replace. The first Braathens DC-6B had entered service in 1961 and the classic piston-engined airliner was to remain a feature of the Norwegian airline's scheduled and charter operations for over ten years.

One service on which the DC-6B had heavily featured was a regular charter from Tromso to Spitzbergen, in the Arctic. Supporting a joint Norwegian/Russian coalmining operation by Store Norske Spitzbergen Kullkompani, landings were at first made on the sea ice, then a gravel strip. Although the DC-6Bs shared the service with F.27s and, later, the F.28s, only the 737 could match the DC-6Bs' load-carrying on the unique service. Both passengers and cargo were carried on the flight, with the 737s freight-carrying capacity being put to especially good use. A tarmac strip was later laid in the mid-1970s, but the special weather conditions and unique operational restrictions still meant that an aircraft of the 737's outstanding capabilities was required.

Irish Deliveries

Aer Lingus, the national carrier of Eire, the Irish Republic, was close on the heels of Braathens in inaugurating its 737 services. The airline's first aircraft, EI-ASA, 'St Jarlath' arrived at Dublin on 2 April 1969, closely followed by two others. The trio began revenue services later that month, flying to London and Paris. Three more 737s, including two convertible 'QCs' were delivered by the end of 1969. The arrival of yet three more in early 1970 saw Aer Lingus able to offer all-jet flights on their European routes, and the withdrawal of their last Vickers Viscount turbo-props. The 737s operated alongside the established short-

Braathens' Boeing 737-200s operated as far north as the Arctic Circle and as far south as Mediterranean resorts. Steve Bunting

New Zealand National Airways' 737s brought jet comfort to their domestic routes. Jenny Gradidge

haul jet fleet of four BAC One-Elevens and were also supplemented by larger 707s when loads demanded it.

A 737 simulator was added to Boeing 720 and BAC One-Eleven examples already in service at the airline's Dublin head office. With more and more 737 operators starting to come on line, some of them with comparatively small fleets, Aer Lingus was increasingly leasing out unused training hours on its simulator. This was the beginning of a whole new source of income for the airline, with third-party maintenance and even short-term crew and aircraft leasing gaining in importance over the next few years.

The 'QC' aircraft were not only utilized on night-time cargo services. 'Combi' passenger/cargo flights operated on some scheduled services to regional points in the UK. The Dublin–Bristol–Cardiff–Dublin route was one such schedule, with the extra freight sales capacity supplementing lower passenger loads at certain times of the day. All-cargo services also included a number of bloodstock charters, flying racehorses from the Irish studs to race meetings and sales around the UK and Continental Europe.

A large programme of IT services from Dublin and other Irish cities kept the 737 and One-Eleven fleets busy around the clock over summer weekends, when there was less demand on the business traffic-based scheduled routes. Aer Lingus had operated substantial numbers of both charter and scheduled flights to Tarbes, transporting pilgrims to the Catholic shrine at Lourdes, in southern France, for many years and the 737s were soon regularly assigned to these services. During the busier months, daily utilization of up to 18 hours a day was getting to be the norm.

The Dutch Twin-Jet Option

The long-established aircraft manufacturer, Fokker, based in the Netherlands, had a very different concept for its offering in the short-haul twin-jet market. Deliberately aiming at a small capacity replacement for its F.27 Friendship, the Fokker jet design, when it did finally emerge, was originally configured for up to sixty-five passengers, about half that of the Boeing 737. Fokker also declared from the beginning that it preferred steady sales over a long-term period, rather than a greater number of orders over a shorter production life.

Powered by two Rolls Royce Spey engines, the F.28 received its first production order in November 1965, some three years after the project was officially announced by the company. The production of the aircraft was an early example of inter-European collaboration, with Short Bros and Harland, of Belfast, producing the outer wings and undercarriages and Germany's MBB and VFW manufacturing the centre and rear fuselage sections, tail units and engine nacelles.

The first order was placed by the West German charter airline, LTU. However, Braathens was the first carrier to place the aircraft into revenue service, on 28 March 1969. Orders followed from operators in Australia, Argentina, Columbia, Spain and the Netherlands, from operators as diverse as Iberia, Spain's national carrier, the Argentine government and Aviaction, a small start-up charter operator in West Germany. All had a variety of uses for the versatile Fokker jet's high performance, especially from short or rough runways. Larger and more powerful versions of the F.28 were offered later and the type became popular as an economic mainline and feeder airliner, as well as its 'outback' perfor-

The Fokker F.28 'Fellowship' enjoyed a moderate success as an economic jet alternative to earlier turbo-props. Via author

mance. The F.28 series was later totally redesigned and updated as the Fokker 70 and 100 types, with new engines and updated flight-deck systems and equipment. The new types remained in production until Fokker succumbed to economic pressures and was forced to cease all manufacturing operations in the late 1990s.

The Aer Lingus 737s were originally ordered specifically for the busy Dublin–London route and were to be seen at London/Heathrow for many years. Malcolm L. Hill

The Series 200 Carries On

Once the outstanding orders for the Series 100 had been delivered to Avianca and Malaysia-Singapore Airlines in 1969, the Series 200 was the sole offering from the 737 stable. Although various combinations of passenger/cargo configurations and rough-field-equipped versions were available, there was only the one basic 737 to hand.

As well as the aerodynamic improvements already made to reduce drag, and the option of the later, more powerful, versions of the JT8D engine, from the 280th aircraft much more substantial improvements were introduced to the production standard Series 200 aircraft. The extra changes included more aerodynamic refinements, especially concentrated on the wing design, including a thickening of the engine strut and a minor repositioning of the slats.

Improvements in short-field take-off and landing characteristics had been brought about by refining the flaps system and the installation of an automatic braking system.

There was an increase in the droop of two slat sections, the extension of the Kreuger flaps inboard, sealing the gap between spoilers and flaps and smoothing the leading edge that was exposed behind the flaps when deployed. One result of the refinements incorporated in the 'Advanced' 737 was an increase in range to 2,370 miles. All Nippon Airways, the Japanese domestic carrier, placed the first 'Advanced' 737-200 in service in June 1971.

Significant as the improvements were, although kits were made available to customers for converting their earlier aircraft to the new 'Advanced' standard, none were sold. Instead, the operators shunned the extra expense and continued to operate the unmodified aircraft under their original performance criteria, ordering new 'Advanced' aircraft in any repeat or new orders.

A Day-to-Day Success

The 737 in 1968 and 1969 established itself in service with several airlines around the world, operating a staggering variety of operational scenarios. For the most part, the airlines and their pilots were pleased with the aircraft. One pilot commented that it was: 'A great aeroplane. It just goes and goes!'

Malaysia-Singapore Airlines was one of the few customers for the smaller 737-100. Aviation Hobby Shop

(*Below*) **United's 737-200s were soon scheduled on busy inter-city routes throughout the airline's network, linking smaller airports to major cities around the USA.** Aviation Hobby Shop

CHAPTER FIVE

Improving the Breed

Worldwide Distribution

While Boeing was developing the 'Advanced' version, the original 737 models were continuing to spread their wings over an increasingly wide range. New operators were as scattered as South African Airlines, Aloha Airlines, Frontier Airlines and All Nippon Airways. Many of the new the Aloha One-Elevens had been popular with passengers and crews alike. However, weight limitations had meant that Aloha had been forced to operate under severe restrictions from some of the smaller airports, with usable traffic loads making the One-Eleven services less economic. The 737s, with their better runway performance, were acquired to counteract these with the Denver, Colorado-based airline since 1966. Frontier had a classic US regional carrier history, its antecedents having begun operations shortly after the Second World War, with fleets of ex-military DC-3s. The first of three small airlines whose merger resulted in the formation of Frontier, Monarch Airlines, inaugurated scheduled services over the Denver–Durango route

South African Airways was to become a long-term 737 customer. Seen in a later livery, 737-200 ZS-SIJ displays its Afrikaans titling on its starboard side. MAP

737 customers had operated jets on their short-haul networks before. The 737s were intended either as replacement for earlier jets, such as Aloha's One-Elevens, or to supplement larger 727s on shorter or less-travelled routes into smaller airports, as was the case with SAA and ANA.

Aloha had been operating a fleet of three BAC One-Elevens on their inter-island Hawaiian network since April 1966. Introduced to compete against DC-9s of their arch rival Hawaiian Airlines, restrictions. Although the One-Elevens were disposed of as soon as the 737s entered service, Aloha continued to operate a small fleet of Vickers Viscounts on local and supplementary flights.

Rocky Mountain Boeings

Frontier Airlines actually ordered their first 737s as replacements for their fleet of Boeing 727-100s, five of which had been in use with a single DC-3 on 27 November 1946. The next spring, another DC-3-equipped airline, Challenger Airlines, based at Salt Lake City, operated its first scheduled services to Denver via several small cities in Southern Wyoming. Arizona Airways began its DC-3 schedules at the same time, flying from Phoenix to cities in the Grand Canyon area.

All three airlines struggled, although they also managed some limited expansion to their small route networks. By 1949,

Frontier's first equipment comprised a fleet of tried and trusted DC-3s inherited from the three local carriers that merged to form the new airline. Aviation Hobby Shop

Challenger had reached Billings, Montana and Arizona flew as far south as El Paso. With Monarch's network neatly sandwiched in the middle it soon became clear to all three that a merger would create a more viable carrier. Approval for the merger was granted by the Civil Aeronautics Board in 1950 and the new company was named Frontier Airlines, serving routes that stretched from Montana to Mexico via seven states in the Rocky Mountain and Southwest regions. Operations began under the new name on 1 June 1950.

A period of steady growth followed, Frontier utilizing a fleet of trusty DC-3s throughout the network. Although stretching over a large territory, the airline still served a region where populations could be sparse, with few big cities. However, growth in exploration for oil, natural gas, uranium, plus reclamation dam projects and tourism to National Parks in the area provided a desperate need for transportation where little other public transport existed and road conditions could be difficult. Growing use of the airline was made by businessmen, construction firms, the military and vacationers.

In late 1958, Frontier's hard work was rewarded with the award of routes to no less than twenty-four new cities in Nebraska, Missouri, Wyoming, Colorado and North and South Dakota. The next year, four more cities were added in Montana.

New Management, New Equipment

The expanded network called for more modern aircraft and the first of what was to grow into a large fleet of second-hand Convair 340s entered service on busier routes in the summer of 1959. The 44-passenger Convairs brought great improvements in passenger comfort over the DC-3s. They were pressurized, which allowed the aircraft to operate at altitudes above most of the rough weather, especially important on the Rocky Mountain services. Their increased cargo and passenger capacity was useful and attracted further revenue where the DC-3s had struggled to accommodate available traffic.

A new management team took over Frontier in 1962, headed by Lewis W. Dymond. Improved schedules, new 'standby' and generous family fares were introduced, resulting in a 26 per cent growth in passenger boardings for the last six months of 1962. Dymond also signed contracts for the conversion of the CV-340 fleet to turbo-prop power, the first of the regional airlines to do so. The re-engined Convairs, redesignated CV-580s when fitted with the Allison 501 prop-jets, were placed into service on 1 June 1964. The 'new' CV-580s could operate 100mph faster than the CV-340s. The extra power provided by the Allisons was greatly appreciated at the small airports served by Frontier, many of which were at rarefied altitudes that had restricted the piston-engined aircraft's operations.

1963 and 1964 boardings had continued to increase and new non-stop authority was granted between several of the larger cities on Frontier's network. This prompted Dymond to place an order for the five Boeing 727-100s, at a cost of $55 million. The first two of the 99-passenger jets were introduced on busier routes from Denver and Salt Lake City in 1966. By the time the 727s were in service, eighteen Convairs had been converted to 580 standard. Non-stop flights were inaugurated between Denver and St Louis by the 727s, with the CV-580s flying new Denver–Kansas City–St Louis services, on 13 June 1967. Trans World Airlines took a very dim view of Frontier's entry into its traditional markets at St Louis and Kansas City and trebled its own competing jet services to Denver.

Other new routes awarded to Frontier at the time were non-stop Denver–Las Vegas

IMPROVING THE BREED

The Convair CV-340s in Frontier's fleet were converted to turbo-prop power to improve performance. The increased speed and smoother ride of the redesignated CV-580s was much appreciated by their passengers. Crews appreciated the extra available power at high-altitude Rocky Mountain airports with short runways. Aviation Hobby Shop

(*Below*) The 727-100s were to be ousted by the 737s from 1969. Via author

services and the extension of routes from Wichita and Topeka to Chicago. The airline began to apply for several more route extensions, including services to Seattle, Houston, New York and Washington, citing their use of 727s which allowed Frontier to operate non-stop between most of the cities concerned. Frontier also claimed that the addition of the extra services to its network would allow the airline to forego its need for its $7 million annual subsidy. However, the CAB refused most of the more ambitious requests, such as non-stop California–New York flights, claiming that 'route strengthening does have its limits'!

The Central Airlines Merger

On 1 October 1967 Frontier took over Fort Worth, Texas-based Central Airlines. Central had been founded in 1944, but did not begin scheduled service until September 1949, using a fleet of small Beech Bonanzas on routes from Fort Worth to Dallas and points in Oklahoma State. DC-3s had entered service in late 1950, with CV-240s following in the early 1960s when Central took over a number of local routes from American Airlines and Eastern Airlines. Central had also opted for turbo-prop conversion of their Convairs, although they chose to fit British Rolls Royce Darts. As such, their 'new' Convairs were designated CV-600s and marketed on Central Airlines services as 'Dart 600s'.

Thus, when Frontier merged with Central, two different versions of Convair turbo-prop were in use on the network. The resulting fleet consisted of five Boeing 727-100s, twenty-two CV-580s and eleven CV-600s, as well as no less than seventeen surviving DC-3s that were still in use with both carriers at the time of the merger. The DC-3s were soon to be disposed of as more jets allowed the transfer of Convairs to their routes. Within a couple of years, the CV-600s were replaced by more CV-580s, to standardize the turbo-prop fleet on one type.

Changes at the Top

Nineteen sixty-eight saw the arrival of the larger Boeing 727-200s and the award of new routes into Memphis from Little Rock. Thus, Memphis became the 116th city and Tennessee the 16th state to be served by Frontier. In terms of the number of cities served, Frontier was now the second largest air carrier in the USA.

The following year Lewis W. Dymond resigned from Frontier and was replaced by E. Paul Burke as President and Board Chairman. One of the new management's first decisions was to replace the original Boeing

727-100s with more economic Boeing 737-200s. The first aircraft was delivered to Frontier that summer and by the end of 1969, ten 737s were in use. The smaller, more flexible, 737 was able to operate from smaller airports than the 727-100s had and introduced jet service to more cities on the Frontier Airlines network.

The 737 was also more economic on some of the non-stop flights between larger cities and proved useful on new routes awarded in 1969, such as Kansas City–Dallas and Salt Lake City–Denver–Dallas, operating alongside the Boeing 727-200s when loads might not justify the use of the bigger aircraft. In total contrast, in 1970, a small fleet of 19-passenger de Havilland Canada Twin Otters was introduced on local flights in northern Montana and North Dakota.

Financial Problems

Generally, 1970 had been a bad year for the airlines, with a sharp slow-down in traffic growth, brought about by inflation and excessive competition. However, Frontier fared slightly better than some carriers, although it was unable to produce a profit that year. New route awards were still finding their way to the airline, with jet service inaugurated between Omaha, Chicago, Denver and Phoenix, amongst others.

The steadily increasing fleet of Boeing 737s was useful on the new routes, being better able to operate profitably with the lower loads encountered whilst traffic was built up. The four main elements of the Frontier fleet, the Twin Otters, the CV-580s, the 737s and the 727-200s provided a wide range of capacity and performance well suited to the airline's varied network.

However, during 1971/72, following another management change, increasing financial problems led to the disposal of the 727-200s to Braniff Airways. Other internal changes were made and the service standards were overhauled in an effort to reverse the carrier's decline. The measures were highly successful and Frontier Airlines carried 13 per cent more passengers in 1972. The revenue loads increased again in 1973 and the CAB statistics showed that Frontier Airlines received fewer passenger complaints than any other regional carrier. With the departure of the 727s, the versatile Boeing 737 fleet had become Frontier's front-line jet equipment. Its ability to operate both local, regional and trunk line was a major factor in Frontier's being able to survive a difficult time in the industry.

Repeat Business

Repeat orders saw original 737 customers such as United, Lufthansa, Piedmont, Britannia, Aer Lingus and Braathens fleets increasing on a yearly basis as the airlines came to rely on the 737 on more of their services. Piedmont retired the last of their piston-engined Martin 404s in 1970, operating to their network of seventy-eight cities with a fleet of 737 jets, supplemented by FH-227B and YS-11A turbo-props. They carried 2,234,999 passengers in 1969. Services had been introduced into Chicago that year and more new services were opened to Charleston, South Carolina. By 1972 Piedmont was able to report record earnings and a net profit of $3,323,317 in its 25th year of operation.

Britannia and Braathens, in particular, appreciated the increased range and improved short runway performance offered by the later, 'Advanced' 737-200 models. As well as being able to offer non-stop services to further ranging points, travel companies were able to develop new resorts and offer their customers increased choice to points only served by basic airport facilities.

Cargo operations also featured more heavily in the charter carrier's 737 services. The ability to convert the 737 to all-cargo, or even 'combi', configuration allowed increased utilization during traditionally slack times when the aircraft might otherwise be idle. Britannia introduced its first convertible aircraft, G-AXNA, into service in early 1970 and the aircraft was kept especially busy with bloodstock charters between the UK, Eire and France. Britannia 737s were also used to carry the British Show Jumping Team from Luton to Kiev.

As their last turbo-prop Bristol Britannias were withdrawn, the Britannia Airways 737s began to operate much longer-ranging

Frontier's 737s filled a vital niche between the larger 727-200s and the turbo-prop fleet of CV-580s. Jenny Gradidge

passenger flights, albeit with necessary refuelling stops, including services from Luton to both North America and the Far East. Bangkok, Colombo, Hong Kong and Kuala Lumpur were all served on affinity group charters from the UK, although fuelling stops had to be made en route, usually at Zagreb, Damascus, Dubai and Karachi.

Braathens also exploited the convertible 737s, taking delivery of cargo-door-equipped 'Advanced' examples in 1971. When not operating passenger flights on the Norwegian airline's scheduled and charter network, the Braathens convertible 737s flew cargoes throughout the world. A regular operation was the airlift of oil-drilling equipment and personnel, from Norway to

IMPROVING THE BREED

(*Top*) Piedmont based a considerable expansion programme around the 737-200 as more were delivered to supplement the original aircraft. Aviation Hobby Shop
(*Middle*) Bolder, updated, colours were seen on United's '737 Friend Ships' from 1972. Jenny Gradidge
(*Bottom*) The flexibility of convertible 737s, such as G-AXNA, allowed Britannia Airways to increase utilization in the quieter winter months when passenger charter work traditionally decreased. Via author

The large cargo door of the convertible 737 allowed the easy loading of awkward and outsize loads, such as this dismantled helicopter being transported from London/Gatwick to Greenland by Braathens. Ivar Hakonsen

Air Algérie was an early client for Aer Lingus's leasing out of spare 737 capacity. EI-ASB is seen in Air Algérie's Caravelle-era livery. Aviation Hobby Shop

IMPROVING THE BREED

Sporting Aer Lingus's later tail livery, EI-BDY wears Eastern Provincial Airlines' red cheatline, the legacy of an off-season winter lease. Via author

West Africa. With weather in the North Sea too rough for oil exploration drilling in the European winter, operations were moved to the West African coast. As their 737 fleet increased, Braathens also posted two or three aircraft in neighbouring Sweden on a year-round basis, flying IT to Mediterranean resorts in the summer and to the Canary Islands in the winter.

Seasonal Leases

Early on, Lufthansa had leased out at least three of their Series 100s to its charter subsidiary, Condor Flugdienst. The 737s operated alongside six Boeing 727-100s, also leased from Lufthansa, on IT charters from a number of West German cities. The Condor 737s replaced the airline's last Vickers Viscount turbo-props and allowed the carrier to claim to be one of the first all-jet charter airlines in Europe.

As well as longer-term leases, like that from Lufthansa to Condor, a number of carriers managed to lease out their spare 737 capacity in their less busy seasons. Aer Lingus, which had pioneered such undertakings with their Boeing 720, 707 and BAC One-Eleven fleets in the past, was one of the first to exploit the 737 in this way. The very first winter of Aer Lingus 737 operations, 1969/70, saw EI-ASB leased to Air Algérie for three months, supplementing the North African airline's fleet of Caravelles.

Later winter contracts usually saw at least some of Aer Lingus' 737s returning regularly to the African continent and also migrating to Canada, the Caribbean and the USA on short-term seasonal leases. Those that remained in Eire continued operating on the Irish airline's scheduled services, although frequencies on some routes were much reduced in the winter months. IT charter flying was almost non-existent until the summer and these combined factors allowed the releasing of otherwise idle aircraft for lease work.

These highly profitable arrangements usually took effect between the end of December and early March, when the aircraft would return to Aer Lingus and their regular scheduled routes from Eire to Europe. Often, the 737s that had been leased out would be seen back on the Aer Lingus services still wearing at least partial liveries of the lease customer, there not having been time to completely repaint the aircraft.

737 Newcomers

Not all of Boeing's customers for the 737 were established operators. A brand new carrier started their operations with the aircraft in June 1971. The road to the inauguration of Southwest Airlines intra-state services within Texas had been a long one, but their successful struggle was to prove important to Boeing over the following decades.

It had been as early as 1966 that the idea of a low-fare, frequent-service airline serving Texas had first been mooted. At the time Rollin King was considering closing down a commuter service that he owned and operated, also called Southwest Airlines, that was losing money on scheduled services from San Antonio, Texas, to small cities such as Laredo and Eagle Pass. The tiny airline operated a collection of small eight-passenger aircraft, mostly Beech and Piper aircraft. Considering his next move, King eventually hit on the idea of a bigger commercial operation, serving Texas's biggest three commercial cities, Dallas, Houston and San Antonio.

A year later King presented a feasibility study to his lawyer, Herbert D. Kelleher. Kelleher helped King incorporate the new company, originally called Air Southwest, and dispose of the loss-making commuter carrier. Kelleher was not keen on the proposal at first, but agreed to undertake the legal work free of charge. Kelleher then started checking out similar operations, such as that of Pacific Southwest in California, and started investing in the idea, and, more importantly, persuading others to do the same.

Most of the first $100,000 raised went on the cost of preparing an application and producing a proper prospectus. An option was also taken out with American Airlines for three of their surplus Lockheed Electras, with financing from Allstate Insurance. The new company managed to attract extra financing from several important Texas concerns that bought stock in Air Southwest, raising $543,000.

unanimously, on 20 February 1968, to back Air Southwest. However, the next day the established carriers, in the shape of Braniff Airways, Trans Texas Airways and Continental Airways obtained a restraining order, prohibiting the commission from delivering the certificate. The case was referred to the Austin State District Court that summer.

The major airlines argued that they already provided adequate service between the cities concerned and that there was no room for any more competition. Air Southwest actually lost the first trial and had to resort to appealing to the Texas Supreme Court. All the $543,000 raised had been spent on the court cases and Allstate Insurance had withdrawn their financing for the Electras. However, in March 1970, the Texas Supreme Court overturned the decision of the lower court, and in December that year, the US Supreme Court refused to hear an appeal by the rival airlines.

flights, the Air Southwest board was also faced with having to refinance the airline if it was to have any chance of starting operations. Trained accountant and ex-president of a number of airlines, M. Lamar Muse was hired in January 1971 and given the task of getting the company airborne. As well as hiring an experienced management team, Muse used every skill and contact he had acquired in his long career to gather together the desperately needed funds.

Gradually, the new finance package was assembled by Muse and veteran airline executives were hired to organize the new airline. The man who had come up with the whole idea in the first place, Rollin King, became executive vice-president for operations. Kelleher continued to participate on a part-time basis as he was still working for his law firm. Although the Allstate deal for the three Electras had now lapsed, this turned out to be a blessing in disguise. Boeing was not only willing to look at an order from Air Southwest for four Boeing 737-200s, but they were prepared to finance 90 per cent of the purchase cost. These were unheard-of financial terms and it was to be the beginning of an excellent relationship between customer airline and aircraft manufacturer.

In March 1971, during the height of the legal wrangling, the airline quietly changed

Pacific Southwest's successful California operation was to provide the model for a Texas-based imitator. MAP

Legal Wranglings

As with PSA and Air California further west, as long as Air Southwest confined their operations to within the borders of their home state, they would not require federal approval from the Civil Aeronautics Board. The company would only need the go-ahead from the Texas Aeronautics Commission, with whom the application to begin commercial operations was filed on 27 November 1967. The TAC voted

Certified – but Broke!

Even now, the rival carriers were still trying to sabotage Air Southwest, attempting to dissuade underwriters from buying stock and filing spurious complaints to the CAB. Although it was now free to begin revenue

its operating name from Air Southwest to Southwest Airlines, King's original company now being defunct. Wearing titles to that effect, the first of the order for four 737s was delivered to Dallas in June 1971. The company adopted a bright eye-catching livery in orange, red and 'desert gold'. Other innovations introduced included pre-punched IMB-card packets of tickets for regular customers, monthly billing and stewardess uniforms that included hot-pants or red vinyl mini-skirts.

Underway but Still under Fire

Scheduled operations finally began on 18 June 1971. The 112-passenger 737 'Love Birds', christened to reflect Southwest's choice of home base at Dallas's Love Field, operated twelve round-trips daily between Dallas and Houston and six a day from Dallas to San Antonio. Fares were pitched as $40 round-trip, undercutting Braniff and Texas International, as Trans Texas had become in the meantime, by $14 and $16, respectively. The inaugural flights had been able to take place despite yet another eleventh hour attempt by Braniff and Texas International to enforce a restraining order that would have prevented services beginning. Only the afternoon before, Kelleher managed to have the order overthrown by the Texas Supreme Court in Austin.

Repeated fares wars, especially with Braniff, dogged the airline over the next few years, as it struggled to establish itself as a profit-making business. At one point, Braniff had reduced their fare on the Dallas–Houston route to $13, half that of Southwest. Although Braniff, with their large domestic network and international services would be able to absorb the loss, at least in the short term, Southwest would have bankrupted itself trying to match it. Instead, Muse devised a programme whereby passengers were still charged $26, but were offered a gift. Anyone declining the gift was entitled to a refund of the fare difference. Initially, 76 per cent of the passengers took the gift, and Southwest could pocket the extra revenue. The percentage later dropped considerably as the novelty wore off, but the promotion lasted long enough for Southwest to win that particular skirmish in the fares war.

Loads had taken a while to pick up, with some early flights operating with only a handful of passengers. Some rescheduling and revamping of the fares structure followed and passenger boarding figures started to show some improvement. One more major change was to switch the Houston terminal from the new Intercontinental Airport, miles outside the city, to the old Hobby Airport, much closer to downtown. This served the needs of Southwest's largely commuting passengers much better and was a popular move. Southwest steadily began to establish itself in the minds of the Texas public as a practical, cheaper, alternative to the big-name airlines in the area.

One of the four original 737s had to be sold after a federal district court judge pronounced that Southwest could not legally fly charters outside Texas. This robbed the airline of a potential source of income and also left them with an idle aircraft at quiet times in the schedule. Although a $500,000 profit was made on the sale of the aircraft, to Frontier Airlines, Southwest was left with the problem of covering all the scheduled flights on the network.

A solution was found by introducing the 10-minute turnround, which was to become a legend in the industry. Such fast turnrounds had been common in the days of the DC-3, or even some of the later turbo-prop operations, but unheard of with the larger jet aircraft. With turnround times slashed, the remaining aircraft were able to maintain the published schedule minus the sold aircraft. The speedy turnrounds continue to this day, enabling the airline to schedule more trips per day per aircraft, as well as saving on the capital cost of extra aircraft that would be required to maintain a more leisurely programme. The success of the short turnround system spoke volumes for the perceived reliability of the Boeing 737 in high-pressure operations.

Southwest Airlines' brightly painted 737-200s finally started revenue services within Texas in June 1971.
Martyn East

The Love Field Factor

One dispute that was guaranteed to keep Southwest's lawyers in steady employment was the problem of Love Field versus Dallas–Fort Worth.

In 1968, all the airline operators then using Dallas original airport at Love Field, signed an agreement, the 1968 Regional Airport Concurrent Bond Ordinance, to move to a new airport being built near Grapevine, Texas, to jointly serve the cities of Dallas and Fort Worth. Situated roughly halfway between the two cities, the costly new facility would have to attract all the airlines to use it for it to have any hope of being profitable. The airlines who signed up for the bond were not only obliged to move to the new airport, but were also liable for any losses it incurred. However, Southwest Airlines was not in existence when the bond was set up and was not about to sign up to it, with its expensive conditions.

As Love Field was only ten minutes from downtown Dallas, Southwest also recognized its convenience for its business commuters, which would give it a major commercial advantage over its larger competitors. In 1972, the cities of Dallas and Fort Worth brought the first of a series of lawsuits in an effort to make Southwest move. Several years of litigation later, Southwest was told that it could operate from Love Field as long as it was an airport. Southwest had actually been told this after the first hearing, but appeals from the cities and larger airlines had kept the case in the courts for years. When the other airlines moved out of Love Field, Southwest took over the prestigious gate positions previously occupied by giant American Airlines. The little airline was growing up.

Southwest Airlines resisted moves to make it transfer operations to the new Dallas/Fort Worth Airport. Instead, it headquartered itself at the downtown Love Field near Dallas. Tim Kincaid Collection

Slow Expansion

One 'advantage' of Southwest Airlines finding itself in almost continuous legal dispute with the larger airlines was that it had to curb any temptation to expand too quickly. This was a common trap that many other inexperienced carriers had fallen into in the past. However, the frequent court cases kept the Southwest management's attention focused on maintaining standards and maximizing revenues on the existing network.

By 1973 though, Southwest's operations were starting to show a profit and some modest expansion was considered feasible. First targeted was the Rio Grande Valley area, served by the airport at Harlingen. Texas International already served routes from Harlingen and would, normally, have been expected to put up a fight against Southwest's application to the Texas Aeronautics Commission. Unfortunately for Texas International, they were suffering from industrial action at the time and their flights were strike-bound. Therefore they were unable to put up much of an argument and the judge decided that any service was better than none, and threw their objections out of court.

As it was, the legal dispute had delayed Southwest beginning service from Harlingen until 1975. Their presence in the area was immediately felt though. The year before, 1974, had seen 123,000 passengers flying from the Valley to Dallas, Houston and San Antonio. Eleven months after Southwest introduced their service, this had risen to 325,000.

Encouraged by the success of the Rio Grande Valley flights, Southwest applied to introduce similar flights from Corpus Christi, Austin, Midland-Odessa, Lubock and El Paso, in March 1976. Initial services began on the new expanded intra-Texas network that winter and were increased in the spring of 1977, as more 737s were delivered from Boeing to operate them.

With its colourful presence now being felt throughout its home state, Southwest would have to start looking further afield for any future development of the network. Muse began studying the possibility of setting up a new subsidiary of the company, to provide a Southwest Airlines style of service from Chicago's Midway Airport. Once the main airport for Chicago, Midway had been eclipsed by the opening of the new facility at O'Hare and was, by the 1970s, very little used. However, moves were being made in Washington that would release Southwest from its intra-state shackles and allow new routes to be opened without the need for out-of-state subsidiaries to be formed.

Southwest and Muse Air

On 28 March 1978, M. Lamar Muse suddenly resigned as Southwest Airline's President and CEO. In the interim, Herb Kelleher was appointed as a temporary replacement, until Howard D. Putnam, the VP-Marketing Services at United Air Lines accepted the permanent post, three months later. Putnam was to remain until 1981, when he left to take the reigns of the, by then, ailing Braniff International. Herb Kelleher was finally persuaded to replace him on a full-time basis. Practically since Day One, Kelleher had been an important influence on Southwest Airlines, but only as an outside advisor and legal representative. Now he was to lead the airline he had been instrumental in founding.

Lamar Muse's departure from Southwest was followed by that of his son, Michael, who had been vp-Finance under his father. A non-competition clause was written into the agreements reached over their leaving Southwest, but within days of this expiring a new airline, Muse Air, came into existence in 1981. Under the control of father and son, Muse Air immediately began rival services over Southwest's core Texan routes.

There were significant differences in the style of operation adopted by Muse. Aiming for a more select clientele, Muse offered assigned seating, with three facing-seat lounge areas in the cabin, extra cabin attendants and upgraded refreshment services. Interestingly, Muse Air was the first US carrier to operate a full non-smoking policy on its aircraft. The Muse Air fleet comprised brand-new, 159-passenger MD-80s, of various marks, later joined by slightly smaller, 130-passenger DC-9-50s, bought from Swissair. The all McDonnell Douglas-built fleet was painted in a unique livery with Muse's signature across the fuselage.

Rather than try to compete by spending money on upgrading their own passenger amenities, Southwest responded with its strengths, and increased frequencies on routes where the two airlines were now competing head-to-head. Although Muse Air managed to make a dent in Southwest's traffic and even experimented with expanding its route system within Texas and to inter-State points, the Southwest philosophy of frequent, low-cost travel with basic amenities won through. Muse Air never made a profit and eventually, in 1986, Lamar Muse took up Herb Kelleher's offer to buy out the company.

Rather than just absorb Muse Air's operations, the airline was reorganized. Renamed TranStar Airlines and with its fleet painted a striking 'Empyrean Blue' livery, the 'new' airline became Southwest's longer-ranging associate, offering premium-grade services. Soon, TranStar's route network stretched from Texas to California, Florida, Louisiana, Nevada and Oklahoma as well as still offering flights linking the main Texan cities.

Old Dog, New Tricks
The new arrangement worked quite well for the first year, Southwest and TranStar serving their different customer bases in their own way. Unfortunately, TranStar became embroiled in a vicious war of fares with Continental Airlines. In 1982, Texas Air Corporation, the owners of Texas International Airlines, had acquired Continental Airlines, which could trace its operations as far back as 1937. Despite continuing unrest within its employee ranks, much of the merged workforce objecting to a somewhat Draconian new management style, Texas Air Corporation merged the two operators under the older and larger airline's name.

After the bankruptcy of Braniff International the same year, the 'new' Continental, by then operating under 'Chapter 11' bankruptcy protection and now headquartered in Houston, was anxious to establish itself as the major operator both within Texas and from the state to the rest of the US. Continental saw TranStar as a threat to their ambitious plans, the smaller carrier having built up a considerable traffic share on competing routes from Houston. Continental introduced much reduced, non-refundable, 'MaxiFares', countered by TranStar's 'StarFares' and 'MediFares' programmes. TranStar also offered improved, two-class, service with a new Business Class upgraded to a First Class in an attempt to improve revenue yields. However, losses mounted to unacceptable levels and Kelleher finally gave up the fight in 1987, closing down TranStar in August that year in an effort to protect Southwest Airlines.

The McDonnell Douglas MD-80 was Muse Air's choice for its regional Texan services.
Tim Kincaid Collection

(continued overleaf)

Southwest and Muse Air continued

Southwest acquired control of its Muse Air rival in 1986. Tim Kincaid Collection

Muse Air was reorganized as TranStar Airlines, replacing Muse Air's 'signature' livery with a new 'Empyrean Blue' design. Tim Kincaid Collection

IMPROVING THE BREED

Texas International's arguments against Southwest's expansion into the Rio Grande Valley fell flat, as Texas International was grounded by a strike at the time. Via author

New Services Worldwide

The Boeing 737 was, by the 1970s, becoming a common sight at airports in every corner of the world. Malaysia-Singapore Airlines became the first Far Eastern operator of the aircraft on 21 August 1969. Their initial fleet of Series 100s was introduced on scheduled flights from Singapore to Kuala Lumpur, Penang, Bangkok, and Kota Kinabula, ousting the long-serving Comet 4s. More 737 routes were introduced as the later order for Series 200s arrived and the aircraft were soon operating over much more of MSA's Asian network.

In 1972 though, MSA was split up, the six-year agreement between the two countries to operate their airline services as a joint venture having expired. From October, MSA became Singapore Airlines,

Singapore Airlines 'inherited' the MSA Boeing 737 fleet when the original carrier was split into two airlines. Aviation Hobby Shop

77

(*Above*) **Malaysian Airline System acquired Boeing 737-200s to operate regional schedules from its Kuala Lumpur base.** Steve Bunting

(*Below*) **Avianca's 737-100s were only to serve for two years before being sold on.** Aviation Hobby shop

based in Singapore, and the Malaysian Airline System, based at Kuala Lumpur. Singapore Airlines took over most of the jet equipment, Boeing 707s used on long-haul flights, and the 737s. Malaysian took over most of the fleet of F.27 turbo-props, operated on local flights, eventually leasing in Boeing 707s, and ordering new 737s, to open their own jet service throughout the region.

Among an increasing number of new operators, South African Airways introduced their fleet in 1969 as part of a general modernization plan for their short- and medium-haul routes. Boeing 707s had operated on long-haul services to Europe for many years and the 727 had also been introduced on major domestic and regional flights in 1965. The 737s were intended 1969/70. Both carriers had previously been operators of first- and second-generation European jet airliners. VASP already flew a pair of BAC One-Elevens, and continued to do so for many years after the VASP 737 fleet had been considerably expanded. The contract for the five VASP 737s had replaced an order for five much larger Boeing 727-200s, the contract for which had been signed in 1968. Aerolineas Argentinas operated several Caravelles and DH Comets on domestic and regional flights – both types were fated to be disposed of as the 737s entered Aerolineas's service.

Avianca had actually withdrawn their 737-100s from service after only two year's use, in late 1971, deciding instead to concentrate on the Boeing 727 for domestic continent in 1970/71. Indian Airlines had operated a small fleet of Caravelle jets on major routes for several years, with turbo-props such as the Viscount, F.27 and HS-748 operating on local routes. The 737, with its improved runway performance over the older Caravelle, was able to introduce jet flights to more cities.

More 'Rough Field' 737 Sales

As well as having established itself early on in rough-field operations with the likes of Wien Consolidated, renamed Wien Air Alaska Inc in May 1973, Nordair and Pacific Western, suitably modified 737s were also soon demonstrating their unique talents elsewhere in the world.

Renamed Wien Air Alaska, the Alaskan pioneer airline made good use of its convertible 737-200Cs throughout the northern state. Jenny Gradidge

to supplement the 727s and replace a sizable fleet of Vickers Viscounts operating on domestic routes.

The Brazilian domestic airline VASP (Viacao Aerea Sao Paulo) and Argentinean national carrier, Aerolineas Argentinas, had followed Avianca's example and placed Series 200 Boeing 737s in service on their South American routes in and regional jet service. The 737s were originally sold to the West German Air Force, but were soon sold back to Boeing. The two aircraft were eventually bought by Aloha Airlines in 1973.

Back in Asia, the state-owned Indian Airlines Corporation had introduced a fleet of Boeing 737-200s on to its huge domestic network throughout the sub- In the more remote parts of the African, Asian and Central/Southern American continents there was as much need for high-capacity aircraft capable of operating economically and safely from very basically equipped airports, as there was in Alaska or arctic Canada.

The enhanced performance advantages of the 'Advanced' 737s lent themselves to the more demanding operational environments. Rival types, such as the Fokker F.28 Fellowship, and the much modified Series 475 version of the BAC One-Eleven, designed specifically as rough-field aircraft, were soon eclipsed by the 737 sales figures as it encroached on their targeted markets.

All the rival types were capable of satisfactory operation from difficult environments. They were also modern and comfortable enough to be utilized on more important regional services, even where small fleet of F.28s operated by Braathens was soon eclipsed by the airline's 737s and the Fokkers were sold in favour of more Boeings.

By 1978, the 737 was also serving mixed prestige and 'second-level' services with the likes of Air Algérie, Air Gabon, Air Madagascar, Air Nauru, Air Tanzania, Air Zaire, Cameroon Airlines, China Airlines (Taiwan), DETA (Mozambique), Far Eastern Air Transport (Taiwan), Gulf Air (Bahrein), Iran Air, Iraqi Airways, Kuwait Airways, Nigeria Airways, Royal Air Maroc, programme, the cancellation of the US SST project and a general down-turn in world financial markets was having a serious accumulative effect.

At one point, after 737 sales had plummeted, a task force set up by Boeing in 1973 seriously considered the option of selling the whole 737 programme to Japan. The fact that most of the 737 production jigs were portable led to the choice of the twin-jet as an asset that might profitably be sold off to save money. From a sales high of 114 in 1969, only twenty-two were ordered in

The stretched Fokker F.28 2000 could carry a more economic load of passengers, but still sold in comparatively small numbers against the 737's much more impressive sales figures. Via author

the rough-field capability was not required. This gave a degree of flexibility in styles of operation that precluded the need for different types of aircraft on different parts of the network.

Where the 737 scored over the equally versatile, but smaller, types was its capacity and range. The original Fokker F.28 carried only sixty-five passengers, although this was increased in later versions, still capable of rough-field operations, to seventy nine. The Series 475 One-Eleven could carry up to eighty-nine, in a high-density configuration. A convertible 737 could carry these sorts of loads in the rear cabin and still have the forward passenger cabin in a generous cargo configuration, in addition to the standard below-floor cargo capacity. The Royal Brunei Airlines, Saudia (Saudi Arabia), SAHSA (Honduras), Sudan Airways, TAAG Angola Airlines, Thai Airways, TAN Airlines (Honduras), Yemen Airways and Zambia Airways. Although not all these operators took advantage of the rough-field modifications, they all used their versatile 737s on disparate services throughout their regions.

Coping with Crisis

Despite the steady spread of the 737 throughout the worldwide airline system during the late 1960s and early 1970s, Boeing was going through a financial crisis. The increasing costs of the 747 wide-body 1972 and barely fourteen in 1973. However, a turnround began with the development of the 'advanced' version and orders began to slowly build up again.

Changes Afoot

Despite the ongoing production delays and expensive difficulties in introducing their new giant 747 'Jumbo', the early 1970s saw Boeing with relatively healthy order books for most of their available models. On the horizon though, was a slow-down in air travel generally, massive fuel price increases and a worldwide wave of deregulation, that would change the air transport industry's goalposts for ever. Testing times were ahead.

Carriers as geographically separate as North Africa's Air Algérie and Air Nauru of the Pacific found use for the 737 on their diverse networks. Via author/MAP

Saudia, of Saudi Arabia (*above*) and aircraft of the Indian Airlines Corporation (*left*) were flown into both major cities and remoter points in their respective countries. Both pictures via author

(*Below*) The Boeing 'family' of jet airliners, as offered in the late 1960s. 737-200, PP-SMA, of VASP of Brazil. 727-200, N1783B, eventually destined for Libyan Arab Airlines. PP-VJH, a 707-320C, later delivered to another Brazilian carrier, VARIG, and 747-100, N731PA wearing Boeing titles over its Pan American colour scheme before delivery. Boeing

CHAPTER SIX

Worldwide Influences

The Oil Crisis

One worldwide crisis that not only contributed to Boeing's woes but also affected nearly every industrial undertaking in the civilized world, struck in 1973. That year, the Organization of Oil Producing and Exporting Countries (OPEC) decided to increase the price of the oil they supplied. Fuel prices rocketed in all sectors, trebling within days and plunging the financial world into chaos.

Up until then, airlines had enjoyed the benefit of comparatively cheap fuel for their aircraft and had still been able to operate types with high fuel consumption at a profit. This changed overnight, and aircraft that had previously been viable were found to be an expensive liability. The Convair series of medium-range, four-engined, jet airliners suffered especially. TWA and Delta operated large fleets of the CV-880 in the USA, and withdrew them from service as soon as they could be replaced by more economic aircraft. Suddenly, Boeing and all the other airliner manufacturers around the world were having to pay much more attention to fuel consumption in their designs. Engine manufacturers were under pressure to produce fuel-efficient power plants and the airframe designers were desperately trying to trim as much weight and aerodynamic drag as possible off the forthcoming aircraft.

The oil crisis also affected the airlines' revenues in other ways. Industrial and financial institutions suffered decreased profits as a result of their own, and their suppliers', increased fuel costs. Some companies went out of business, the survivors cutting costs wherever possible, often causing some cutbacks in corporate travel. Where the workforce was hit by redundancies and closures, leisure travel suffered and the airlines were losing passengers from all market groups.

The Ripples Spread

The effect continued into 1974, with poor advance bookings and more rounds of fuel price rises. Europe was as badly hit as anywhere, with the UK suffering a miners' strike as well. Petrol rationing was threatened in the UK; in the end, it did not need to be introduced, although the British public did have to suffer extensive power cuts from the electrical industry.

One important UK charter carrier, Court Line Aviation, ceased operations in the middle of August 1974, at the height of the summer travel season. The Luton-based operator flew a large fleet of BAC One-Elevens and a pair of Lockheed Tristar wide-bodies throughout Europe's holiday spots, as well as some longer-haul flights to Canada and the Caribbean. Forced into a corner by the increased fuel costs and a vicious price-war among the tour companies, including Clarksons Holidays and Horizon Travel, both owned by the same holding company as the airline, the entire group was unable to avoid sudden liquidation when the working capital ran out.

Court Line Aviation's Luton neighbour, Britannia Airways, managed to weather the storm. By now, being a subsidiary of the powerful and much more diverse Thomson Group, the airline was able to survive with only minimal cuts and cost-saving measures. By 1976, their

Lufthansa soon acquired Series 200 737s to operate alongside their original Series 100s. The likes of D-ABHU, 'Konstaz', and its fleetmates, were already established as one of the most popular regional jet airliners, when the oil crisis changed the operational parameters of the airline industry forever. *Lufthansa*

(*Above*) **Britannia Airways managed to survive the turmoil of the fuel crisis, with the backing of its powerful owners and careful management.**
Jenny Gradidge

Mey-Air Transport's attempt to expand into jet charter operations eventually failed. LN-MTD later found a new home with Piedmont as N754N. Jenny Gradidge

recovery saw their fleet of 737-200s increase to thirteen, including two convertible models. A pair of long-range 707s had been operated briefly in 1971–73, on flights to the USA, Canada, the Caribbean and Far East. However, they had been returned to their lessors after changes in US law had made it uneconomic for Britannia to operate their charters there. The all-737 fleet was now operating from a number of UK regional points, as well as the Luton head office.

More European Charter 737s

After being one of the 737s few supporters for all-charter services in Europe, by the mid-1970s Britannia was finally joined by more inclusive-tour operators. Germany's Condor, that had leased 737s from Lufthansa for several years, had returned to only operating 727s for their short-haul fleet.

However, Norwegian carrier Mey-Air, previously an operator of Convair propeller aircraft, took delivery in 1971 of two 737-200s. Operating an extensive IT and *ad hoc* network from Scandinavia, Mey Air was to become a victim of the post-OPEC slump, ceasing operations and undergoing the ignominy of having its jet fleet repossessed by Boeing for non-payment. Despite Mey-Air's disappointment, Belgium's Trans European Airways and the Netherlands' Transavia had both finally opted for the 737-200 to replace their older jet fleets.

Transavia was the longer-established of the two airlines, having been founded in 1965 as Transavia (Limburg) NV. Revenue operations, however, did not begin until 17 November 1966. On that date, supporting personnel and artists of the Dutch Dance Theatre were flown to Naples. Transavia's initial fleet comprised two DC-6s and one DC-6B. The following year the DC-6 fleet consisted of no less than ten aircraft, after the arrival of two convertible passenger/cargo DC-6As and five more DC-6Bs.

Transavia operated its first jet equipment in the shape of a single Boeing 707-320C that flew long-distance charters between May and October 1968. Two Caravelle 3s, leased from the manufacturer, entered service on the IT routes from the Netherlands in 1969. More Caravelles were acquired second-hand, from Swissair and United, replacing the leased examples, as well as the last DC-6Bs, which left the fleet at the end of 1969. More 707s were leased in over the subsequent years.

The fuel crisis hit the Caravelle's economic viability very hard and Transavia began looking for a less thirsty replacement. Twelve of the French twin-jets were in use by 1973, operating over an increasing network of IT charters, as well as being in demand for *ad hoc* and short-term leasing contract work with other airlines short of capacity. This latter operation was to become a Transavia speciality in the years to come.

The Caravelle replacements started to be delivered in May 1974 and by the following May there were seven Boeing 737-200s in service with the Dutch charter carrier. Of the seven, one was leased from Britannia Airways and three were on lease from United Airlines.

Belgian Pace-setter

It was a further two years before another European charter carrier adopted the 737 for its short-haul needs. Trans European Airways, based in Brussels, Belgium's capital, was one of the newer breed of charter airline, without its roots in the propeller era.

Trans European had not been founded until October 1970, to operate IT charters for parent Belgian travel companies TIFA and G.P. Gutelman. Boasting a modern image, in contrast to earlier charter specialists, the airline started operations with an ex-Eastern Airlines Boeing 720 jet. Three early model Boeing 707s later joined the single 720 on IT charter work throughout Europe and also to some longer-haul destinations.

Two Series 200 737s arrived in 1976, following two leased wide-bodied Airbus A300Bs that had joined the 707/720 fleet. With another series 200 on order, Trans European was to find the 737 an ideal aircraft for its needs and was soon planning on acquiring further aircraft to service a major expansion of its operations.

(*Above*) Transavia's Caravelle 3, PH-TRP had previously served with SAS and Swissair. During its time with Transavia it spent time leased out to Tunisair. Aviation Hobby Shop

(*Below*) PH-TVH was one of the first of Transavia's 737-200s that eventually ousted the Caravelles from the Dutch charter carrier's fleet. Steve Bunting

Trans European opted for the 737 to replace larger, but ageing, Boeing 707s and 720s. Via author

Caribbean Lease

France's national carrier, Air France, had joined the ranks of European scheduled 737 operators as early as October 1973. However, it was not the extensive European-scheduled network of Air France that was to see the 737s, but the airline's regional services between the French territories in the Antilles Islands chain in the Caribbean. In addition to providing an important feeder service to Air France's trans-Atlantic flights to and from Paris, the Caribbean network provided regional links to other important islands in the vicinity, as well as to Florida in the southern USA. Air France had previously assigned Caravelles to the area to operate the local network.

Two Boeing 737-200s were leased from Western, the first, N4522W was christened 'Antilles' once it was painted in Air France colours. The second, N4504W, was christened 'Guyane' and arrived in January 1974. Being operated as dictated by Western's practices as agreed with their pilots' unions, the aircraft leased to Air France were obliged to be flown with three flight-deck crew members. The French airline was also intending to use the period of the lease to evaluate the 737 as a possible replacement for the remaining Caravelles on European scheduled services. Air France had already introduced Boeing 727-200s on busier ex-Caravelle routes within Europe.

Once again, though, the three-crew question was raised by the Air France pilots' unions and was to delay the company's decision. Despite the other European operators of the 737 all opting for a two-pilot flight-deck crew, the French unions concerned, SNPL and SNOMAC, both pressured for Air France to adopt the three-crew option. The two organizations disputed Lufthansa's assertion that the two-crew operation was perfectly safe. However, a new joint, 9-month, FAA/NASA study from the USA, presented in 1978, reaffirmed that it 'found no evidence to indicate that a two-man crew aircraft is a detriment to safety'.

The study had reviewed the record of five trunk carrier aircraft, namely the Boeing 727, 737, BAC One-Eleven, DC-8 and DC-9. The further study of three versus two crew members concluded that the records studied:

> precluded making any statement beyond that there is no significant difference in the level of safety between the two and three man operation.

Nonetheless, the lack of an agreement on the matter led to Air France cancelling a lease package for thirteen 737-200s. It was to be December 1981 before Air France was able to announce an order for twelve 737-200s.

Air France's Alternatives

One serious alternative to the 737 for Air France was a French-built option, the Dassault Mercure. Dassault had developed the Mercure as a 'mini-airbus' seating 130–150 passengers, specifically on short-haul operations. The company had discerned that the rival types then in use were basically medium-haul airliners, believing their basic design had been compromised by stretching to provide more capacity over a shorter range. Resembling a much enlarged 737, the Mercure was designed from the beginning as a high-capacity, short-range aircraft and the first prototype first flew on 28 May 1971.

Powered by imported Pratt & Whitney JT8D-15s, the Mercure was offered to many European carriers and marketed as a viable alternative to the American choices. However, the much hoped-for Air France order failed to materialize. Other than an order for ten from Air Inter that placed the first into service on its domestic French network in 1974, there were no other takers for the Mercure. Plans for an enlarged version were soon abandoned. Air Inter later acquired one of the prototype Mercures as well and were very satisfied with their fleet, but there were no more Mercures produced after the initial production batch, a financial disaster for Dassault.

Although a commercial failure for its maker, the few Dassault Mercures built enjoyed long and successful, accident-free, careers with French domestic carrier, Air Inter. Dassault

Deregulation in the USA

The Airline Deregulation Act was passed by the US Congress in 1978, with wide support from most sides of the party political fences. In effect, the American scheduled and charter air carriers had previously been stringently controlled by the CAB and FAA in everything from route licences to fares they could offer. Under deregulation the airlines were to be 'set free', at least domestically, flying where they thought they could make a profit and charging what they thought the market would allow. The carriers had only to prove to the authorities that they were 'fit, willing and able' to conduct their operations safely and in the public interest. On overseas services, for the time being, regulation continued as most foreign routes were governed by international agreement.

The main aim of the act was to reduce airline fares and offer more choice to the travelling public. For many years the prime transcontinental routes were the sole province of the major carriers. America, TWA and United ruled the non-stop coast-to-coast services, with Braniff, Eastern, Delta and National operating the main north–south routes on the east coast and to the south and southwest. Continental, Northwest and Western linked the west coast with the midwest and southwest as well as flying some of the 'thinner' transcontinental flights in the north and south of the country. In between, the major carriers had their 'sphere of influence' in various regions, often in competition with a regional or local service carrier. There were overlaps and inconsistencies – for instance, both Delta and National operated transcontinental routes across the south of the USA, albeit usually with at least one en route stop. Nonetheless there was an established status quo that was about to be seriously upset.

Once the act was law, there was an upsurge in new routes and even new airlines trying to take advantage of the situation. The established carriers were still struggling with the effects of the oil crisis and financial down-turn in the national economy that had left them with half-empty aircraft being flown at a loss. However well-intentioned, some of the new operators found themselves floundering and regional carriers that expanded their networks overnight were having trouble recouping the cost of their actions.

Even the major established carriers were not immune. Competition from new low-fare carriers was one of the factors blamed for the eventual demise of once-giant Braniff Airways, Eastern Air Lines and Pan American World Airways in later years. Even some of the survivors were badly mauled in the fight for revenue. Once-mighty Trans World Airlines eventually found itself shrunk to a shadow of its former self, with the international network especially hit by low-fare competition and worldwide recession.

Air Florida began its short-range, intra-Florida services with a highly unsuitable, long-range, Boeing 707. Via author

Post-Deregulation Scramble

Among the US carriers already in operation that were swift to take advantage of the new rules, Air Florida was, at least for a while, one of the more successful. Originally formed under the old regulations, it was an intra-state carrier, based in Miami. Eager to repeat the California and Texan success of PSA and Southwest Airlines, Air Florida began scheduled services from Miami to Jacksonville and Tampa in September 1972.

Curiously, Air Florida's first aircraft was none other than a Boeing 707-320. Even in pre-fuel-crisis days, this was far from suitable equipment for the brief flights within Florida's borders. In short order, a pair of much more economical Lockheed Electra turbo-props replaced the 707, in March 1973.

Although soon joined by a third Electra in 1974, the small fleet was initially struggling against the local might of Eastern Air Lines and National Airlines. A leased Boeing 727-100 jet was acquired in 1976 and operated alongside the Electras. Steady route expansion brought Gainesville, Orlando, Panama City, Pensacola, St Petersburg and Tallahassee, all still within Florida, into the network. After a change of management in 1977, an injection of investment capital followed and five ex-Air Canada DC-9-15Fs replace the 727 and Electras.

Take-over and Meteoric Expansion

More DC-9s joined the fleet and local commuter operator, Air Sunshine, also based at Miami, was taken over in July 1978. Although the Air Sunshine fleet of DC-3s and Convair CV-440s was not retained, Air Florida added several extra Florida cities to the network via the buy-out. New international routes were also opened from Miami to points in the Bahamas and the Caribbean.

Air Florida joined the ranks of 737 operators in 1979, when the first of four ex-Singapore Airlines Series 100s arrived at Miami. Over the next two years the company undertook an explosive expansion programme, taking full advantage of the new freedoms available under deregulation. More 737s, all Series 200s, were acquired, with twelve 'Advanced' aircraft on order. In addition, second-hand aircraft were acquired to speed up the expansion. As well as nine ex-United aircraft, two of which were leased from Transavia, another two were contracted in from leasing companies.

The much enlarged fleet was soon opening new scheduled services from Florida to neighbouring southern states, the Midwest and the Great Lakes. Most importantly, destinations in the affluent northeast, such as Boston, New York, Philadelphia and Washington were also served by the 737s. New destinations in the Caribbean and Central America also came on line as soon as aircraft could be found to open the routes. To aid the growth of the network, Air Florida also acquired half a dozen Boeing 727-200s from a cancelled Braniff Airways order.

The modest Caribbean and Bahamian international network was soon eclipsed by the opening of trans-Atlantic schedules to Amsterdam, Brussels, Dusseldorf, Frankfurt, London and Madrid. Long-range, wide-body, DC-10-30s were leased in to operate the long-haul schedules.

Pride before the Fall

As its tenth anniversary approached, Air Florida was able to boast a fleet that had increased from one 707, to three DC-10s, six 727-200s, four 737-100s and nineteen 737-200s, with five more 737-200s on order. There was also an order for three of Boeing's new high-capacity twin-jet model, the 757, in the pipeline. Celebrations for the anniversary took on a decidedly muted air though, following tragic loss of one of the 737-200s at Washington in January 1982.

Already running well behind schedule as a result of exceptionally harsh winter weather in the northeast, Air Florida's 737-200, N62AF, was one of the ex-United aircraft. It was operating Flight 90 on 13 January, a Washington–Fort Lauderdale service, with seventy-four passengers and five crew members on board. Washington National

Ex-SIA 737-100s heralded the arrival of the many -200s, both new and second-hand, with Air Florida. Aviation Hobby Shop

The Boeing 727-200 provided more capacity as routes expanded throughout the eastern USA. Via author

Airport had reopened at 15.00hrs, following snow clearance that had closed it down for an hour. Following de-icing, N62AF was pushed back from the terminal and awaited its turn for departure with several other aircraft, mostly also delayed.

N62AF sat on the taxiway for nearly another hour before finally being given clearance for take-off. In that time, snow had built up on the wing surfaces and ice had also built up in the compressor inlets of the engines. Blockage of the inlet tubes would give false indications of thrust, showing a higher amount than was actually being developed. On take-off, the anomalous readings from the blocked tubes led the crew to believe that they had reached a safe take-off speed before they actually had. In addition, the renewed snow and ice on the wings and empennage that had built up again as the aircraft waited on the taxiway, caused the aircraft to pitch up as soon as it was airborne and the aircraft was soon in a dangerous stalling condition.

In a nose-high attitude, with the undercarriage down and flaps still partially extended, N62AF barely reached 300ft (90m) in altitude before starting to descend again. In a slight left turn, the crew tried to raise the nose and apply power, but their efforts were in vain. The aircraft crashed into the 14th Street Bridge, about a mile from the end of the runway. Sliding over the roadway on the bridge, packed with early rush-hour traffic, N62AF plunged into the iced-up Potomac River.

As well as killing the flight-deck crew, Capt Larry Wheaton and First Officer Roger Pettit, two of the flight attendants and sixty-nine of the passengers, four persons unfortunate enough to have been in vehicles on the bridge also perished. All the survivors from the aircraft, one flight attendant and four passengers, had been in the rear section of the cabin, which had broken away and remained partly above the ice and water in the river. The survivors were hoisted or towed to safety by a US Park Police helicopter that had managed to reach the crash site in twenty minutes. When a female survivor lost her grip on a rescue rope, two bystanders from the bridge, including a US Congressional Budget Office clerk named Lenny Skutnick, jumped into the freezing river to help her. One passenger, who had survived the initial impact, had been seen to unselfishly assist others reach the helicopter's rescue line, before he slipped beneath the water and drowned.

The Aftermath

In the subsequent inquiry, a number of unfortunate factors were found to have contributed to the crash. The initial de-icing was criticized as having been undertaken with an incorrect mix of glycol and water. Even so, human error was deemed to have been a major factor, with some seriously flawed judgements on the part of the operating crew being accredited with much of the blame. The airline itself came in for some criticism with regards to training procedures. However, the controller at Washington had asked the crew of N62AF for 'No delay on departure', as another aircraft was about to land on the runway behind them. The pressure this put on the crew to clear the runway for the approaching Eastern 727 was cited as a possible cause of the crew missing signs that all was not well with the engine thrust readings and perhaps choosing not to give as much attention as they should have to the build-up of snow on the aircraft's wings.

Air Florida had always operated to a slim profit margin in an effort to be able to offer the cheap fares it had built its reputation on. The inevitable dip in passenger boardings, following the accident at Washington, hit the company hard, financially. Although some improvement was eventually achieved as time went by, Air Florida never managed to fully recover from the adverse publicity and finally closed down in the summer of 1984.

The People's Champion

While Air Florida had been an established carrier that took advantage of deregulation to change itself beyond recognition, another feature of the post-deregulation era was the formation of brand new airlines, established to make their mark under the new rules.

Formed in 1980, PeoplExpress Airlines was the brainchild of Don Burr, a Harvard MBA, who had been President of Texas International Airlines. Burr had a vision of a new low-fare airline, with a unique management style. Having pioneered discount 'peanut fares' at Texas International, Burr

WORLDWIDE INFLUENCES

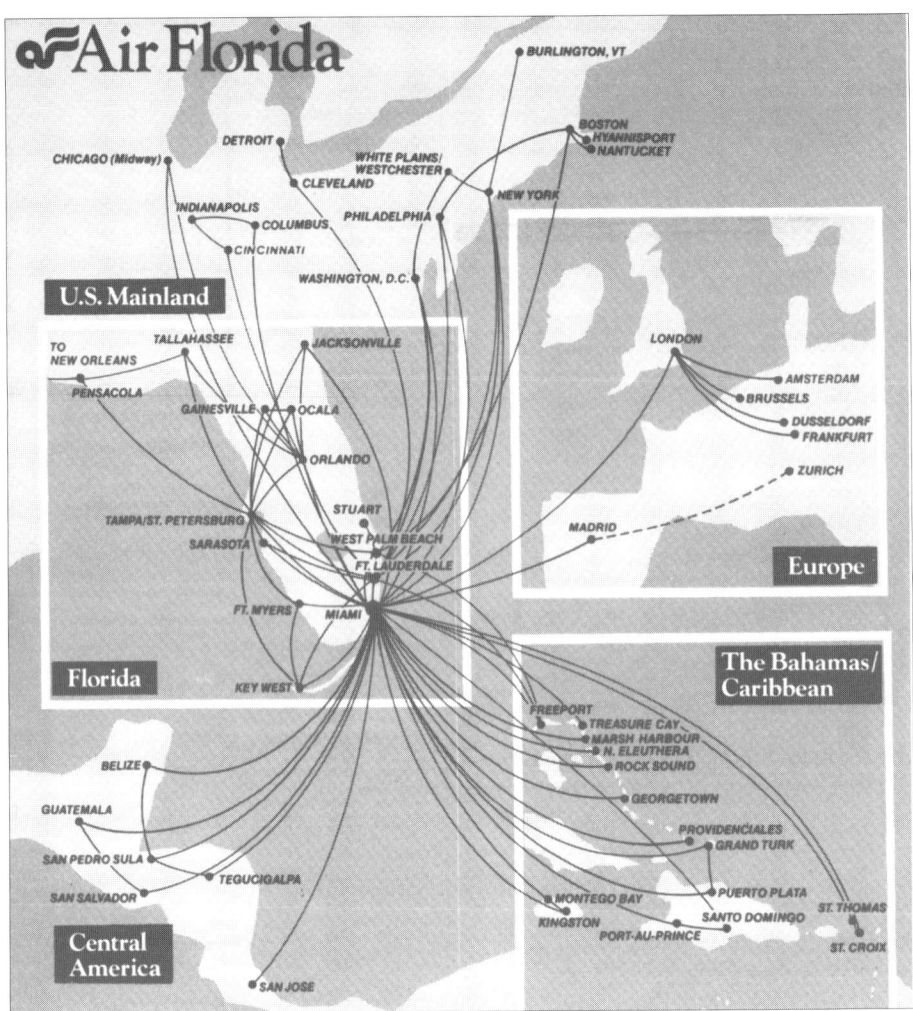

Air Florida's carefully built empire was to slowly crumble in the wake of the Washington tragedy. Via author

When Lufthansa delivered the last of PeoplExpress's -100s, the German airline's engineers painted farewell tears on the aircraft's tail logo. Via author

90

was well aware that the paying public would forgo expensive amenities in return for cheap, frequent, reliable air service. In particular, he had a vision of maximum responsibilities to the employees, for minimum supervision. This was unlikely to be approved by his then boss, Frank Lorenzo, the entrepreneur who owned Texas Air Corporation that controlled Texas International.

Burr, and two other Texas International associates, Melrose Dawsey and Gerald Gitner, resigned from the Texas carrier and set about gathering finance for their new venture. From several options, the base for the new carrier was narrowed down to the then much under-used Newark International, in New Jersey. Initial stock offerings gained the company $25 million to finance its start-up and several other talented executives defected from Texas International to join PeoplExpress.

Lufthansa's Series 100s Come Home

Lufthansa had been offering its early Series 100 Boeing 737s for sale, as more, larger, 'Advanced' Series 200s arrived from Seattle. The offers Lufthansa received for the aircraft varied from the sublime to the ridiculous. One prospective purchaser wanted one aircraft to ferry his casino's clients free of charge, another wanted 'over-favourable' credit facilities for eight aircraft over ten years. One presented a contract full of holes and the next 'candidate' wanted an astronomical commission paid to him personally 'under the counter'.

PeoplExpress were willing to pay $51.8 million for a lease-purchase agreement for fourteen of the aircraft. Well experienced in selling off surplus members of their fleet, Lufthansa knew a good deal when it was presented and, after protracted negotiations, involving dozens of contract rewrites, an agreement was reached. The deal included modification of the 737s into a high-density, 118-passenger configuration, pre-delivery overhauls, cockpit instrument conversions back to US standards and the repainting of the aircraft into PeoplExpress's cream, burgundy and brown livery. A further three aircraft were added to the order at a later date, the last five Lufthansa 737-100s being sold to Far Eastern Air Transport of Taiwan later in 1981.

The first three 737-100s were delivered to Newark ready for service inauguration in early 1981, with routes opened from Newark to Buffalo, New York, Columbus, Ohio and Norfolk, Virginia, with a typical one-way fare of $35. More routes opened as the rest of the Lufthansa aircraft were delivered over the next twelve months and PeoplExpress began its meteoric rise. From the start, the new airline targeted first-time flyers as a major part of its market base. Burr wanted to attract passengers off the buses, trains and even out of their cars, and make air transport accessible to all.

The unique administration style of the airline saw substantial staff salary savings by 'cross utilizing' aircraft crews on ground-based jobs in addition to their flying duties. Other ground-based functions were undertaken in a similar manner and other money-saving moves included the charging of passengers for any baggage carried, at $3 a piece. All refreshments on board were charged for as well, and most of the ticketing activities were undertaken on board by the cabin crews. New staff were required to buy a minimum of 100 shares of PeoplExpress stock. As long as the airline was making money, the quarterly profit-sharing payout went a long way towards bringing their significantly lower salaries nearer to the industry norm.

Explosive Expansion

Despite the rather basic nature of their service, PeoplExpress's flights were soon among the most popular in the industry. In July 1983, an incredible load factor of 83.6 per cent was achieved. On 6 May 1983, an

Ex-Braniff International Boeing 747, N602BN, was one of several operated on PeoplExpress's much expanded transcontinental and trans-Atlantic low-fare network. Aviation Hobby Shop

The Boeing 727-200 became the most common type in the PeoplExpress fleet, outnumbering the 737-100s and -200s. Malcolm L. Hill

ex-Braniff International Boeing 747, with 485 seats, was placed into service on a Newark–London (Gatwick) trans-Atlantic schedule, with similar low-fare features. Five slightly larger 737-200s had been acquired from CP Air in early 1982, as the original seventeen -100s were stretched to their operational limits. The extra 737s were soon eclipsed by the arrival of eighteen 185-seat Boeing 727-200s.

Eventually, the 727 was to outnumber the 737 in PeoplExpress service, with no less than fifty-one being acquired, along with an eventual total of nine 747s, as routes were extended from coast to coast, south to Florida and even a further trans-Atlantic route, from Newark to Brussels was opened. Unfortunately, the explosive expansion soon began to take a toll on PeoplExpress service reputation. The airline's claim to 'Fly Smart', no longer always lived up to expectations.

Burr's revolutionary staff empowerment philosophy also became unwieldy as the carrier grew. Abuse of the system was widespread, a lack of accountability to a supervisory body causing incompetence to go unchecked and even criminal abuse of the in-flight ticketing, and other revenue-gathering systems, becoming rife. While most of the employees were intensely loyal and trustworthy, the actions of a few opportunists within the organization were draining badly needed funds from the airline. Within four years PeoplExpress had certainly grown beyond its founders' wildest dreams, and even proved the concept of airline seats as a commodity to be sold at the cheapest rate the profit margin would bear. Nonetheless, Burr and the PeoplExpress management were sailing the airline very close to the wind, financially, and it would take just one mistake to bring about disaster.

Denver Ambitions

Burr's old boss, Frank Lorenzo, of Texas Air Corporation, had recently merged Texas International with Continental Airlines after a hostile takeover. The takeover was hostile to the extent that the Continental employees had been treated to an unpleasant example of Lorenzo's management style when drastic reductions in pay and benefits had been forced upon them, despite vociferous union objections. In an attempt to further expand his airline empire, Lorenzo had made a bid for Denver-based Frontier Airlines.

Frontier had continued to serve the Rocky Mountain area of its origins, eventually serving twenty-six states, as well as international flights to four cities in Canada. The Convair 580s were slowly replaced by more 737-200s, and, later, MD-80s, until the last were retired on 1 June 1982. A new holding company, Frontier Holdings Inc, took over the airline as its prime subsidiary. Unfortunately, the economic downturn in the USA followed soon afterwards and, in 1983 the airline posted its first annual loss for a decade, of $13.8 million. The results in 1984 were even worse, with projections for 1985 not showing any sign of improvement.

As one option, in early 1985, the airline's owner offered Frontier Airline's employees the chance to buy the carrier for $211 million, at $17 a share. However, Lorenzo stepped in and offered substantially more to the shareholders, leaving the employees hopelessly outbid. The employees, fearful of Lorenzo's reputation, tried to block the move by threatening court action, citing the monopoly that would be created by the enlargement of Continental's already sizable presence at Denver. In the meantime, Burr and PeoplExpress offered $24 per share and, to the Frontier employees' relief, finalized the deal in the autumn of 1985.

False Optimism

Frontier continued operations, now as a subsidiary of PeoplExpress, for the time being. Burr did intend to eventually operate as one carrier, the Frontier route system giving PeoplExpress a welcome expansion into Western markets. Nevertheless Burr intended to operate Frontier as a separate division for at least five years before attempting full integration. This was because Frontier's more traditional approach, with a heavily unionized workforce, contrasted starkly with Burr's system of 'staff empowerment'. Unfortunately, Frontier continued to lose money at an alarming rate, reaching over $1 million a day at one point. PeoplExpress's substantial investment in the carrier was starting to look very risky. It was becoming clear, by the summer of 1986, that Frontier could not survive and it looked as though it might take PeoplExpress down with it.

In a desperate bid to keep Lorenzo at bay, an attempt was made to sell Frontier on to United. However, the United employees' unions objected to the plans put forward for integrating the Frontier staff and the deal never materialized. Once the talks with United broke down, Frontier was forced to stop flying and Frank Lorenzo made his move. Texas Air Corporation purchased the assets of both Frontier and PeoplExpress; by now both were on the brink of insolvency. The absorption of the two beleaguered airlines into Continental took effect on 1 February 1987.

Another Texas Air Corporation airline, La Guardia Airport-based New York Air was also absorbed into Continental at the same time. Founded by Texas International, initially as a rival to the long-established Eastern Air Lines 'Shuttle' between La Guardia, Boston and Washington, New York Air had started low-fare scheduled services on 19 December 1980. The initial fleet of three ex-Texas International DC-9s had grown as the network expanded into further New England points and as far south as Florida and Louisiana. Over thirty aircraft were in use by the time of the consolidation into Continental, mostly DC-9 and MD-80s, but a handful of 737s were in service as well.

Texas Air Corporation also later acquired Eastern itself, but prolonged disputes with its employees prevented any thoughts of integration into Continental. Instead, Eastern's few profitable assets were disposed of or transferred to Continental and the remainder was allowed to slip into bankruptcy and eventual liquidation in January 1991.

Continental had only recently become a 737 operator itself, shortly before the multi-mergers. As well as suddenly taking on the ex-Frontier, New York Air and

Frontier had continued to operate a mixed fleet of Convair CV-580s and Boeing 727-200s, both types taking on a brighter, modern, red and orange livery in later years. Malcolm L. Hill

Despite the best efforts of its staff and management, the sale of Frontier to PeoplExpress failed to save the carrier from economic oblivion. Jenny Gradidge

Northern Stars

While new 737 operators were using the aircraft in a leading role in exploring new forms of commercial air transport, it also continued to make its mark in more rugged fields, literally, with its Alaskan and Canadian operators.

Wien Air Alaska had continued to operate its socially vital scheduled network throughout Alaska during the 1970s and early 80s. By 1982, the fleet consisted of thirteen 737-200s, ten of them convertible to 'combi' passenger/freight operations, five of which were of the 'Advanced' model. The remaining three were early models leased in from United. The airline also flew five 727-100s, one of them an all-cargo freighter. The carrier had been the subject of speculation regarding a possible takeover by Western Air Lines in the early 1980s, as its one-time neighbour Pacific Northern had once been. On this occasion, however, the merger talks came to nothing. Unfortunately, Wien Air Alaska began to suffer from financial problems and, with no other viable purchaser on the horizon, succumbed to the pressures in 1984 and ceased operations, bringing to an end nearly sixty years of service to Alaska.

Alaska's other major carrier, Alaska Airlines had based their jet fleet on a variety of options over the years. Initially, Convair 880 and 990As had replaced the piston-powered DC-6 on main routes from Alaska to Seattle and Portland. Eventually, the Convair jets were joined by Boeing 707s and 720s on the 'Golden Nugget Service' and Boeing 727-100s joined Alaska Airlines in 1966. The 727 was much better suited to Alaska's operations, with its ability to operate from more airfields on the airline's local network than the larger jets. For the first time, jets could serve out-of-the-way cities like Nome, Kotzebue and Unalakleet. The airline introduced its first 737, a leased 'Advanced' convertible aircraft, in January 1981. Two more, new, convertible aircraft arrived from Seattle a few months later.

In Canada, the 737 was proving as useful a transportation tool as ever. On both intercity commuter, holiday flights to sunnier climes and Arctic services to remote communities, the aircraft was invaluable. Nevertheless, company politics began to intervene and the aircraft's operators were to go through a series of changes.

Pacific Western Airlines had already absorbed the fleet of fellow 737 operator, Transair, in 1979. In 1986, CP Air had reverted to its original operating name, Canadian Pacific Air Lines. Shortly after this, Pacific Western Airlines' parent company acquired control of the larger airline in 1986. This and later moves also brought 737 operators Eastern Provincial, Nordair and Quebecair under the control of the same group and the surviving operations of all the airlines were merged under a new name, Canadian Airlines International. Some of the less economic regional services were assigned to new subsidiary airlines. However, the combined fleets still consisted of more than eighty aircraft, of which sixty were Boeing 737-200s.

Transair had been absorbed by Pacific Western in 1979, their 737 fleets combining to create an impressive operation.
Jenny Gradidge/Aviation Hobby Shop

Alaska Airlines operated a mixed fleet of 727s and 737s. Via author

Another round of mergers, acquisitions and renaming brought Eastern Provincial into the new Canadian Airlines International. Steve Bunting/Martyn East

Continental added the PeoplExpress/Frontier/New York Air 737s to its already over-diverse fleet, in 1987. Martyn East

PeoplExpress Boeing 737s (of three different marks), Boeing 727s, 747s, McDonnell Douglas DC-9s, of several models, MD-80s and DC-10s made up the highly diverse fleet. In addition, ex-Eastern Airbus A300Bs were shortly to make their own maverick contribution. The varied network serviced not only local domestic routes, but also transcontinental, trans-Atlantic and even trans-Pacific longer-haul services. Few of the routes were making much, if any, money and the now highly unwieldy Continental Airlines entered its second period of Chapter 11 bankruptcy protection within months of the mergers taking effect.

Air Florida Aftermath

With the demise of Air Florida, there was a gap in the low-fare market in the 'Sunshine State'. Quick to step in to try to fill the breach was Chicago-based Midway Airlines, which took over some of the assets, including the more profitable local routes. Midway also took over some of the ex-Air Florida Boeing 737 fleet, offering employment to many of the defunct airline's staff.

Midway Airlines had begun operations from Chicago's older airport in November 1979, operating a fleet of DC-9s on services to Cleveland, Detroit and Kansas City. Expansion followed with new routes opening to Newark, New York and Washington, with the Chicago operations eventually being rebranded as 'Midway Metrolink'. These offered all business-class facilities, while the Florida-based 737s flew all economy-class flights, as 'Midway Express'. Eventually, the two operation were merged into one. The airline continued its expansion, replacing the 737s with more DC-9s, of various marks, until mounting losses caused the company to cease all operations in 1991.

Another concern also took over a number of Air Florida's aircraft. Veteran long-haul carrier Pan American World Airways, had already introduced a handful of 737-200s on their Internal German Network. Leased-in from 1982 to replace less fuel-efficient Boeing 727-100s, the 737s flew from West Berlin to Frankfurt, Hamburg, Munich, Nuremburg and Stuttgart, as well as appearing on some international European routes. Pan American's buy-out of Miami-based National Airlines in 1980 had brought a number of short-haul Floridian routes into the network, where the 737s also proved more economic. Five ex-Air Florida 737s were acquired to increase the Boeing twin-jet fleet and the aircraft served in West Germany as well as Florida.

The reunification of Germany, in 1990, saw Pan American eventually withdrawing from Berlin. Pan American itself was now in decline system-wide, struggling against serious mismanagement, unable to cope with low-fare competition from deregulated carriers. The 737s returned to Miami where they replaced more 727s. A total of sixteen 737s were to be operated by Pan American.

Pan American acquired 737-200s to replace 727-100s on West German and US domestic services. N388PA 'Clipper Reinickendorf' was leased in for the Berlin-based operations in 1983–84. Via author

Originally delivered to Western in 1969, 737-200, B-12001 operated VIP services for the Mexican Air Force from 1980 until 1999. The aircraft was written off in a landing accident at Loma Bonita. *Steve Bunting*

Delta ordered a fleet of 'Advanced' 737-200s to replace older DC-9s. N303DL was one of the first, arriving in 1983. *Via author*

Another ex-Western aircraft, 737-200, B2613 flew for Far Eastern Air Transport of Taiwan from 1979 to 1996. *Aviation Hobby Shop*

G-BADP was named 'Sir Arthur Whitten-Brown' in Britannia Airways service. *Steve Bunting*

Belgium's Sabena operated several versions of the 737 on its European network. Steve Bunting

(*Above*) Delivered to the Imperial Iranian regime in 1977, Boeing 737-200, EP-AGA continued to operate VIP services for the post-revolutionary Islamic Republic government. MAP

(*Below*) Bahamasair has flown several 737s, in various versions of its blue and yellow livery, on different leasing contracts over the years. C6-BEX flew for the airline from 1983 to 1991. Steve Bunting

(*Right*) USAir's N247US began life in 1982 as N793N, 'Suwanee Pacemaker' with Piedmont Airlines. The aircraft was transferred to US Airways Metrojet in 1998. Steve Bunting

(*Below*) F-GLXG was operated by Trans European, Rotterdam Airlines, TEA (UK) and GB Airways before joining Europe Aero Service in 1993. MAP

(*Bottom*) Air Malta's 737-200s fly an extensive IT charter programme to the Mediterranean island, as well as vital scheduled services. Martyn East

(*Above*) N307AC was retained by American Airlines for just over three years after the airline took over AirCal. American Airlines C.R. Smith Museum

Air Holland operated 737-300, PH-OZA on IT charters from Amsterdam in the early 1990s. Malcolm L. Hill

(*Below*) EC-EBY was delivered new to Hispania in 1987. It later served with Transwede, TEA (Switzerland), Air Europa, TAESA, NordicEast and Western Pacific, before becoming N334AW with America West in 1999. Richard Howell

(*Top*) A Maersk Air 737-300, on lease to British Airways, shares the Bristol, UK, ramp with a GB Airways 737-200 in 1989. Martyn East

(*Above*) Inter European's leased 737-300, G-MONP on turn-round at Bristol with Paramount's -300, G-PATE in 1990. Martyn East

United has flown 737-300, N33OUA since its delivery in 1988. Steve Bunting

(*Below*) Deutsche BA has based its post-reunification success around the 737-300. Deutsche BA

Denver-based Frontier Airlines' 737s feature colourful designs on their tails, unique to each individual aircraft. Aviation Hobby Shop

(*Above*) Aer Lingus has operated a large fleet since 1968, eventually replacing them with European-built Airbus variants. Martyn East

(*Below*) Fly Cruise was a specialist cruise line charter subsidiary of Carnival Air Lines that took over the latter's charter services as Carnival increased its scheduled network. Carnival later merged with a briefly revived Pan American, before ceasing operations. -400, N402KW is pictured taxying at Miami. Steve Bunting

(*Above*) 737-500, N507SW is one of several Southwest Airline's aircraft to wear the special 'Shamu' livery, promoting Seaworld's famous killer whale attraction. Steve Bunting

(*Below*) France's Air Outre Mer operates a number of 737 versions on its scheduled and charter services. 737-500, F-GINL was delivered on lease in 1998. MAP

(*Below*) Maersk Air (UK) operated its 737-500s in full British Airways 'World Images' livery. Aviation Hobby Shop

(*Top*) **British Midland's new image as british midland bmi was unveiled in 2001. 737-500, G-BVZH was one of the first to wear the revised livery.** Aviation Hobby Shop

(*Middle*) **Lufthansa operates its 737-300QCs on night-time cargo and mail services around Europe.** Lufthansa

(*Bottom*) **Maersk Air operate 'Next Generation' 737s, including 737-700, OY-MRC, alongside earlier versions.** Aviation Hobby Shop

Following Pan American's withdrawal from Berlin, the 737s returned to the USA. N68AF, 'Clipper Rainbow', an ex-Air Florida aircraft, carries the final 'Billboard' livery, on push-back from Tampa for a short flight back to Miami. Malcolm L. Hill

Beginning by selling off its Pacific network, Pan American continued to sell off assets and close routes in an effort to save money. New, smaller, Airbus types had been imported from Europe to replace 747s on domestic trunk routes, and were later seen on some of the international flights. The sale of the prime US–London/Heathrow routes followed, also sold to United.

A deal was reached with Atlanta-based Delta Air Lines, whereby Delta would acquire the remaining trans-Atlantic network and domestic 'Shuttle' operation between Boston, New York and Washington, one of the few profitable parts of the airline. Pan American would continue on services to the Caribbean and Central and South America, based at Miami. The 'tactical retreat' to Miami was seen as the chance for a new start, and the only chance for the carrier to survive in any substantial form.

However, at the last minute, Delta withdrew vital funding. The 'Shuttle' and the remaining trans-Atlantic routes had already been transferred to Delta, but the expected life-span of the rest of Pan American could be counted in hours. The tattered remnant of the historic carrier was forced into an ignominious bankruptcy on 4 December 1991. The very last commercial flight by an aircraft of the original Pan American World Airways was operated later that day by a Boeing 727-200 on a scheduled service from Barbados to Miami. Ironically, the 727 was named 'Clipper Goodwill'.

More New Operators

An interesting addition to the ranks of US 737 operators was scheduled Air Express carrier, Federal Express. A small fleet of convertible 737-200Cs were delivered to Federal Express from 1979, and operated on their extensive night-time cargo network. The convertible version had been chosen as, at the time, the carrier was considering diversifying into passenger charter or low-fare scheduled services, to occupy the aircraft when not required for the freight work. However, these plans were soon abandoned and the 737s disposed of by 1981, in favour of larger all-cargo aircraft.

In the Middle East, Egyptair leased two Air Lingus 737-200s in 1975, prior to taking delivery of their own fleet of eight new aircraft on order from Boeing. The 737s were to replace the airline's ageing fleet of Comet 4Cs and Russian-built Il-18 and AN-24 turbo-props on local and regional flights. The Egyptair 737s joined others already in service in the region with Gulf Air, Iran Air, Iraqi Airways, Saudia and Sudan Airways. Egyptair later leased aircraft from their 737 fleet to associate airline, Air Sinai, that operates scheduled flights domestically with Egypt and internationally on schedules to Israel, as well as charters to Europe.

In Europe, among others, Greece's national carrier, Olympic Airways placed the 737-200 in service on their domestic and European schedules. Belgium's Sabena had replaced their last Caravelles and Boeing 727-100s with 737-200s, beginning in 1974. Sabena also leased aircraft to their IT charter subsidiary, Sobelair, in competition with TEA's Boeing 737 operations. Abelag Airways, a new Brussels-based carrier, operated 737-200s alongside 707s, before changing its name to Air Belgium. Neighbouring Luxair replaced their own Caravelles with 737-200s, flying them on European schedules, as well as a popular programme of ITs from its Luxembourg base.

Air France's own, long-awaited, Boeing 737-200s finally arrived in Europe in December 1982. They replaced the last of the airline's surviving Caravelles, a type that had been in service with Air France since 1959!

Low-Fare Hopefuls

PeoplExpress, and its initial success, soon found some disciples around America. One to take up much of the PeoplExpress philosophy, including a version of the staff-empowering concept, was America West Airlines, based at Phoenix, Arizona.

Founded as a company in 1981 and beginning operations in 1983, America West initially operated a trio of Boeing 737-200s on routes from Phoenix to Colorado Springs, Kansas City, Los Angeles and Wichita. By the end of the first year's operations, ten 737s were in use servicing twelve cities from Phoenix. International operations, with routes opening to Canada, followed shortly afterwards, as did seasonal ski-flight schedules to Colorado.

Further east, Presidential Airways began operations from Washington's Dulles International Airport in October 1985. High frequency, low-fare, flights served Boston, Hartford, Cincinnati, Cleveland, Miami, Orlando and West Palm Beach with a fleet of twelve 737-200s. A small fleet of British-built BAe 146-200s began joining Presidential in mid-1986, on lower-capacity flights.

Plans to replace the 737s with an all-BAe 146 fleet were speeded up as the company continued to lose money and entered Chapter 11 bankruptcy protection. Eventually the company was reorganized as a United Express carrier, operating on behalf of the larger airline on routes from Dulles. Even this support failed to save Presidential and, after yet another reorganization and renewal as Presidential Express, operating BAe Jetstream commuter turbo-props, Presidential finally ceased operations for good in December 1989.

America West Airlines managed to survive, despite experiencing its own growing pains. The Phoenix-based airline was forced into Chapter 11 itself a number of times, for the first time in 1991. In what was seen later as a classic case of overexpansion, a pair of second-hand Boeing 747 wide-bodies had been placed in service on short-lived, loss-making, schedules to Hawaii. For once, as with other less fortunate airlines, this did not foretell the beginning of the end. America West used its periods of bankruptcy protection as a useful breathing space in which to reorganize and, where necessary, reinvent itself.

(*Above*) America West's initial growth at Phoenix was based around the 737. Steve Bunting

(*Below*) Originally Britannia airways G-AVRO, Presidential Airways N313XV is pictured at Luton before its trans-Atlantic delivery flight. Steve Bunting

WORLDWIDE INFLUENCES

(*Above*) Federal Express only operated the 737 for a short time, replacing them with larger 727-200 freighters when plans to operate passenger services were dropped. MAP

(*Below*) The single aircraft fleet of Air Sinai, operating a limited domestic and regional network, contrasted dramatically with Sabena's wide-ranging use of its numerous 737s, of various versions, throughout Europe. Both pictures courtesy of Steve Bunting

WORLDWIDE INFLUENCES

(*Left*) Sabena's charter subsidiary, Sobelair, operated its 737s to resort areas around the Mediterranean. Via author

(*Below left*) Air France finally placed their own 737s into service on European routes in 1982. F-GBYP is pictured during a turnround at Geneva. Malcolm L. Hill

Deregulation Aftermath

Although the debate will certainly rage for years as to the benefits or otherwise of the deregulation of the US airline industry, there is no doubt that it had a dramatic effect of the travelling habits of America. While some operators thrived under the new conditions, some faltered and many failed in short order. Similar reforms were soon to be copied the world over in the following decades, with varying degrees of success.

Throughout the upheavals, the Boeing 737 had played a part, both plying its traditional trade with the established carriers and blazing pioneering trails with the new breed of low-cost airlines. As the regulatory changes began to make their mark on the airlines, Boeing was looking closely at the basic 737. Was it to be seen as having served its purpose and confined to history as a 1960s and 70s phenomenon? Or was there life in an updated design?

(*Below*) Luxair's busy fleet of 737-200s flew both scheduled and IT charters within Europe. Luxair

CHAPTER SEVEN

The Baby Grows

Britannia airways updated their 737-200 fleet over the years, replacing older aircraft with more modern versions. G-BJCV, 'Viscount Trenchard' was delivered in early 1982. Via author

What Next?

With the 1980s approaching, the 737 sales figures had maintained their recovery from the early 1970s slump. With the 'Advanced' version making its mark, Boeing was finally able to start looking to the future of the 737 programme.

A major factor to be considered was that of fuel economy. Since the original OPEC crisis in 1974, the price of aviation fuel had leapt up several times. The comparatively thirsty JT8Ds were becoming less economical as the years went by. New noise pollution legislation was on the horizon as well that would eventually restrict operations of both the early model 737s and the larger 727s. There were at least only two thirsty and noisy JT8Ds on the 737, compared to three on the 727.

Development of an even more stretched 727-300 series was finally abandoned, although it had found favour with several airlines. United, in particular, had co-operated with Boeing on the design studies for the proposed 727-300, that would be a further 18ft 4in (5.6m) longer than the -200 and the airline came close to placing a production order. However, an all-new design, originally designated the 7N7, was finally chosen for development by Boeing. This eventually emerged as the twin-engined 757. The last new 727 rolled off the production line in September 1984.

Although the 727 had eventually been completed replaced, Boeing opted to study an upgraded 737, as an alternative to designing a whole new type. The 737 studies centred on re-engining the design, preferably with more fuel-efficient high-bypass turbofans, then under development. As well as offering the required fuel economies, the new engines would be much quieter. Further improvements looked at for the new 737 versions included a modernized flight-deck, revised systems and refined aerodynamics.

Go Ahead for the -300

Boeing finally made its decision to proceed with an improved 737 in January 1979. The established design would form the basis of the company's offering for the 100–150 seater, short/medium-range market. The first public reference to the new type, now known as the 737-300, was made at the Farnborough Air Show in 1980. At the time, Boeing was still negotiating with the two main candidates to supply the new engine designs, CFM International, with their CFM56, and Rolls Royce with the proposed RJ500.

CFM International finally won through and, when the 737-300 was formally launched with the first production order in March 1981, the aircraft would be CFM56 powered. CFM International was jointly owned by General Electric of the USA and SNECMA of France. The CFM56 was first developed as a possible replacement for older types of engines on the Boeing 707. Boeing had planned to offer new 707 airframes fitted with the engines, as well as retrofitting existing aircraft. The civil programme was later cancelled, although the engine was used to re-engine many military 707s and KC135s. An updated flight-deck for the new 737 saw the use of more modern instrumentation and new technology systems such as digital avionics, up to the standard on Boeing's new 757 and 767 models.

The 737-300 flight-deck incorporated many advances originally designed for the then new 757 and 767 models. Lufthansa

The CFM56 was a very different engine design from the JT8D. Much bigger, the high bypass ratio engines could not be hung below the 737 wings as with the earlier versions of the aircraft. Instead, they had to be cantilevered out ahead of the wing's leading edge. The original 737 design's inherent lack of centre of gravity problems made this fairly major re-design possible. Any other engine location would have made use of the much larger CFM56 difficult, if not totally impossible. To solve the problem of ground clearance with the wider engine, the lower section of the engine nacelle was slightly flattened at the bottom and even some parts of the engine were repositioned.

The power added by the 22,000lb thrust of the CFM56 allowed Boeing to initiate the first major stretch of the 737 since the -200. Two fuselage plugs, one of 3ft 8in (1.1m) forward of the wing, one of 5ft (1.5m) at the rear, increased the overall length to 109ft 7in (33m). In a high-density configuration, this would allow the seating of up to 149 passengers.

Bigger Yet

The initial stretch that produced the Series 300 was not to be the end of the story. Boeing continued to study whole new designs in the 150-seat range through the mid-1980s, evaluating airline reaction to a '7-7' design, to be powered by IAE V2500 engines. Later this design was refined into the '7J7' proposal that was expected to be built in close co-operation with Japan. Despite, or possibly as a result of, being powered by propfan engines and incorporating fly-by-wire, totally electronic controls, the 7J7 received a fairly cool reception from the airlines.

Nonetheless, Boeing kept the 7J7 proposal alive and offered a further stretch of the 737 as a 'stop-gap' until the 7J7 technology was perfected into a more practical airliner design. The airlines had been pressuring Boeing to make a decision and the Series 400 was finally announced in late 1985. Further stretched by 6ft (1.8m)

Better Late Than Never

Although Britannia Airways' success with the 737 had not gone unnoticed with the United Kingdom's national carrier, it was to be over ten years before British Airways was to put their own aircraft into service. BA's predecessor, British European Airways had lobbied for permission to order the 737 for many years. Operating as a nationalized corporation at the time though, there was a great deal of political interference in the airline's operations. As a result, locally produced aircraft such as the Hawker Siddeley Trident and BAC One-Eleven had to be favoured, even though they were less economic to operate.

By the time the two national airlines were merged into one company, British Airways, in 1974, the British aerospace industry was in serious decline, which occurred as a result of political interference. As such, its proposals for new aircraft for British Airways European Division, as BEA had initially become, were for the most part uncompetitive. Yet further enlarged versions of the Trident and One-Eleven were proposed, but soon rejected, as was the French-built Mercure.

Once freed from its government chains, BA was able to actively consider US aircraft for its short-haul needs. In late 1977, under the pretext of a capacity shortage, British Airways leased in both McDonnell Douglas DC-9-51s and Boeing 737-200s, from Finnair and Transavia respectively, to assess the performance of both types on their short-haul network. The Finnair DC-9s only operated on the London–Helsinki service. The Transavia 737s, initially wearing BA stickers in addition to Transavia's colours, were used on flights from London to Amsterdam, Brussels, Frankfurt, Hamburg, Istanbul, Stavanger and Stockholm, as well as also appearing on the Helsinki route. As the study continued, the Transavia aircraft were eventually repainted in full BA livery. Also evaluated at the time was the Boeing 7N7 project that BA later ordered as the Boeing 757.

As a result of the assessments, British Airways placed an order for nineteen 737-200s in July 1978. To be promoted as the 'Super 737s', by BA, the aircraft were an updated version of the 'Advanced' 737, with CAT 3A autoland certification, matching the autoland capabilities of the Tridents that they were to replace. The flight-deck layout was upgraded and the avionics incorporated a new digital Automatic Flight Control System.

British Airways' own 737s entered service in February 1980, and the Transavia aircraft were returned. Coincident with the arrival of the 737, a massive 70 per cent fuel price rise was imposed, making their arrival even more welcome as it allowed the swift retirement of more thirsty Tridents and One-Elevens. The fact that the new aircraft could be operated with two flight-deck crew, as opposed to the Trident's three, also added to cost savings that arrived with the 737s.

Nine more 'Super 737s' were ordered to re-equip BA's charter subsidiary, British Airtours. Originally flying ex-BEA Comet 4Bs, as BEA Airtours from 1968, the charter arm had taken on a new identity with the emergence of BA after the merger. A fleet of ex-BOAC Boeing 707s had already replaced the Comets, but these were becoming uneconomic on the shorter European charters. Lockheed Tristars took over the longer-ranging flights and the 737s were to finally replace the ageing 707s from 1980–81.

British Airways itself ordered a further sixteen 737-200s that, along with the arrival of Boeing 757s, would accelerate the retirement of the last Tridents and One-Elevens.

(*Above*) British Airways own 737-200s were operated from February 1980 on both domestic and international services from London/Heathrow. Malcolm L. Hill

(*Below*) BA subsidiary, British Airtours, specialized in IT charters with its 737-200s that had replaced older 707s. Steve Bunting

(*Above*) Southwest's 737s steadily expanded their sphere of influence under deregulation. Tim Kincaid Collection

forward and 4ft (1.2m) aft, the 737-400 fuselage was only 5in (12.5cm) shorter than the original 'Dash Eighty', the prototype Boeing 707/KC135.

The 7J7 was officially 'indefinitely postponed', while the supposedly 'stop-gap' 737-400 was launched into production with the first orders received in June 1986. Over 170 passengers could now be accommodated in the stretched 737-400.

The Series 200 into the 1980s

Even as Boeing was refining the proposed Series 300, the Series 200 continued to attract customers. The Series 300 was not intended as an immediate replacement for the Series 200. Indeed, the Series 200 and 300 were to be produced side by side for some years.

Established US operators of the 737 continued to expand their fleets of Series 200s. Southwest Airlines had been swift to take advantage of deregulation and expand out of its Texan confines. Others had stumbled into the post-deregulation era and overstretched themselves. Nonetheless, under Herb Kelleher's direction, Southwest had controlled their growth, while still sustaining a healthy expansion. As well as extending the established network to the east and west, eventually reaching Arizona, California, Nevada and Tennessee, new Kansas City services were extended northwards to St Louis and Chicago/Midway.

USAir took delivery of 737-200s as part of a modernization programme, beginning the gradual process of replacing older DC-9s and BAC One-Elevens. Steve Bunting

Unlike other US pioneer 737 operators, California's Pacific Southwest Airlines had eventually disposed of their fleet. After a financially disastrous attempt to operate wide-bodied Lockheed L-1011 Tristars on their high-pressure, inter-city network, PSA had standardized on the Boeing 727-200. Over thirty were operated by the airline at the trijet's PSA zenith. Later, even the 727s were replaced by more economical MD-81s and several DC-9-30s were acquired second-hand. A number of UK-built BAe-146s were also introduced, as frequency of service became a priority over aircraft capacity.

Other long-term 737 operators, United, Western and Piedmont, were still steadily increasing their fleets of Series 200s. Second-hand aircraft were often acquired, as well as new examples off the production line. Even Lufthansa was still taking delivery of 737s, taking their 70th aircraft on charge in March 1985. All these operators were showing a healthy interest in the Series 300/400 developments, as was Southwest Airlines.

USAir, the renamed Allegheny Airlines, whose takeover of Lake Central in 1968 had led to the cancellation of the latter's own 737 order, finally took delivery of the type in 1982. Another takeover in 1972 had seen the network and fleet of New York State-based Mohawk Airlines being integrated into Allegheny. The much expanded carrier had changed its name to USAir in 1979 in order to give the airline a less parochial image and reflect its ambitions to expand nationwide.

As a result of the Mohawk acquisition, Allegheny operated a number of the, basically similar, American-built DC-9-30s and British-built BAC One-Eleven jets, the latter inherited from Mohawk. The jets were supplemented by a large fleet of Convair CV-580 turbo-props. The first of an initial order of seven 737-200s joined the USAir fleet to begin the replacement of the older One-Eleven and DC-9s, with new 727-200s also joining the airline's inventory for new Pittsburgh–California longer-range services.

More UK Charter 737s

Despite the post-fuel-crisis depression, the seemingly inexorable rise of the inclusive tour market in Europe was to lead to further expansion of the 737's presence on the continent in the early 1980s. Established operators found themselves in the position of having to lease in extra capacity to cater for the demand as the holiday industry recovered. Some new carriers quickly stepped in to exploit opportunities in the growing market and were soon showing their colours on airport ramps around Europe. Cost-cutting was still a high priority and charter operators of older, less fuel-efficient aircraft were starting to look seriously at their options for replacing their thirstier fleets.

The first of the 'new breed' of British charter carriers to emerge was Air Europe, which began operations in May 1979. Established with the backing of Intasun, then one of the largest UK IT travel companies, both organizations had entrepreneur Harry Goodman as their chairman. The original founders of the airline, Errol Cossey and Martin O'Regan had both been with leading British independent, Dan-Air Services, as Commercial Director and Group Finance Director respectively. They decided to strike out on their own after the Dan-Air management rejected their proposals for modernizing the fleet to make it more economic and attractive to potential charterers. Goodman had been interested in their ideas and offered backing to establish Intasun's own 'in-house' airline.

Getting Air Europe Underway

The strong financial backing meant that Air Europe was able to go straight to Boeing for a brand new fleet. The whole pretext behind Casey and O'Regan's plan had been to introduce modern aircraft with lower operating costs and operational reliability. As a result, they felt that they would be able to offer a cost-effective, reliable service with increased aircraft utilization, thus allowing lower rates to be offered to charterers. The older fleet operated by Dan-Air was unable to offer the lower seat-mile costs increasingly demanded by Intasun and other tour operators.

A deposit was paid to Boeing for three new 737-200 'Advanced' aircraft. The aircraft's financing came via a Japanese investment group and involved a 10-year lease-purchase agreement. Then still a novel idea, but now a standard industry practice, the arrangement was a natural evolution of earlier styles of leasing practices. In addition to the initial three aircraft, two more 737s were on order for delivery in time for the 1980 season.

Late 1978 to early 1979 was spent in a flurry of organization, recruitment and training. Determined to lay to rest the old charter airline's reputations for old, unreliable aircraft and indifferent service, Air Europe's management laid great emphasis on employing a cadre of professional people who took pride in their work. The new base at London/Gatwick became operational when the first aircraft, registered G-BMHG (after Mike Harry Goodman), was delivered on 10 April 1979. Soon joined by G-BMOR (after Martin O'Regan) and G-BMEC (after Errol Cossey), commercial operations began

Air Europe's brand new fleet was one of the most modern available for IT work in the UK. MAP

with a Gatwick–Palma IT charter on Friday 14 May, carrying 130 Intasun customers.

Another Holiday Flight Newcomer

As Air Europe was getting itself geared up for its first summer season, another UK tour operator was also setting up its own 737 airline. Horizon Travel had been one of the pioneers of the industry, flying its first IT passengers from Britain to Corsica in 1949. Expanding steadily over the years, the inevitable corporate 'ups and downs' included the company being a part of the giant Clarksons organization when it entered bankruptcy in 1974. However, Horizon survived, being sold on to new owners by the official receiver.

Horizon soon regained its place among the busiest tour companies. Like Intasun, Horizon became dissatisfied with the service offered by established charter airlines and looked to provide a superior service while being able to reduce costs by operating its own airline division. The new airline, Orion Airways, was formed in late 1978, but was not to begin operations until the 1980 summer season.

Staff and crews were recruited and trained throughout 1979, in preparation for the 1980 summer season. Unlike Air Europe that based itself at London's Gatwick Airport, Orion Airways adopted East Midlands Airport as its headquarters. East Midlands Airport, near Castle Donington, had been opened in 1964 to serve the metropolitan areas encapsulated by Derby, Nottingham and Leicester. Up until the opening of East Midlands Airport, the area had been dominated by Birmingham's Elmdon Airport, much further to the west and inconvenient for the population of the more eastern cities in the region.

Orion's first three Boeing 737-200s were delivered in February and March 1980.

Orion Airways had the backing of Horizon, one of the most distinguished and longest established IT holiday companies. Steve Bunting

Operations were initially undertaken solely for Horizon, eventually serving twenty-five holiday destinations in nine countries. When three more aircraft were delivered in time for the 1981 season, operations were also being undertaken from Birmingham, Luton and Manchester, with other regional points eventually joining the IT charter network.

One Pilot's View

Among the pilots recruited was Chris Harrison, originally with British Midland Airways, the only carrier with any significant presence at East Midlands up until the arrival of Orion Airways. Although Chris's introduction to the Boeing 737 was to be some time after the type made its debut, his experience of transition from propeller to jet was to be typical of many over the years.

I gave up a command on Viscounts with BMA to go fly 737s as a First Officer (something I now advise F/Os *never* to do – sometimes it is very difficult to get back in the left hand seat!). Apart from single engine jets in the Royal Air Force, this was the first type of jet aircraft I had flown. I was amazed at how much further ahead of the aircraft I had to think. For instance, having to plan Top of Descent points, dependent on winds, aircraft weight, ATC altitude restrictions, etc., mostly up to 130 nautical miles from the airport!

The aircraft, as are all jets, became a big glider with the engines at idle power. Of course, on the Viscounts, propellers could provide enormous amounts of drag to slow down and descend, but could also provide instantaneous response to deliver power. This was not so on the JT8Ds, on which an eight second spool-up time from idle to full power could be expected. This could be potentially disastrous at low height, low power configuration, if immediate full power was required. Hence, high drag against high power approaches were much safer. The 737 was one of the first aircraft to incorporate high lift devices and if all were extended – slats, flaps and if, upon landing, the speedbrake was extended, it looked as though there was hardly anything on the wing that was not extended or moving, as you could see right through it!

The Orion 737s were used extensively on holiday IT work. Because of the high density configuration of 130 passenger seats for flights of up to four hours, with reserves, this meant sometimes having to include technical, refuelling, stops on flights to and from the Canary Islands, especially from airfields further north in the UK. Operating the aircraft to the maximum extent of its range and field performance, with temperatures in the holiday destinations often being very hot in summer, up to 30–40°, meant that we were becoming very adept at squeezing the last kilo out of the weight and balance calculations.

More IT Interest in the 737

As well as Air Europe and Orion's use of the aircraft as the basis of their new operations, a number of other charter operators around Europe started taking interest in the type as a replacement for their older fleets. In the UK, established operators

Dan-Air Services, based at Gatwick and Monarch Airlines, Britannia Airways' neighbour at Luton, both introduced 737-200s into their fleets in late 1980.

Dan-Air had finally recognized that their fleet needed modernization. Its charter operations were based mostly around fleets of second-hand Comets and BAC One-Elevens, with larger Boeing 727-100s and -200s. Despite having been comparatively cheap to acquire, the Dan-air aircraft were increasingly expensive to operate and maintain. The tour companies were also becoming reluctant to accommodate their clients on Dan-Air's older aircraft and were threatening to take their business elsewhere. As the last of the Comets was finally withdrawn from service, at the end of 1980, Dan-Air took delivery of its first 737. The single Series 200 was operated on lease from the Danish airline, Maersk Air.

Maersk Air, a subsidiary of the giant A.P. Moller Group, owners of the Maersk Shipping organization, had begun operations as a flight service division of its parent company. Fokker F.27s had opened general charter flights in 1979, later undertaking domestic schedules and ITs for a number of local tour companies. As the IT market expanded in Denmark as swiftly as anywhere else, Maersk replaced the Fokkers on the holiday charters with second-hand Boeing 720Bs, resplendent in their all-blue colour scheme.

Maersk began to replace the 720Bs with 737-200s in 1978. like other carriers before it, Maersk started leasing out spare capacity

(*Above*) Maersk began large-scale IT services with Boeing 720Bs, eventually replacing them with 737s. Leasing contracts soon became a large part of the airline's operations. 737 OY-APG was contracted out to Tunisair in 1978. Jenny Gradidge

in the off-season. Soon, Maersk was specializing in longer-term leasing, buying aircraft specifically to undertake leasing contracts, using them only briefly on their own charter services.

Dan-Air only operated one 737, G-BICV, through 1981. Initially, it was mainly used on ITs for the Thomas Cook travel organization, for whom the aircraft flew holiday passengers throughout Europe. It was not until 1982 that another aircraft, also leased from Maersk, joined the first 737. However, further leased aircraft soon followed from various sources.

G-BICV was the first 737 to wear the famous Dan-Air 'Compass Rose' logo. Via author

Monarch Joins the Club

Monarch Airlines had intended their 737s to replace their fleet of BAC One-Elevens that operated alongside Boeing 720Bs on European ITs from bases at Luton and Manchester. Like Air Europe and Orion, Monarch had been set up by a tour company, Cosmos Holidays, in 1968. Originally operating a fleet of Bristol Britannia turboprops, Boeing 720Bs and BAC One-Elevens had eventually replaced the prop-liners.

The first pair of Monarch 737s were also leased in, as was the increasingly popular fashion, this time from Bavaria Fluggesellschaft. Although originally a charter carrier, flying BAC One-Elevens from Munich, Bavaria had sold its commercial airline operation to another operator, Germanair. However, Bavaria continued to exist as a separate company and began specializing in leasing aircraft to other airlines.

The first of a pair of Bavaria 737-200s arrived at Monarch Airline's Luton base in late September 1980, followed by the second a month later. Joining Britannia's 737s at Luton that had already been flying from the Bedfordshire airport for twelve years, the new 737s began operation on Monarch's inclusive-tour network soon afterwards.

Seasonal Swaps

Air Europe pioneered a new leasing arrangement with foreign carriers, in an effort to boost utilization in the winter months. As already mentioned, leasing contracts were undertaken by a number of airline operators. Aer Lingus, Britannia and Transavia, among others, had all sent aircraft off to temporary new homes in their slack traffic periods. The lucrative contracts were often repeated over several years, but were usually a one-way street.

As well as enjoying a steady influx of new aircraft of its own most years, Britannia often leased in extra aircraft to cover seasonal shortages. Among the sources for Britannia's extra seasonal aircraft were Pluna of Paraguay, Quebecair of Canada and Eagle Air of Iceland, all in variations of their combined liveries.

Air Europe, however, came to a firmer, more regular, agreement with Air Florida, whose slackest time, the summer, Florida's low season, was Air Europe's busiest. This worked both ways, with Air Europe having spare capacity in the winter, when thousands were trying to escape the potentially harsh northern American winter and head south to the 'Sunshine State'.

Two of Air Florida's Boeing 737-200s spent the summer of 1981 operating Europe-based inclusive-tour charters from the UK alongside Air Europe's fleet of six similar aircraft. When they returned in the autumn, three Air Europe aircraft joined them and spent the winter operating on the Florida-based scheduled flights of Air Florida. Although a convincingly 'tidy' arrangement, the operation was not without its problems, not least with America's Federal Aviation Administration and Britain's Civil Aviation Authority. Both official bodies found objections to the 'foreign' aircraft. For example, the UK-registered

Monarch Airlines leased in 737-200s from Germany's Bavaria. MAP

aircraft were fitted with 'stick-pusher' stall warning devices that were not approved by the American authorities.

This 'swap' was repeated the next two years, until Air Florida ceased operations. As Air Florida lurched into its final financial crisis, Air Europe insisted it be paid every 48 hours for the continued use of their 737s. When the end came for the US carrier in 1984, its sudden demise into bankruptcy left Air Europe with a serious capacity shortage as the promised aircraft were no longer forthcoming. The airline was forced to lease in extra aircraft at short notice, a rather expensive exercise, to cover the shortfall.

Air Europe, under the wings of its parent company, the Intasun Leisure Group, later retitled the International Leisure Group, or ILG, survived the loss of Air Florida's loaned equipment and continued its apparently unstoppable expansion. Brand new Boeing 757s, among the first in Europe, had joined the fleet in 1983. Long-haul flights had been introduced, with the 757s operating over the Atlantic to Florida. Orion, still deriving much of its income from Horizon, steadily expanded its 737-200 charter operation, with several new bases opening around the UK.

Leasing False-Starts

Although the increasing use of leasing contracts instead of outright purchases by airlines was a popular one, it did not always work out. As a number of leasing operators increased, GATX/Booth were soon joined by the lines of International Lease Finance Corporation (ILFC), Bavaria, Ansett Worldwide, Guinness Peat Aviation (GPA), American Finance Group, Pacific Aviation Holding Co., Integrated Aircraft Corporation and others, as well as airlines such as Maersk Air acquiring aircraft specifically to lease out at a profit. The more favourable economic terms meant that the smaller airlines no longer had to wait for the bigger carrier's 'cast-offs'. The established airlines also saw the advantages to themselves of leasing in their fleets from financial and leasing companies. They no longer needed to have such large sections of their capital tied up in owning their aircraft outright.

Not all the customer airlines were financially stable enough to support their 737s though and soon fell by the wayside. In 1980, GPA leased 737-200s to French charter operator Aerotour, that had previously flown Caravelles. The lease was short-lived, however, as the aircraft were returned at the end of the 1980 season following Aerotour's financial collapse. The usually astute Maersk Air also lost out occasionally. In November 1980, a new German charter airline, Supair, had their aircraft repossessed by Maersk within a month of delivery after the airline failed to begin operations.

The Series 300 Debuts

The first Series 300 Boeing 737 took to the air for the first time on 24 February 1984. Orders were already flooding in for the aircraft, the customers being impressed with the promised increased performance, economy and reduced noise and emission levels of the new engines. By the end of the year, orders for the Series 300 had reached no less then 252 from twenty-six customers bringing the total for the 737 series as a whole to 1,418.

One of the first 737-300s flew in the colours of USAir, the launch customer, with Boeing titles, and was displayed as such at the 1984 Farnborough Air Show in the UK. By then end of the following year the new version had been delivered to AirCal (the rebranded Air California),

An early production 737-300 was displayed at Farnborough in 1984, wearing basic USAir colours. Jenny Gradidge

Non-Airline 737s

Despite Boeing's traditional military connections, the 737 remained a largely civilian project, as had been intended from the beginning. However, long-standing Boeing customer, the US Air Force, did place an order for nineteen specialized navigation trainers, to be based on the 737-200 airframe. The aircraft was designated the T-43A by the USAF. With most windows removed, the cabin rearranged to accommodate up to twelve trainee navigation stations and four astrodomes fitted to the top of the fuselage, the first T-43A was delivered in July 1973.

From 1992, at least five of the T-43As were transferred to a civilian operator, E.G. & G. Inc, who operate them alongside ex-airline 737-200s on 'Special Projects', personnel and equipment shuttles from Las Vegas, in connection with US government work at the remote Roswell Air Force base.

Ten years later, the Indonesian government also ordered specially modified 737s for military use. Designated Boeing 737-2X9s, the three aircraft are equipped with Motorola side-looking, multi-mission radar installed in distinctive housings above the rear fuselage. The aircraft are used to patrol the Indonesian Islands to detect illegal maritime activities.

The USAF T-43A navigation trainer was based around the 737-200 airframe. Jenny Gradidge

Indonesia's 737-2X9s feature radar housings built into the fuselage. Boeing

(*Below*) **N1288 was a 737-200 supplied to Essex International as a private corporate jet in late 1969.** Via author

The 737 was also adopted as a VIP or corporate transport by a number of civilian operators, as well as providing luxury accommodation for military organizations and government heads throughout the world.

Some companies also operated airline-style configured aircraft on private 'scheduled' services carrying company personnel between far-ranging plants and locations. Range could be extended to 4,606 miles by the addition of extra fuel cells in one of the lower cargo holds. The more luxurious executive interiors, where required, could be installed by Boeing, but in many cases the customers preferred to use outside craftsmen. Civilian customers for private 737-200s included Dome Petroleum, Eldorado Oil, Essex, Maritime, Noga and Petrolair. Military operators of both new and second-hand 737s included the air forces of Brazil, India, Mexico, Peru, Thailand and Venezuela.

THE BABY GROWS

(*Above*) JAT's 737-300 operations were stalled following the violent break-up of the former Yugoslavia. Steve Bunting

(*Below*) Aviogenex's main IT charter market, to and from Yugoslav resorts on the Adriatic Riviera, vanished overnight when war broke out between new rival states in the region. Richard Howell

America West, Cameroon Airlines, Continental, CP Air, Dan-Air, Jugoslovenski Aerotransport (JAT), Maersk Air, New York Air, Orion, Pakistan International, Piedmont, Southwest, Sunworld International, United, USAir and Western.

Many of these customers were new 737 operators. In the case of JAT, New York Air and Sunworld International, their previous main equipment had been DC-9s. JAT's efforts to replace its medium/short-haul fleet with the 737 were to be temporarily curtailed and most of the fleet disposed of. Limited charter services later restarted with a single 727-200 once some semblance of peace returned to the region.

New York Air was to be merged into Continental by the two airlines' owner, the Texas Air Corporation, when PeoplExpress was taken over. Sunworld International, a low-fare scheduled and charter carrier based at Las Vegas, operated three leased 737-300s only briefly, supplementing its DC-9 services throughout the west of the

The 737 in Wales

One of the Sunworld International aircraft found a temporary home at Cardiff, the capital of the UK principality of Wales. Airways International Cymru (Wales International Airways) had begun operations in 1984 with a pair of BAC One-Elevens. Owned by a local travel company, Red Dragon Travel, IT charters operated from Cardiff and the nearby English city of Bristol to European resorts. One of the

Monarch's 737-300 services encompassed most of the main holiday airports of southern Europe. G-MONH is pictured at one of the busiest, Palma, Majorca. Martyn East

halted when Yugoslavia was broken up into several states, following the fall of Communism in Eastern Europe. JAT's once extensive network was closed down, or severely curtailed, for long periods and the fleet either stored or leased out. Another Yugoslav 737 operator to suffer as a result of the political unrest in the country was Aviogenex. Formed as the country's IT specialist, Aviogenex operated a pair of 737-200s alongside a fleet of Tupolev Tu-134As and Boeing 727-200s, on IT charters from the Adriatic resorts to Western Europe. When the Yugoslav tourist industry collapsed with the violent break-up of the country into independent states, Aviogenex operations were greatly

USA. The DC-9s only continued in service for a short while before the airline ceased operations due to financial problems.

In high-density, inclusive-tour, configuration, the Series 300 carried 148 passengers, eighteen more than the -200's maximum. This increased revenue potential, linked to lower fuel costs, attracted the cost-conscious charter carriers in particular. Monarch took delivery of their first -300 in 1986, supplementing their earlier Series -200s and hastening the retirement of the last of their One-Elevens. New Boeing 757s had replaced the last of Monarch's high capacity 720Bs and were used on long-haul flights as well as supplementing the 737s on European ITs.

One-Elevens was leased out to British Midland Airways, but was replaced in 1985 by an ex-Britannia Airways 737-200, G-BAZI, obtained via Havelet leasing.

Although attracting a number of contracts from important tour operators, such as Cosmos, Air Cymru, as the company name tended to be shortened to in everyday use, had a chequered reputation. Popular with passengers for its friendly service, and with its staff as a pleasant company to work for, the daily operations tended to suffer from an unusual number of technical delays and operational problems. The airline's situation was not greatly helped when the Sunworld aircraft arrived in 1986. The operational fleet then consisted

G-BAZI came to Airways International Cymru from Britannia Airways, via a leasing company. Richard Howell

Airways International Cymru operated a large proportion of their flights from Bristol/Lulsgate, across the Severn Estuary from its main base at Cardiff. G-PROK, the second 737-300, is seen here, taxying away from the old Bristol terminal. Martyn East

HIGH FLYERS FLY AIC
Airways International Cymru

A cartoon 737 featured in Airways International Cymru's promotional material. Via author

(*Below*) **The larger 737-300 provided Orion, and its other operators, with increased revenue potential for similar costs.** Steve Bunting

of three aircraft, one One-Eleven, one 737-200 and the 737-300, all with totally different seating configurations (89, 130 and 148, respectively).

Should any technical or operational problems occur, none of the aircraft could cover the other's flights, even if available. The first ex-Sunworld aircraft was returned to its owners, ILFC, at the end of the 1986 season, with the -200, G-BAZI, going to Aer Lingus on lease for four months in the winter, leaving the One-Eleven alone in Air Cymru service. After G-BAZI returned in early 1987, it was joined by two other ILFC 737-300s, one of them also an ex-Sunworld International aircraft. This at least gave the fleet some semblance of standardization. At the end of 1987, the 737-300s were returned to ILFC and the Series 200 was subleased to a new US start-up to be based in Miami.

Unfortunately, the contract went sour, with the US airline failing to begin operations and stranding the aircraft, along with its seconded Air Cymru crews, in Miami amid the legal wrangles. An ill-advised,

As well as Europe's charter carriers suddenly finding the Boeing 737 the answer to their re-equipment prayers, even more scheduled carriers were seeing the light.

As already related, Air Algérie had been an early lease contract customer for Aer Lingus's 737s since the late 1960s. Air Algérie later went on to operate a not inconsiderable fleet of their own, finally replacing their ageing Caravelles. Tunis Air had introduced their first 737-200 in 1979, serving an extensive regional network that extended to Europe, as well as neighbouring North African states. With Tunisia boasting a number of popular coastal resorts, Tunis Air's 737s were soon chartered out to tour operators for IT flights, especially from northern Europe.

Already popular with Arabian carriers, the type was also adopted by the Israeli national airline, El Al. Previously almost solely an operator of longer-range aircraft, El Al leased in two 737-200s from Trans European, of Belgium, to evaluate the aircraft for use on regional schedules from Tel Aviv. The pair of leased 737s joined El Al in October 1980 and were operated on schedules to Europe and around the Mediterranean. An order was placed for two of their own 737-200s, delivered in January 1983, replacing the leased aircraft.

The independent Israeli airline, Arkia, also took delivery of Boeing 737-200s, its first, a second-hand ex-Wien Air Alaska aircraft arriving in 1981. When two new aircraft were delivered to Arkia in 1983, the original aircraft was sold. The aircraft were operated on scheduled domestic and regional flights, as well as an extensive programme of charters to Europe. Unfortunately, Arkia suffered financial problems after much of their scheduled network was closed down for political reasons, and the aircraft were sold or leased out in 1984.

Air Malta took delivery of their first 737 in 1981, leased in from Transavia of the Netherlands. The first of Air Malta's own order, for six 737-200s, was delivered in 1983. Operating on scheduled and IT charter services throughout the Mediterranean region and to Europe, Air Malta's 737s were acquired to replace the company's first aircraft, a fleet of second-hand Boeing 720Bs.

In 1983, the Boeing 737-200 also joined the fleet of the Portuguese national carrier, TAP-Air Portugal. The new aircraft were replacing older Boeings, in the shape of 727-100s on TAP-Air Portugal's scheduled and holiday charter network. The airline's charter subsidiary, Air Atlantis, based at the southern resort of Faro, also operated 737s from 1985. Air Atlantis, too, flew a handful of 727-200s and even long-range 707s on higher-capacity and further-ranging flights.

OPPOSITE PAGE

(*Top*) **Air Algérie built up a considerable 737 fleet for domestic, regional and trans-Mediterranean scheduled services.** Steve Bunting

(*Middle*) **Arkia flew its first 737s only briefly on IT charters and scheduled services in 1983/84. Other versions were acquired by Arkia some years later.** MAP

(*Bottom*) **The 737-200 joined Air Malta in 1981, with leased aircraft replaced by their own fleet in 1983.** Richard Howell

New Mediterranean Operators

unofficial attempt to repossess the aircraft caused even more legal expenses for Air Cymru. Without suitable aircraft for the forthcoming season, and the US legal bills eating into its operating capital, the company was forced to cease operations in early 1988.

Air California Progress

In the hands of new majority shareholders, the Westgate-California Corporation, since 1970, Air California had continued a steady expansion throughout the decade, carrying its ten millionth passenger in 1976. As a result of deregulation, Air California was able to expand outside California's borders, initially beginning interstate service to Reno, Nevada, in December 1978.

By 1979, nine 737s were operated alongside three Electras, the latter type reintroduced into the fleet in 1975 to operate services to ultra noise-sensitive Lake Tahoe. Also in 1979, an order was placed for five 162-passenger McDonnell Douglas MD-80s, with options for up to eight more. Two more Boeing 737-200s arrived in 1980, as the last of the Electras were finally disposed of.

More interstate flights were added, with service opening to Seattle and Phoenix. Shortly before the introduction of the MD-80s, in 1981, the company identity was amended to AirCal, with a smart new modern logo and colour scheme. The airline was purchased from Westgate California by a new company, AirCal Investments Inc, for $61.5 million.

Twelve Boeing 737-300s were ordered in June 1984, with options taken out on a further eleven, as part of a large fleet replacement programme. Nine of the firm orders came from AirCal itself – the remaining three were for aircraft to be leased from ILFC. The -300s were intended to eventually replace the then entire fleet of fourteen 737-200s, two leased -100s and seven MD-80s.

The New Boy on the Block

Although advanced electronic flight systems were to be introduced on the 737-300, the earliest examples were built with established analogue technology. Once it was more widely available though, the airlines and their pilots were soon enthusing about the new systems and their advantages over older versions.

Chris Harrison flew both the Series 200 and 300 with Orion and, from 1986 onwards, other operators:

> I found the workload much lower on the 300 due to the assistance of INS, automated power settings and calculations in the climb. Eventually, when the 'glass cockpit' came out, one could have a much better 'situational awareness'.

A typical UK airport line-up in the 1980s. No less than four different UK 737 operators, Orion Airways, Air Europe, British Airtours and Britannia Airways all share the Manchester ramp. Steve Bunting

> It gave one the ability to see, almost as on a map, your reference to waypoints, track, thunderstorms, airports and, eventually with TCAS (Terrain Collision Avoidance System), other aircraft around you.

The forthcoming Series 400 promised even more technical advances, linked to the higher capacity offered by the yet-further stretched fuselage. However, as well as being a natural development of the 737 breed, the Series 400 was developed in response to a growing threat to the type's sales from Europe. Would it rise to the challenge?

CHAPTER EIGHT

A New Lease of Life

The Next Big One

As the Series 300s began rolling off the Renton production line, beside the still popular -200s, Boeing was refining an even larger 737. The 9ft 6in (2.9m) longer -400 was fitted with extra over-wing emergency exits, two each side instead of one, and stronger wings and landing gear were fitted to cope with the increased gross weight of up to 142,000lb (64,410kg). The first Series 400 flew on 29 April 1988, all-metal-based livery. The latter company had acquired Piedmont, after purchasing a majority shareholding. However, with protracted legal wrangles and operational problems, it was to be another eighteen months before the Piedmont identity was to be fully absorbed into USAir. In the spring of 1988, USAir further expanded its swiftly growing network by acquiring Pacific Southwest Airlines, giving it a badly needed foothold in America's western states.

been taken over by Atlanta-based Delta Air Lines, and AirCal had been bought out by American Airlines.

Western had struggled in the post-deregulation era. As a cost-cutting measure, emphasis was diverted away from larger, expensive bases, such as Los Angeles, where cut-throat competition was wiping out what small profits there were. The airline began concentrating flights at less expensive 'hubs' such as Salt Lake City, in Utah. Still a large, important airline, operating DC-10 wide-

The arrival of the even further stretched Series 400 saw the 737 finally losing its 'Baby Boeing' tag. Boeing

the first production delivery being made to launch customer, Piedmont Airlines, on 15 September the same year. Piedmont placed the aircraft into service on 1 October 1988.

The Piedmont Airlines 737-400s were delivered in a hybrid Piedmont/USAir,

Californian Merger Mania

The loss of Pacific Southwest Airlines was the latest in a series of mergers and acquisitions that saw the disappearance of no less than three of California's 'home based' carriers. In 1987 Western Air Lines had

bodies to Hawaii and Mexico, alongside Boeing 727-200s and 737-200s, Western had begun introducing the 737-300 alongside the older versions. Delta Air Lines saw the chance to extend its network westwards, and took over the ailing 62-year-old airline as of 1 April 1987.

117

The Rise and Rise of the Pacemakers

Since its introduction of the 737-200, in 1968, Piedmont Airlines had never looked back. A sustained programme of growth and expansion had seen the once humble Local Service Carrier that had struggled to link the Ohio River Valley to the Atlantic coast, become one of the US's leading regional airlines. The remaining vintage Martin 404s had left the fleet in 1970 to be replaced by the Japanese-built YS-11As. In 1972, the airline's 25th year of operation, Piedmont reported record earnings and a profit of $3,323,317.

In 1979, Piedmont had fought off a hostile takeover bid by the then expansive Air Florida and in 1981 a new hub operation was opened at Charlotte, North Carolina. This was followed a year later with another new hub being inaugurated at Dayton, Ohio. The last turbo-prop YS-11As were sold off by 1982, and Piedmont became an all-jet airline, operating the now long-established 737-200s, alongside a mixed fleet of 727-100s that had re-entered Piedmont service in 1977, and 727-200s that had arrived in 1981.

Yet another new hub operation was opened at Baltimore in 1983, with twenty-nine daily flights to fourteen destinations. Henson Airlines, a small commuter airline based in Salisbury, Maryland, was taken over in 1983. Henson was then operated as a 'Piedmont Regional Airline', the beginning of a network of smaller, associated airlines that were to feed traffic into Piedmont's mainline network as 'Piedmont Commuter' carriers. The following year, a transcontinental service was opened to Los Angeles and San Francisco. In

1984 – a landmark year – the airline carried 13 million passengers and exceeded $1 billion in revenues, thus officially becoming a 'major' airline. In January 1985, Piedmont was named 'Airline of the Year' by the influential magazine, *Air Transport World*.

May 1986 saw Piedmont acquiring New York State-based Empire Airlines that operated a fleet of Fokker F.28 jets from Syracuse. The addition of the Dutch jets brought Piedmont's fleet up to 149 aircraft. This consisted of sixty-three Boeing 737-200s, thirteen 737-300s, thirty-four 727-200s (the 727-100s had left Piedmont in 1983), twenty Fokker F.28-1000s and nineteen F.28-4000s. The 1,177 daily departures served eighty-seven airports in twenty-seven states, the District of Columbia and two international points in Canada.

International expansion plans were implemented, with new wide-bodied Boeing 767-200s opening a Charlotte–London service in June 1987. The 767s also operated on transcontinental service from the hubs in the eastern states. New international flights also opened to Nassau, in the Bahamas in November. By then though, negotiations were well underway for the USAir purchase of Piedmont and, on 5 November, the airline became a subsidiary of USAir Group Inc.

Operations continued independently for a while, as the full merger of the two sizable airlines was engineered. However, finally, on 4 August 1989 the last Piedmont flight ever left Dayton for South Bend, Indiana. The next day, Piedmont ceased to exist and all operations were conducted under the USAir name. At the time of the final merger Piedmont Airlines was flying sixty-two 737-200s, forty-two 737-300s, eight 737-400s, six 767-200s, thirty-four 727-200s, twenty F.28-1000s and twenty-five F.28-4000s.

The 737-200 had proved itself the ideal aircraft for Piedmont's network, leading to sustained growth for the airline. Jenny Gradidge

---

American's intention to buy AirCal was announced in November 1986 and the deal was closed in April the next year. As with Delta and USAir, American felt the need to increase its profile in the western half of the USA, hence its interest in AirCal's successful network. The merger became effective on 1 July 1987, with AirCal's identity being replaced by American Airline's image from that date. The orderly integration of AirCal employees and aircraft into American was to make the merger 'nearly invisible' to passengers. Of the 3,700 AirCal employees, over 95 per cent were offered jobs within the new operation.

American's Chairman and President, Robert J. Crandall was expansive in his praise for the AirCal staff as he welcomed them into American Airlines:

> Both American and AirCal are winners. Both are can-do, quality orientated organizations, full of talented people who believe they can achieve anything they set out to do.

Post-Merger Operations

Following the acquisition by their new owners, both the fleets of Western and AirCal started appearing in 'hybrid' schemes, usually comprising a new name painted over their old liveries. Delta had actually been in the process of introducing their own fleet of 'Advanced' 737-200s, to replace older DC-9s, when the Western 737-200s and -300s were added.

American Airlines, though, had not previously been a Boeing 737 operator.

Western's attempts to survive after deregulation were doomed to failure. Its second 737-200, N4502W, was still in the fleet and taken over by Delta in 1987, nineteen years after it had been delivered. Via author

(*Below*) **Delta had ordered their own 'Advanced' 737-200s to replace older jets. The ex-Western 737-300s, like N303WA, soon appeared throughout the Delta network in full colours.**
Via author/Steve Bunting

Eventually, the ex-AirCal 737s were gradually disposed of or returned to lessors as contracts came up for renewal. American took delivery of further MD-80s, their preferred twin-engined jet, to replace them in Californian service as soon as it became practicable to do so.

The ex-Piedmont aircraft suffered no such ignominy. The length of time it had taken for the two airlines to merge had allowed them to co-ordinate their fleets well before they became one. PSA's MD-80s and DC-9s were fitted into the combined fleet as well, although, in time, the British BAe 146s were stored and then disposed of, after USAir had decided to cut back its West Coast presence after all.

Braniff Revival, and Revival

Some of the ex-AirCal/American and Western series 200 737s found temporary new homes with the re-established Braniff Inc. After a dramatic cessation of operations by the original Braniff Airways in 1982, the company remained dormant until a new financial package was put together under new ownership. Braniff reopened services from Dallas with a much reduced fleet of Boeing 727-200s in March 1984. Later, Orlando-based Florida Express Airlines was taken over and their fleet of BAC One-Elevens joined the 727s. After a period of reorganization and retrenchment, Braniff closed down the Dallas operation and moved home to a smaller hub already established at Kansas City, retaining Orlando as a southern base.

The 737-200s were leased in from the Polaris Aircraft Leasing Corporation in late 1987, to supplement the 727s and One-Elevens. A large order was placed for leased Airbus A320s, intended as the new standard aircraft for Braniff. Unfortunately, shortly after the first of the A320s entered service from Kansas City, Braniff Inc ceased operations in September 1989.

Once again though, Braniff reappeared. The operating authority of a small charter carrier, Emerald Airlines, was purchased by new owners and it was turned into the new Braniff. Once more flying Boeing 727-200s,

Both AirCal's 737-200s and -300s were to acquire American Airline's titles as soon as the merger took effect. Both pictures courtesy of American Airlines C.R. Smith Museum

the 'new' airline was contracted for a number of charter services by travel companies around the USA. An attempt to return to scheduled services, from Dallas to New York and Los Angeles, was initiated in 1991, and the network was later expanded to include Fort Lauderdale, Islip and Newark. However, scheduled services were closed down as uneconomic later that year and, in July 1992, the third Braniff followed its predecessors into bankruptcy.

Air Europe – and Family

Air Europe had followed Orion by introducing the Boeing 737-300. An Orion 737-300 was leased-in for crew training before the type entered charter service with Air Europe in 1987. Orders were placed at the

(*Top*) American Airlines retained the ex-AirCal 737s long enough to justify repainting, but they were disposed of as more MD-80s arrived to replace them.
American Airlines C.R. Smith Museum

(*Above*) Braniff's ex-Western 737-200, N4509W is seen at Tampa on the afternoon of 27 September 1989. Within a couple of hours of this photograph being taken, Braniff had ceased operations.
Malcolm L. Hill

Air Europa was Air Europe's first attempt at establishing a 'family' of airlines. Its 737-300s operated their first Spanish-based IT charters in November 1986.
Richard Howell

same time for five more 757s, as well as five 737-400s, for 1988/89 delivery.

Not all the Air Europe orders were intended for UK-based operations though. In June 1986, ILG had invested a 25 per cent holding in a new Spanish IT operator, initially entitled Air Espania. The operating name was changed to Air Europa before operations began in November 1986, with their aircraft flying in an only very slightly modified Air Europe livery. The adoption of the new title and identical livery would enable swift transfer of the aircraft between the two companies, with only one letter of the title and the national flag needing to be changed.

The 'Airline Family' Concept Spreads

Air Europe was far from the only charter carrier to embrace the 'family' concept of linked airlines. In 1988/89, Trans European Airways had established both a new Turkish subsidiary, TUR, and a UK-based operation, Trans European Airways (UK) Ltd. New 'TEAs' were also set up in Cyprus, France, Italy and Switzerland, with various levels of shareholding by the Brussels-based 'parent' airline.

Air Europa inherited Air Europe's 'mission' to establish more professional, modern, airline practices within the independent Spanish airline community. Its 737s were to join those operated by long-established charter specialist, Spantax, and relative newcomer, Hispania that had begun IT charter operations with a fleet of Caravelles in 1983. Hispania initially leased in 737-200s, and later -300s. The Spantax aircraft were part of a modernization programme that was intended to see the replacement of an ageing fleet of Convair CV-990As. Unfortunately, Spantax's attempts at reorganizing and its eventual sale to new owners failed to revive its fortunes and the airline ceased operations in 1988. Hispania survived long enough to introduce Boeing 757s alongside its 737-300s, but also ceased trading, due to financial problems in 1989.

Other Spanish Hopefuls

Universair was a new IT operator formed by the Spanish hotel group, Hola. With backing from the UK's Orion Airways and Belgium's Air Belgium, both 737 operators in their own right, Universair opened its Palma, Majorca base in 1987. The fleet had grown to three 737-300s by 1988. In 1990, Universair merged with two other Spanish operators to form Meridiana SA, a new scheduled carrier, and ceased to be a 737 operator.

VIVA (Vuelos Internacionales de Vacaciones SA) was set up in 1988 and was owned by Iberia and Lufthansa, with a modern fleet of four 737-300s. The first flight, a Nuremburg–Palma charter, took place on 15 April. Initially concentrating on the traditional IT charter markets, VIVA began undertaking scheduled services on behalf of Iberia, especially after Iberia bought out Lufthansa's share in 1990. Eventually VIVA opened a scheduled network of its own, centred on Palma, Majorca and Malaga on the mainland. At its peak the VIVA 737 fleet stood at nine Series 300s. The scheduled services operated from 1991 to 1996, when Iberia took over the routes and VIVA reverted to an all-charter operation. In 1999, Iberia decided to close down the airline and integrated its aircraft and staff.

Shorter-lived was Nortjet, a new Spanish charter operator that began IT services in 1990 with the first of three Boeing 737-400s leased from GPA. However, Nortjet's fleet was repossessed by GPA in February 1992, after the airline ceased operations. Much more successful was Futura, established in 1989 with backing from Aer Lingus and Banco de Santander. Using a single Boeing 737-400, operations began on 17 February 1990. With its solid financial backing, Futura survived and was flying six 737-400s by 1993, from bases at Palma and Tenerife. Throughout, Aer Lingus maintained a 85 per cent shareholding. In May 1997 a Palma–London/Gatwick schedule opened under the name of Futura Direct.

Air Europe Acquisitions

Air Europe's 737-400s started to enter service in the 1989 summer season. The high-density configured, 170-passenger 737-400s joined the airline's -300s and replaced the last of the -200s, which were disposed of or leased out. A single Boeing 747 had also been leased in for a year and flew to US, Caribbean and Far Eastern destinations.

The establishment of the Spanish sister company was the beginning of ILG's 'Airlines of Europe' policy that envisaged a European network of airlines. Other subsidiaries were opened in Italy and Germany, both operating Boeing 757s on charter services. A Norwegian charter carrier, Norway Airlines, was purchased and its Boeing 737-300s painted in Air Europe's full livery. Initially the Oslo-based airline was renamed Air Norway, then Air Europe (Scandinavia). As well as continuing to operate IT charters from Oslo, Air Europe (Scandinavia)'s aircraft were also used to open scheduled services to London/Gatwick.

Change of Direction

Air Europe had started to add scheduled services to its UK operations since the early 1980s. At first, leisure-orientated destinations were served, but from 1988 more business traffic-based services, from London/Gatwick to Amsterdam, Brussels, Copenhagen, Frankfurt, Geneva, Munich, Paris and Zurich were opened. A small Gatwick-based commuter carrier, Connectair, was acquired in 1989 and rebranded as Air Europe Express, flying Shorts 330s and 360s. Guernsey Airlines was later bought out and merged into the new 'Express' operation that operated scheduled flights from points in the UK to the Channel Islands and from Gatwick to Antwerp, Dusseldorf and Rotterdam.

Still led by Harry Goodman, ILG, the airline's owners, were very keen for Air Europe to establish itself as a major UK scheduled operator. Goodman's ambitious scheduled service plans eventually led to Air Europe's original founders, Errol Cossey and Martin O'Regan, leaving the company. They grew increasingly wary of Air Europe's owners' apparent determination to leave its original specialization, the holiday charter, and concentrate on the much riskier scheduled network.

A fleet of Fokker 100s was in the process of being acquired for use on the less busy scheduled flights from late 1989. For the longer term, Air Europe had ordered no less than eight wide-bodied MD-11s from McDonnell Douglas, as well as still further 737s and 757s. However, the end came suddenly, on 8 March 1991. On that day, a number of banks and other creditors took steps to retrieve £160 million owed to them by the financially overstretched ILG group. That morning, Air Europe's aircraft were impounded and the whole organization was placed under administration.

Various 'rescue' plans were put forward, but ILG collapsed and Air Europe never took to the skies again. The German and

Although Universair was luckier than some Spanish charter hopefuls in that it survived through merger, the resulting carrier disposed of the 737-300s. Richard Howell

Air Europe utilized its 737s on new scheduled services as well as the original IT charter programme. Steve Bunting

The European Challenge

By the 1980s, Europe's first bid to rival the 737, the Dassault Mercure, had proved a financial failure, attracting only one customer, and the quantity production of the earlier European jet airliner types was drawing to a close. The larger-capacity, medium/short-range jet market seemed to be firmly in the hands of America's Boeing and McDonnell Douglas. The new -300 and -400 Boeing 737s and the new MD-80 series of enlarged DC-9s from McDonnell Douglas were attracting orders from airlines and leasing agents worldwide. The Fokker F.28 and BAe 146 were selling in respectable numbers, but were of a considerably lower capacity than the larger American aircraft and aimed at a more specialized market.

Recognizing that the smaller aerospace companies of Europe had no hope of producing serious rivals to the giant American concerns, the European industry had already taken steps to combine forces and offer competitive products. As early as 1970, an Anglo-French study into medium-haul wide-bodied types had led to the formal establishment of Airbus Industrie, a multinational consortium of aerospace and aircraft manufacturing companies. Eventually, Airbus comprised contributions from Aérospatiale of France, British Aerospace (originally Hawker Siddeley) of the UK, Deutsche Aerospace of Germany, Fokker of the Netherlands and CASA of Spain.

The new consortium's first commercial project, the wide-bodied Airbus A300, first flew in October 1972. Although initial sales were slow, the A300 eventually established a substantial customer base for the aircraft. A major breakthrough was achieved with the sale of A300s to US-based Eastern Air Lines, with later US sales of developed versions to American Airlines and Pan American World Airways.

Airbus had always planned to offer a portfolio of airliner types and the first new variant, the slightly smaller Airbus A310, followed in 1982. Airbus's first narrow-bodied type, the A320, was formally launched into development in 1984 and the first flight occurred in February 1987. The A320 was a direct rival to the enlarged 737 models, with similar capacity to the 737-400. The sale of the A320 to long-established 737 operator United Airlines, as well as a large order placed by Minneapolis-based Northwest Airlines, an operator of a substantial fleet of DC-9s of different variants, set alarm bells ringing in the Boeing and McDonnell Douglas sales offices.

(*Below*) Although initially selling only slowly, the Airbus A300B eventually established itself as a serious contender in the international airliner market. Malcolm L. Hill

(*Bottom*) The acquisition of large fleets of Airbus types (A320 illustrated) by major US carriers, such as Northwest Airlines, made Boeing examine its own offerings very closely. Northwest via author

Norwegian subsidiaries also ceased operations. Nonetheless, the Spanish and Italian operations found new owners and eventually thrived as Air Europa and air Europe (Italy). Air Europe Express eventually re-emerged as a new commuter carrier, Euroworld, later renamed CityFlyer Express.

More UK Comings and Goings

Orion Airways had disappeared in 1989. Its parent company, Horizon Travel, had been taken over by the Thomson Travel Group that year. Horizon's operations were merged into Thomson Holidays and, not surprisingly, Orion's services were merged into Thomson's own established airline subsidiary, Britannia Airways. At the time of the merger, Orion was operating its 737-300s and a pair of wide-bodied, Airbus A300Bs. As Britannia was operating the similar Boeing 767, the Airbus A300Bs found themselves surplus to requirements and were returned to their owners. Orion's 737-300s were retained for a while though and were flown alongside the long-serving 737-200s.

In April 1988, a new airline had risen from the ashes of Airways International Cymru. The ex-AIC 737-200, G-BAZI re-emerged as G-BOSA in the livery of Amberair, the operating name of Cardiff-based Amber Airways. A second 737-200, G-BKMS, was also leased in and the pair operated IT charters from several UK points. Amberair barely operated for one season before it was taken over in October 1988, by Bristol-based Paramount Airways. Paramount flew mostly MD-80s, although a single 737-300 was also operated. The ex-Amberair 737-200s were eventually returned to their owners. Paramount itself ceased operations in 1990, following a financial scandal involving its owner's group of companies.

Inter European Airways had started Cardiff-based 737-200 IT charter operations in May 1987. Utilizing a single leased, ex-Maersk Air aircraft, Inter European had been founded by a Cardiff travel company, Aspro Holidays. Owned by the Asprou brothers, Aspro Holidays specialized in tours to Greece and Cyprus, as well as serving traditional Spanish destinations. The 737 flew from Cardiff and Bristol for the 1987 season, being returned to its owners at the end of that summer's flying programme. IEA remained dormant for the winter, but came back in style in 1988, leasing in two brand-new 737-300s.

This time, operations continued through the winter months and over the following years more 737-300s were acquired, as was a single 737-400. In addition to Cardiff and Bristol, new bases were set up at Manchester and London/Gatwick as Aspro Holidays greatly expanded its successful tour programme. Airbus A320s began to replace the 737-300s in 1993, joining Boeing 757s that had entered service the previous year.

As with Orion though, IEA was to vanish as the result of tour company mergers. Manchester-based Airtours took over Aspro Holidays in 1993, rebranding the tour company as its low-cost subsidiary. Inter European's 757s and A320s were taken over by Airtour's own airline operation, Airtours International. The remaining IEA 737s were returned to their owners once their last Aspro contracts had been completed.

Air UK Goes 'Leisure'

While Air Europe was struggling to move from charter to scheduled services, a British scheduled airline, Air UK, was moving in the opposite direction. Air UK operated a network of scheduled commuter and trunk services throughout Britain and to nearby points in continental Europe with a large fleet of F.27 turboprops and BAe 146 jets.

In June 1987, Air UK and Viking International, a charter brokerage company, became the major investors in a new IT charter company, to be named Air UK Leisure. Basing itself initially at London/Stansted, Air UK Leisure took delivery of three second-hand Boeing 737-200s in time to commence operations in May 1988. The first commercial services were charters from Stansted to Faro, Gerona and Rome, departing on 1 May. Services also opened from Manchester and East Midlands the next day, with flights to Rhodes and Palma, respectively.

The 737-200s were replaced in October 1989 by the first of an eventual fleet of seven Series 400s. As well as operating on Air UK Leisure's expanding network of ITs, seasonal leasings saw some of the aircraft take up

Orion's 737-300s took on Britannia's identity following the merger of the two airlines in 1989. Jenny Gradidge

Inter European Airways began operations with a single 737-200, G-BNGK, leased in for the summer of 1987. Richard Howell

with SEEA from March 1993 to April 1994, before the Greek company ceased operations. Virgin then took over the route itself, with Airbus equipment.

In 1992, Air UK Leisure was joined by a subsidiary company, Leisure International Airways. LIA was established to operate long-haul charters with a small fleet of wide-body Boeing 767-300s, based at London/Gatwick. For a while, operations continued separately, but in 1996, Air UK Leisure was merged into LIA. LIA was now part of the Unijet travel group, a major IT holiday operator. The 737-400s were eventually disposed of, in favour of more long-haul aircraft, although Airbus A320s and A321s were later acquired to operate European IT charter services. LIA lost its identity when Unijet was bought out by First Choice, another IT operator, and LIA was merged with First Choice's own in-house airline, Air 2000.

other airlines' liveries, especially in the quieter winter months. Malaysian Airlines, Indian scheduled carrier Modiluft and Canadian charter operators Odyssey International and Vacationair all took out short leases on Air UK Leisure's Series 400s. G-UKLB was leased out on a longer contract, to South East European Airways, of Athens. SEEA operated a small network of domestic flights in Greece, with Fokker F.50 turboprops, but its main activity was providing aircraft and crews for Virgin Atlantic Airway's Athens–London scheduled service. Flying in full Virgin livery, the 737-400 flew

More Stansted 737s

Titan Airways, based at Stansted, specialized in contract, *ad hoc* and short-notice charters, the latter often on behalf of other airlines. Beginning operations in 1988 with a small fleet of Cessna twins, Titan grew to fly Shorts 360 and ATR-42 turboprops, as well as BAe 146 jets. A single

G-BNZT 'Flagship St Andrew' was one of the trio of 737-200s used to inaugurate Air UK Leisure's IT services in 1988. Via author

737-300 was acquired in 1999, soon finding itself in demand with Titan's clientèle. A two-class layout was adopted for the 737, with eight business-class and 118 economy-class seats, all in leather.

March 2000 saw the 737-300 appear in the colours of British World Airlines. Three aircraft entered service during the year on IT and *ad hoc* flights from crew bases at Stansted, Gatwick and Manchester. British World had previously been known as British Air Ferries, until the airline's name was changed in 1993. BAF owed its unusual title to long-running car ferry scheduled services once operated by the company across the English Channel from Southend.

Airways, taking over the Gatwick-based independent in late 1987, it inherited the latter's order for the rival Airbus A320. Originally intended to replace BCal's fleet of BAC One-Elevens, the A320s were delivered to BA and initially entered service on the Gatwick network. However, the A320s were soon moved to the Heathrow base and replaced at Gatwick by Boeing 737s.

In October 1988, BA placed a large order for up to twenty-four more 737s, with an option to choose which variant would be delivered at a later date. Part of a larger order that included six wide-bodied Boeing 767s and an extra 757, all twenty-four 737s were

Novair's Series 400s

Not part of the BCal buy-out by British Airways was British Caledonian's own charter subsidiary, British Caledonian Charter. Originally formed in 1983, in partnership with the Rank Organization, BCal Charter operated ex-Laker Airways DC-10s on IT charter services originally contracted by Rank to the defunct carrier before its 1982 bankruptcy. In 1984, Rank purchased BCal's remaining shareholding and re-branded the airline Cal Air International, while retaining the BCal 'Scottishness'.

When British Airways rebranded its own charter operator, British Airtours, as

British World spread their small 737-300 fleet between bases throughout the UK. G-OBWZ is seen at London/Gatwick. Aviation Hobby Shop

BAF had turned to more conventional scheduled and charters in the 1970s, replacing their specialized 'Carvair' aircraft with turbo-prop Heralds and Viscounts, before introducing One-Elevens as their first jets in the 1990s. The 737-300s displaced the One-Elevens, which were finally withdrawn in December 2000.

BA 737 Expansion

British Airways had been very satisfied with their 'Super 737-200s'. When BA became the successful suitor for British Caledonian

eventually delivered as Series 400s, the first arriving in 1991. In the meantime, four Series 300s were leased from Maersk Air.

As the newer versions arrived at Heathrow, the earlier -200s were transferred to either Birmingham or Manchester, to begin replacing the airline's surviving One-Elevens. For a while, the aircraft wore either 'Birmingham' or 'Manchester' suffixes to their titles, as the outstations were given more autonomy under the British Airways Regional Division banner. Later, the titles were amended back to their original format, although the Regional Division continued to be responsible for the aircraft's operation.

Caledonian Airways, in 1988, the two similarly Scottish themed carriers briefly operated alongside each other from London/Gatwick. However, in May, Cal Air was renamed Novair International Airways. The next year, a pair of Boeing 737-400s was delivered to Novair International and operated on IT flights from Gatwick, Birmingham, Glasgow, Manchester and Newcastle, supplementing the DC-10s.

Unfortunately, Rank was not impressed with the profitability of the airline and put Novair up for sale. After failing to find a buyer, Rank decided to cut its losses and all operations were closed down in May 1990.

Novair International operated its 737-400s for only a year before the Rank Organization closed down the carrier when it failed to find a buyer. Aviation Hobby Shop

BA's Dan-Air Buy-out

British Airways found itself the new operators of a whole new fleet of 737s from October 1992, following its purchase of ailing, Gatwick-based, Dan-Air Services. A leading independent airline, first established in 1952, Dan-Air had suffered severe financial problems throughout the 1980s. An attempt to switch the company's focus from charter to more scheduled services that had been part of the company's activities for many years on a much smaller scale, proved expensive. Even once Dan-Air had started to make much-needed changes in its commercial operations, it soon became clear that it was a classic, sad, case of 'too little, too late'.

Both the BAC One-Eleven and Boeing 737 fleets were used on new scheduled routes from Gatwick to Brussels, Dublin, Lisbon, Madrid, Nice and Paris, with new BAe 146 jets on less-busy flights. Dan-Air found it very hard-going competing with the established national carriers, despite gaining an enviable reputation for professional customer service. Dan-Air actually gained a breathing space with the demise of Air Europe, against which it had competed on a number of important Gatwick-based scheduled routes. The transfer of Air Europe's displaced passengers to Dan-Air gave the latter a welcome revenue

Dan-Air's 737 fleet grew steadily over the years, operating on an expanding scheduled network in addition to charters. Via author

The 737-300 featured in the Dan-Air fleet from 1985. G-BOWR was an ex-Orion/Britannia Airways Aircraft. MAP

(*Below*) **British Airtours' 737-200s were transferred to 'new' charter subsidiary, Caledonian Airways, reviving a respected airline name from the past.** Richard Howell

boost, when it had been within days of insolvency itself.

The Dan-Air management had finally recognized the hopelessness of the situation and began looking for prospective buyers for their airline. Richard Branson's Virgin group came close to buying the scheduled operation, but, eventually, British Airways bought Dan-Air for a token one pound. Hardly the bargain it sounds, British Airways also took on the obligations for Dan-Air's not inconsiderable debts, as well as responsibility for the welfare of its staff. Only Dan-Air's Gatwick-based scheduled network was of interest to BA and all charter work would cease.

At the time of the takeover, Dan-Air was operating a diverse fleet of twelve BAC One-Elevens, seven Boeing 727-200s, four BAe 146s, four BAe 748 turbo-props and no less than nineteen Boeing 737s of various marks. Only three 737-300s and nine 737-400s were to be retained by BA. The rest of the fleet, their crews and support staff would be rendered redundant.

As their IT charter contracts ran out for the 1992 summer season, the Boeing 727-200s and most of the One-Elevens were placed into storage. The 748s, 146s and the remaining One-Elevens were disposed of as their scheduled routes were either closed down or taken over by BA. The end finally came for Dan-Air on the evening of 8 November 1992. The very last Dan-Air flight was operated by Boeing 737-400, G-BNNK, on flight DA689, a scheduled service from London/Gatwick to Madrid. Departing Gatwick at 20.20, the aircraft night-stopped at Madrid and returned the next day as a BA operation.

The few retained aircraft and crews were combined with BA's already established Gatwick short-haul base. The amalgamated operations were organized as a new subsidiary, 'British Airways European Operations at Gatwick', later thankfully shortened to 'EuroGatwick'. The ex-Dan-Air 737-300s were only retained for a short while, being returned to their owners at the end of their lease contracts, in 1993 and 1994. More 737-400s were transferred from Heathrow though, to replace them and increase the BA profile at Gatwick as the hub was developed. As well as new aircraft ordered from Boeing, BA also acquired second-hand Series 300s and -400s, as their use of the type increased.

GB Airways' smart livery was to disappear after the airline signed up to become a 'franchise carrier' for British Airways. Martyn East

BA's 'Associated' 737s

The British Airways takeover of British Caledonian also led to drastic changes in the operations of British Airtours. The charter subsidiary was rebranded as 'Caledonian Airways', taking on the identity of one of BCal's original constituent airlines. With cabin crews taking over BCal's Scottish tartan themed uniforms and image, British Airtours fleet of Lockheed L-1011 Tristars and Boeing 737-200s were repainted in their own version of the grey-topped BA livery, complete with a heraldic lion painted on the tail. The 737s were eventually replaced by larger Boeing 757s and were disposed of.

For many years, BA's predecessor, BEA had been associated with a small airline based at Gibraltar, a British territory on the southern tip of Spain. Gibraltar Airways, its title shortened in daily use to Gibair, had been founded locally, in 1931, to operate scheduled services to neighbouring Spain and Morocco. Postwar, BEA took a 51 per cent share in the airline and Gibair continued to provide vital local links for the island, as well as feeding traffic from North Africa to BEA's services from Gibraltar to London. Small twin-engined types had steadily been replaced by single leased DC-3s and turbo-prop Viscounts over the years. Gibair later became GB Airways and, from April 1979, services were operated from Gibraltar to London/Gatwick. The new service utilized 737-200s leased from Britannia Airways, replacing a previous pooling arrangement using BEA/BA aircraft to London/Heathrow.

The contract with Britannia was replaced by GB Airways flying their own 737-200s, initially with three leased in via British Airways. From 1989 the airline had moved its headquarters and main base to London/Gatwick, although Gibraltar was still an important point on the network. More leased 737-200s replaced the original aircraft and GB Airways expanded quickly with flights to Casablanca, Funchal, Marrakech, Tangier and Tunis from Gatwick, with some services also being scheduled from Heathrow. A Manchester–Gibraltar schedule was operated, as well as scheduled services from Gibraltar to Casablanca, Marrakech and Tangier. In the summer of 1994, two of the airline's 737s were given 'GB Leisure' titles and operated IT charters from Gatwick and Manchester.

From 1995, GB Airways began operating as a BA 'franchise' carrier, adopting BA's livery, uniforms and flight prefix. BA had actually sold its last shareholdings in GB Airways that year, but maintained an influence under the franchise contract. Two ex-BA Series 400 737s were transferred to join GB's own five 737-200s and new routes opened from Gatwick to Murcia and Valencia, in Spain.

Elsewhere in Europe

The Trans European 'family' concept fared as well as that of Air Europe. The group suffered financial collapse in 1991. The Belgian and UK operations had added Series 300 737s to their original fleets of Series 200s. TUR, in Turkey, TEA Italy, TEA Switzerland, TEA Cyprus and TEA France initially survived the group's collapse, although the Cypriot, French, Italian and Turkish companies later suspended operations. After TEA UK ceased operations its operating authority was later used to establish a new company, Excalibur Airways, which operated Airbus A320s. The original Belgian company was quickly revived as EuroBelgian Airlines, again operating 737s.

In the Netherlands, Transavia steadily expanded their all-737 fleet, eventually adding Series 300 737s and 757s. As well as their own IT charter services, Transavia continued to be active in the leasing market, operating both Series 200s and 300s for the Dutch national carrier, KLM. The flag-carrier that had taken a financial interest in Transavia was to eventually take delivery of its own 737-400s, replacing a long-standing fleet of DC-9s.

A very short-lived Dutch 737 operation saw a single Series 200 operated by Rotterdam Airlines. The aircraft was leased from TEA and flown on scheduled Rotterdam–

(*Above*) **Transavia was to base its prosperity on the 737 for many years, -300s joining the original -200s at Amsterdam.** Malcolm L. Hill

(*Below*) **Lufthansa utilized the 737-300 on their European services.** Lufthansa

London/Gatwick services several times a day from November 1983, as well as some IT work. The aircraft was far too large for the available market on the London route, especially during the traditionally quiet winter season, and all operations ceased in March 1984. Air Holland had been established in 1985, operating IT charters with a pair of Boeing 727-200s. During a chequered career, Air Holland halted operations for reorganization several times, but survived long enough to operate three 737-300s over its various incarnations.

In Germany, although an early customer for the rival Airbus single-aisle types, Lufthansa continued to utilize their large 737 fleet, throughout their European and domestic network. Also in Germany, both new and established charter operators had begun to introduce 737s into service. Condor reintroduced the type, eventually with both Series 200s and -300s being operated at various times in the 1980s and 90s.

Hapag Lloyd replaced their last Boeing 727s and BAC One-Elevens with 737s and Germania, previously founded as SAT with Caravelles and 727s, introduced 737-300s.

All Change at Berlin

The reunification of Germany led to fundamental changes in the airline services offered from Berlin. At the end of the Second World War Berlin had been divided up, with its western half buried within the boundaries of East Germany. Originally, Air France, American Overseas Airlines and Britain's BEA had taken on the task of linking West Berlin with the rest of the new Federal Republic. Later, American Overseas was taken over by Pan American and Air France operated its Berlin flights in association with BEA, later British Airways, under a pooling agreement. As long as East Germany existed as a separate country, West German registered aircraft were forbidden in its airspace and, thereby, denied access to Berlin.

Air France eventually returned to the Berlin market though, with the founding of a new carrier, EuroBerlin France, in partnership with Lufthansa. Services opened in 1988 from Berlin-Tegel to Dusseldorf, Hamburg and Stuttgart, eventually utilizing seven 737-300s. IT charters also operated from Berlin to southern Europe at weekends. Over 885,000 passengers were carried in 1991, of which 850,000 were carried on the scheduled services. EuroBerlin was closed down in 1994 after German reunification had removed its main reason to exist.

Pan American's Berlin services had been disposed of as part of its cost-cutting measures, but British Airways had continued to operate a Berlin base. However, BA eventually took steps to withdraw, but still maintained a commercial presence under the new regime.

A consortium, comprising BA and three German banks, acquired a small West German commuter operator, Delta Air, founded in 1978. By 1992, Delta's fleet of SAAB 340s was operating several routes from its base at Friedrichshafen in southern Germany. A co-operation agreement had been signed with Lufthansa covering the Delta Air network from Friedrichshafen and Stuttgart. International schedules served Geneva, Zurich and the Channel Islands.

The acquisition of Delta Air by BA and the banks heralded a major change in the commuter carrier. Renamed Deutsche BA, the 'new' airline began commercial services from Berlin-Tegel to Stuttgart and Munich, in June 1992. An initial fleet of three leased 737-300s was joined by four more later in the year and new routes opened to Dusseldorf and Cologne.

The airline's head office was moved, in 1994, to Munich, although a large programme of scheduled and charter flights still operated from the Berlin base. Smaller Fokker 100s were leased in to supplement the 737s and SAABs that continued in operation. The original turbo-prop network was sold off in January 1997.

Soon replacing BA completely, which closed down or transferred its Berlin-based facilities as Deutsche BA grew, the 737-300 fleet continued to expand. IT charter routes were opened for German travel companies in 1993 and international schedules opened from Berlin to Nice, Oslo, St Petersburg and Stockholm, and from Dresden to Paris. New routes were opened in 1994 from Munich and Frankfurt to Paris and from Munich to Dusseldorf and Madrid. London/Gatwick was linked to Deutsche BA's network in 1995 with flights from Bremen and Munich. Berlin–Gatwick services began in 1996 and the last Fokker 100 was returned to its owner in early 1998. Year 2000 saw Deutsche BA operating eighteen Boeing 737-300s from bases at Berlin and Munich.

Deutsche BA adopted 'Germanized' versions of British Airways new 'World Images' livery for their 737-300s.
Deutsche BA

Originally operating under US registry, Air Berlin greatly expanded their 737 IT charter services from other German cities, following reunification. The reunification also led to Germania taking over Berlin-based Berlin European UK, that had operated ITs with leased 737-300s since April 1990.

Antipodean 737s

The New Zealand National Airways Corporation was merged with New Zealand's long-haul operator, Air New Zealand, in 1978. Ten 737-200s made the transition, along with a fleet of Fokker F.27s. More 737s were delivered in the following years, including several Series 300s. Although NZNAC had been an early operator of the Boeing 737, New Zealand's bigger neighbour, Australia, resisted the arrival of the aircraft for some time.

Originally, the Australian airline industry was heavily regulated, with the two major domestic carriers, Ansett and Trans Australia, being forced to compete under very restrictive conditions. Flights had to leave at identical departure times, using comparable aircraft. Originally, TAA had favoured buying in Caravelles as their first jets, and later lobbied to buy BAC One-Elevens. However, Ansett did not want the European designs and, finally, both airlines ordered fleets of Boeing 727s and Douglas DC-9-30s.

Eventually the regulations were relaxed and the airlines were able to enjoy more freedom in their equipment policy. Ansett originally began importing 737-200s as replacements for their DC-9s in 1981. Newer version Series 300s followed and Ansett also bought Airbus A320s to operate on their domestic network alongside them. Ansett bought shares in a local New Zealand-based carrier, Newmans Air, renaming it Ansett New Zealand and re-equipping the airline with 737s to better compete against Air New Zealand. BAe146s eventually replaced the 737s, and another change of ownership and name change saw Ansett New Zealand become Qantas New Zealand in 2000.

Trans Australia changed their name to Australian Airlines in 1986, the same year they introduced the first of a large fleet of Boeing 737-300s to replace their own earlier jets. However, in September 1992, Australian Airlines was bought out by Qantas Airways and became the domestic arm of what had previously been Australia's international specialist.

A NEW LEASE OF LIFE

Ansett chose the 737 to modernize its fleets in the 1980s. MAP

Hong Kong's Dragonair began operations with a small fleet of 737-200s. MAP

Eastern Growth

Elsewhere in the Asian and Pacific regions, rapid financial growth had seen several new operators emerging, with both them and established airlines choosing the new versions of the 737 as their medium/short-haul airliner.

In Korea, a brand new carrier, Asiana Airlines began regional and domestic operations with a fleet of 737-400s. As well as the 737s, a new international and long-haul network was established with Boeing 767s.

The network and fleet later grew rapidly as Asiana was encouraged by the Korean government to be the country's 'second designated carrier' after Korean Air Lines.

In Hong Kong, Dragonair was founded in 1985 and began flights to Kota Kinabalu, with a single Boeing 737-200 leased from Guinness Peat. New route licences saw the airline opening services to eight points in mainland China and to Phuket, in Thailand. Cathay Pacific, the major airline in Hong Kong, took a financial interest in the budding carrier and Lockheed

L-1011 Tristars were transferred to expand the network. The original 737 was joined by five more leased aircraft, before the type was discarded in favour of a standardized fleet of Airbus aircraft.

Long-established Thai Airways took delivery of their first 737-200 in 1977, supplementing a fleet of HS-748 turbo-props. Other 737s followed, as well as Airbus A310 wide-bodies, as Thai's original domestic network was expanded to include regional international points. However, Thai was merged into the country's flag carrier airline,

133

Thai Airways International, in 1988. Thai Airways International continued to expand the 737 fleet, taking delivery of its first Series 400s in 1990.

Air Pacific, of Fiji, regularly upgraded their small 737 fleet, operated on regional flights, with new versions replacing older aircraft as leases came up for renewal. Air Vanuatu and Solomon Airlines also joined established operators such as Air Pacific and Air Nauru in operating small fleets, or even single 737s, of various marks, on their Pacific region services.

Japanese use of the 737 had waned slightly after All Nippon Airways disposed of their fleet in favour of larger types. However, ANA subsidiary, NKK (Nihon Kinkyori Airways), continued to operate a small fleet of 737-200s on domestic services, alongside YS-11A turbo-props. NKK was later rebranded Air Nippon. Southwest Airlines, based at Naha on the island of Okinawa, operated 737s on regional flights and to the main Japanese islands. Later renamed Japan TransOcean Air, Japan Air Lines took a major shareholding in the company.

The Future?

As the 1990s ran their course, many of the Boeing 737's operators were having to rethink their operation. In particular, they were having to address the worldwide obsession with deregulation and cost-cutting, linked with often difficult financial circumstances. To conquer these challenges, both Boeing and the operators had to make fundamental, dramatic changes to both their basic philosophies and daily operations. Nothing was likely to be the same again.

The -300 and -400 versions of the 737 became popular and reliable aircraft in daily service worldwide.
Steve Bunting/MAP

CHAPTER NINE

The Last of the Old Generation

A New Short-body 737

The Series 200 version of the Boeing 737 ended its 21-year production run in June 1988. Over 1,000 JT8D-powered 737s were produced, including over 100 convertible aircraft, fitted with cargo doors. Despite its obvious success, the final Series 200 version could no longer be updated, especially with the original engine. Environmental regulations were making it difficult to economically operate the JT8D-powered aircraft within the new restrictions that were becoming prevalent worldwide.

There was still an identifiable market for a lower-capacity aircraft, nearer the Series 200 size, especially with scheduled service operators. So, in 1987, Boeing launched the Series 500, basically a new version of the Series 300, shortened by 94in (239cm) by the removal of fuselage plugs forward and

(*Above*) The 737-500 launch customer was long-term client Southwest Airlines. Steve Bunting

(*Below*) Lufthansa acquired 737-500s to complement the larger -300s and -400s in its fleet, and replace the older -200s. Lufthansa

aft of the wing. The new version incorporated all the larger aircraft's improvements, including the use of the CFM6 engine. Before launching the Series 500, Boeing had actually studied an even smaller version of the 737, originally designated the 737-250. The 100-seater Series 250 failed to attract orders and the proposal was cancelled in 1986, in favour of the Series 500.

Faithful 737 customer, Southwest Airlines, became the launch customer, eventually taking delivery of 25 Series 500s. Braathens, Euralair and Maersk Air soon placed orders of their own. A Series 500 was the 2,000th 737 to be delivered, fittingly to the original programme's first customer, Lufthansa, on 15 February 1991. The aircraft was also the German airline's 100th 737.

The Series 500 soon found a niche for itself in the 737 family of aircraft. As a replacement of the older Series 200, it could be seen as ideal. Not everyone wanted the extra passenger capacity of the larger Series 300 and 400. The CFM6's better fuel consumption and extra power over the JT8D could just as well be translated into more range or better short-runway performance, as into the extra load-carrying of the bigger versions.

Scandinavian Expansion

Braathens certainly appreciated the Series 500's capabilities as a Series 200 replacement. The Norwegian carrier had already placed five Series 400s into service on IT charters and busier scheduled services between its more important points. The Braathens Series 500 fleet was to eventually grow to twenty-one aircraft, ousting the last of their Series 200s. In neighbouring Denmark, Maersk used the Series 500 to expand its scheduled network, especially from Danish regional points such as Billund, as well as finding it a useful aircraft for its long-established charter and leasing business.

Braathens had expanded out of the Norwegian market in 1996 when the company acquired a 50 per cent interest in Transwede Airways of Stockholm. Transwede operated a network of scheduled services as well as charters, with a fleet of Fokker F.100s. Braathens later merged the Transwede schedules with another Swedish carrier that it had acquired, Malmo Aviation, under the name Braathens Malmo. Transwede also flew holiday charters under the name of Transwede Leisure, with Boeing 737-200s, -300s and -500s, leased in for the IT contracts over the years. The Leisure division was not part of the Braathens purchase and eventually ceased operations.

A fleet of Boeing 737-200s was included in the inventory of Time Air Sweden, which also operated much larger Tristars and DC-8s. Time Air Sweden operated IT charters from Sweden and Finland between March 1991 and February 1993, when flights were suspended following financial problems.

The Scandinavian region's largest carrier, the multinational Scandinavian Airlines System, came to operate the 737 almost in passing. Long known for operating a large fleet of DC-9s on its European regional services, SAS took over the operations of Swedish domestic carrier, Linjeflyg, in 1993. Linjeflyg had flown a purely domestic scheduled service network in Sweden since 1957 and utilized a large fleet of Fokker F.28s. In late 1990–early 1991, however, the airline had taken delivery of a number of leased Boeing 737-500s.

As well as the domestic scheduled flights, the 737-500s also operated charters for Linjeflyg to Malaga, Rome and Zakynthos. No less than ten were delivered to Linjeflyg and the last two direct to SAS after the takeover. Prior to the merger, two aircraft were subleased to LOT, the Polish airline. As SAS tried to assimilate the new

Braathens 737-500s operated a growing regional network, including international scheduled services from Norway to Newcastle in the UK. MAP

The convertible 'QC' 737-300s of Falcon Air operate passenger flights by day and carry Sweden's mail at night. Aviation Hobby Shop

Sweden's Postal 'QCs'

In the 1960s, Falcon Air was founded at Gothenburg and flew as an air taxi company with a fleet of Cessna, Piper and Beechcraft light aircraft. The small company's operations were transformed in 1986 when the first of a fleet of three Lockheed Electra freighter turbo-props entered service on cargo and mail-carrying contracts. fleet into its ranks, more of the aircraft were leased out on contracts of varying lengths.

By 1988 the Swedish Post Office had purchased the company to ensure control over its important postal network. A fourth Electra joined Falcon and the operating base was moved to Malmo. In 1990 the air taxi operation was sold and in 1991 the Electras were replaced with three new Boeing 737-300QCs.

Conversion of Falcon Air's 737s from passenger to cargo configuration takes less than an hour. Every evening the aircraft are reconfigured to take up to sixteen containers and the aircraft operate mail services between Stockholm, Gothenburg, Malmo and Umea. Every morning the passenger seats are refitted into the cabins and the aircraft operate IT charters to southern Europe, as well as a scheduled domestic service from Stockholm to Umea, in northern Sweden.

Maersk's British Connection

Maersk Air not only placed their Series 500s into their Denmark-based flights. Since 1993, Maersk had operated a UK subsidiary, Maersk Air (UK) Ltd. The airline was

Maersk Air (UK) operated their new 737-500s on British Airways-branded scheduled services from Birmingham. Via author

formed when Birmingham based-Brymon European Airways was 'de-merged' into its original constituent parts, Brymon Airways and Birmingham European Airways. The two airlines had been joined in 1989, Brymon having operated scheduled services with a fleet of De Havilland Canada DHC-8 turbo-props from Plymouth and Bristol, and Birmingham European operating a scheduled network from Birmingham with a fleet mostly comprised of BAC One-Eleven jets. The merger had not been a success, with both units still maintaining largely separate operations.

Instead, Maersk Air, already a minority shareholder, bought out the Birmingham-based half of Brymon European. The southwest-based division, the original Brymon Airways, reverted to its old name and was bought out by British Airways. It went on to operate its scheduled routes as a wholly owned 'franchise' carrier in BA's name. Maersk Air (UK)'s aircraft also took up British Airways livery, as a contracted 'franchise' carrier, flying from Birmingham. The Danish parent company transferred several Series 500s to the UK service to replace the old One-Elevens. As well as operating the BA flights, Maersk Air (UK)'s aircraft are also used for IT charter work, in their own right.

British Midland's Boeing Twins

UK independent airline, British Midland Airways, was to become the main customer for SAS's excess 737-500 capacity. After a brief period in the early 1970s, when a trio of new BAC One-Elevens were operated, BMA had preferred to operate turbo-prop aircraft on its largely domestic network. The One-Elevens had been disposed of as too expensive for BMA's then modest network. For some years after, apart from a number of second-hand 707s flown on charter and leasing contracts, the airline stuck to propeller aircraft. The Vickers Viscount, along with a handful of Dart Heralds, Fokker F.27s or Shorts turbo-prop types over the ensuing years, formed the backbone of the airline's fleet.

A single leased DC-9 brought the jet back to BMA's scheduled network in 1976. Route expansion into more major domestic services and the eventual opening of a larger international presence from London to Europe saw more second-hand DC-9s joining the carrier. The first appearance of 737s with British Midland titles was in 1987, with the delivery of the airline's first Series 300, for operation on the busier routes from London-Heathrow. Leased Series 200s also operated briefly and BMA's first Series 400 was placed into service in late 1988.

As the British Midland 737 fleet grew, the type was seen increasingly on scheduled services from other bases, as well as an expanded IT charter programme. In addition to flying IT charters on behalf of BMA, spare 737 capacity was sub-chartered to other carriers, in particular Air 2000, an IT charter carrier that then operated Boeing 757s and Airbus A320s of its own.

Air 2000 had actually leased a single Series 300, G-KKUH, from ILFC for the summer season of 1989, and options were taken out on two 737-400s. However, before confirming the order, Air 2000 decided on the Airbus A320 as its smaller jet to supplement the 757s. Coincidentally, G-KKUH went on to be leased to both Linjeflyg, as SE-DLA 'Vaermland II' during 1990, and British Midland, as G-OBML (with whom it often operated Air 2000 sub-charters), from 1991 to 1997. The increased use of the 737s soon led to the gradual rundown and disposal of the DC-9 fleet and the first of the ex-Lin/SAS Series 500s was leased in by BMA in 1993.

Aer Lingus Fleet Update

The Series 500 was taken up by Aer Lingus as replacement for their long-serving Series 200. Having already replaced the leased Series 300s with larger 400 series 737s on their busier routes, the Irish national carrier need a lower capacity aircraft on its European network. The ageing Series 200s would soon fall foul of environmental regulations, as would the airline's quartet of BAC One-Elevens that had been in use even longer than the 737-200s. In fact, the 737-200s had been intended to replace the One-Elevens, but the British jets had continued in use, finding a useful niche on Aer Lingus's less busy routes and as back-ups to the 737s.

The arrival of the 737-500s saw the swift departure of the remaining 737-200s and One-Elevens. It also saw the end of all-cargo and 'combi' services, with the departure of the last 'QC' 737-200s. From then on, the airline's cargo was carried in

Boeing 737s, including -300 G-OBMA, eventually replaced DC-9s with British Midland Airways. MAP

Tragic Lessons at Kegworth

Soon after the first pair of Series 400s entered BMA service, the first aircraft, G-OBME, crashed at Kegworth, while attempting an emergency landing at BMA's home base at East Midlands Airport. The aircraft was operating flight BD092, an evening scheduled flight from London/Heathrow to Belfast. While flying 20 nautical miles southeast of East Midlands, passengers and cabin crew noticed smoke entering the cabin through the air conditioning, as well as sparks coming out of the left engine. The flight-deck crew, Capt Kevin Hunt and F/O David McClelland, also noticed the severe vibration and smell of smoke. As he disengaged the auto-pilot and took control of the aircraft, the Captain asked which engine was causing the problem. By an appalling series of misunderstandings the wrong engine, the right-hand one, was switched off.

Declaring an emergency and turning towards East Midlands Airport, the pilots attempted to increase power on the left engine when the lowered landing gear caused more drag. They were genuinely alarmed to find it gave no response and it was too late to attempt to restart the right-hand, serviceable engine. With the runway agonizingly in sight and lined up, the aircraft was unable to maintain height and glided towards the ground. Even more bad luck came their way as, instead of open countryside that might have made the crash more survivable, directly in the stricken 737-400's path was the M1 motorway.

After it struck the ground and smashed through a fence, the aircraft dropped 30ft (9m) on to the main carriageway of the motorway and continued across it. By incredible good fortune there were no vehicles directly in the aircraft's path as it carried on and crashed into the other side, finally coming to rest, its fuselage shattered, towards the top of an embankment. Forty-seven of the 118 passengers perished in the crash. That figure could have been much higher, but fortunately there was no post-crash fire despite a great deal of leaking fuel around the area. As a direct result of the accident, emergency training was redesigned, with more emphasis on cockpit/cabin communication procedures in a crisis.

G-OBME was in service with British Midland for only a matter of months before forty-seven died on board it in the Kegworth crash. Via author

G-KKUH was intended to be the first of many 737-300s operated by Air 2000 on European ITs. However, the airline elected to order Airbus A320s instead. Via author

Aer Lingus 737-500s displaced the last of the long-serving -200s on the Irish carrier's European and domestic routes. Steve Bunting

the holds of the passenger configured fleets, or contracted-in freighter aircraft.

However, Aer Lingus's apparent faithfulness to Boeing came to an end with the introduction of Airbus A321s in the late 1990s. Airbus A330 wide-bodied airliners had already replaced long-serving Boeing 747s on the airline's trans-Atlantic routes from 1994. The successful introduction of Airbus A321s eventually led to orders for more examples of the Airbus short-haul family, with A320s and A319s being earmarked to eventually replace the remaining Boeing 737s.

More French Interest

Euralair, a French IT charter operator, had operated the Series 200 before taking delivery of its first Series 500 in June 1990. In addition to its own charter and scheduled programmes, Euralair operated a number of services on behalf of Air France's non-scheduled subsidiary, Air Charter. Air France also leased in Euralair's 737s for its own scheduled services and as a result, Euralair's aircraft often wore various combinations of livery and joint titles.

A similar arrangement was contracted by Air France with French independent carriers, Aéromaritime and Europe Aéro Service, for the use of their 737 fleets.

Boeing 737-300s served Aéromaritime on Paris-based charter flights until the fleet was absorbed by Air France. Steve Bunting

Aéromaritime was the non-scheduled subsidiary of UTA (Union de Transports Aériens), Air France's arch rival on long-haul routes. Aéromaritime operated a large fleet of both 737-300s and -400s on its European and North African charter network. UTA was purchased by Air France in 1991 and its fleet, and that of Aéromaritime, was eventually absorbed by Air France and Air Charter. In 1992 Europe Aéro Service flew six 737s, both Series 200s and -500s, four Caravelles and four Boeing 727s, on IT charters and a rapidly increasing scheduled network. However, EAS later ceased operations, following financial problems.

Charter operators Corsair, Minerve and Star Europe also flew the 737 on the French registry. Minerve was later merged with Air Outre Mer to form a new, large, independent, AOM French Airlines. Star Europe leased two Boeing 737-400s in the winter season of 1996/97, but they were replaced by two new Airbus A320s in time for the 1997 summer season. Corsair initially operated 737-200s to supplement their original Caravelle fleet, later replacing them with larger Series 300 and -400s.

Air France itself also took delivery of a fleet of Series 500s, the first arriving in 1991. The original order for twenty Series 500s was later reduced by three, but the remaining seventeen aircraft were quickly put to use alongside the established Series 200s on the European and domestic network. However, Air France had also ordered a large fleet of the Boeing 737's rival, the Airbus A320, instead of the larger 737 variants, and the European type was soon to find favour with the airline. In 1997, Air France absorbed the large, Airbus-oriented, fleet of Air Inter (that had already been renamed Air France Europe), and the Boeings began to be seriously outnumbered.

The French 'Combis'

Before its demise, EAS had participated in the establishment of a new specialist operator. Along with Air Inter and Transport Aérien Transrégional, EAS formed Inter Cargo Service. Operating a pair of Vanguard freighter turbo-props, Inter Cargo had opened scheduled freight services in 1987, flying from Paris to Toulouse, for TAT, and to Marseilles and other southern French towns, for Air Inter and Air France. The Vanguard operation came to a tragic end though, when both aircraft were lost in crashes within weeks of each other in 1989.

ICS was reorganized though and restarted operations with a pair of ex-Lufthansa Boeing 737-200QCs, operating passenger charters and scheduled services on behalf of Air France and Air Inter in the daytime, reverting to cargo/mail operations every night. After slightly reworking the airline's name to Inter Ciel Service, to make it more attractive to customers for passenger work, the company name was changed to L'Aéropostale as more night-time postal contracts were transferred from Air France and Air Inter. The L'Aéropostale fleet grew to accommodate the increased workload, with no less than fifteen 737-300s, all 'QC' versions with large freight doors, operating the extensive passenger and cargo/postal network.

The owners of EAS had also participated in the creation of Air Toulouse, which had operated Caravelles briefly in 1990. The new financing led to the appearance of Air Toulouse International in 1992, using two ex-EAS Caravelles. A single Boeing 737-200, also ex-EAS, eventually took over from the Caravelles and a massive expansion saw six in use by the summer of 1998. The expansion proved to be too rapid, and Air Toulouse International was declared bankrupt in June 1999. Subsequently, a name change followed refinancing and IT charters began under the name of Aéris in July 1999, with four 737-300s.

F-GIXI had been converted to 'QC' configuration for L'Aéropostale after flying with Aer Lingus, Futura and Viva. Steve Bunting

The Series 500 in the USA

Although Southwest Airlines had been a launch customer for the Series 500, there was little other 'home market' interest in the variant. One of the few major customers of the 737-500 in the USA was 737 pioneering operator, United Airlines. The first of an eventual fleet of fifty-seven of the smaller CFM56-powered 737 entered United service in late 1990. United had already taken delivery of the Series 300, of which over 100 were eventually to be delivered. The new 737s operated alongside a fleet of Airbus A320s, later joined by slightly smaller A321s, and a dwindling number of fuel-thirsty Boeing 727-200s, operating times of the PeoplExpress takeover and regular lapses into bankruptcy protection had done little to enhance the reputation of the airline with the travelling public, let alone the rest of the industry.

It was to take a change of ownership and management to begin the turnround, but new initiatives and policy changes finally started to see Continental making a remarkable comeback from the mid-1990s. The much criticized entrepreneur Frank Lorenzo, who had masterminded the original Continental/Texas International merger, sold most of his direct and indirect shareholdings in Continental in 1990. The new management team, led by new CEO Gordon Bethune, concentrated on restoring the eastern half of the country, again aimed at regaining lost traffic. Neither of the 'new' carriers was a success and both were eventually reabsorbed into the mainstream airline.

The 737-500 order was part of a massive re-equipment plan, designed to see the disposal of the older, less reliable and uneconomic types. Continental Airlines' short-haul network was hampered by being operated by a mixed bag of variants of several different airliner types, and badly in need of standardization. The ex-Lufthansa/PeoplExpress 737-100s were among the targeted fleet members, with the Series 500s meant to replace them and older DC-9s as soon as possible. Larger 737 models, as well as Boeing 757s, were also on order with a

Southwest expanded its influence across the USA, especially in California, with three of its busy fleet captured here at San Diego. *Malcolm L. Hill*

short and medium-haul inter-city services throughout United's domestic US network. As well as providing invaluable local communications, the short-haul fleet fed passengers into United's growing international route system. Once replaced by the later 737s and Airbuses, the last of the original Series 200s were finally disposed of after over thirty years of faithful service.

Continental Airlines was the only other major US customer for the Series 500. For many years after its emergence from the 'merger-mania' of the 1980s Continental had struggled to survive. Long-running labour-relation problems, the unsettled Continental's long-suffering reputation as a reliable carrier supplying a quality service to its passengers. More emphasis was placed on higher revenue business-class traffic, with a new 'Business First' service initially introduced on transoceanic flights.

Innovative promotions included the attempt to form new divisions, separate from the mainstream Continental Airlines operation. 'Continental West' was organized to take over the western network and regain traffic lost to an increasingly omnipresent Southwest Airlines, and other new lost-cost carriers. Later, 'Continental Lite' took over more leisure-related routes in view to eventually replacing the remaining Boeing 727s and McDonnell Douglas DC-9s and MD-80s over the following years.

Southwest and America West Go Nationwide

Much more popular in the USA was the Series 300, with Southwest Airlines, in particular, using the type to service its massive expansion through the late 1980s and 1990s. In 1994, Southwest had acquired Morris Air, which operated a fleet of 737-300s. Morris Air, which began services in

The 737 still featured heavily in America West's programme, despite increased use of Airbus types in the Phoenix-based airline's fleet. Aviation Hobby Shop

1992, was based at Salt Lake City and flew low-cost services throughout the western USA. The purchase of their fleet and route network gave Southwest a greatly increased presence in the region. The airline's influence in California was boosted even more by the opening of a hub at Los Angeles/Burbank and Southwest Airline's success was said to account for the progressive reduction of services in the area by USAir and Delta.

The two national carriers had spent a lot of money increasing their own Californian profile by buying out PSA and Western respectively and their reduction of Californian services was a major commercial victory for Southwest. Southwest Airlines also expanded to the north and east, developing new operational hubs at Chicago/Midway and Baltimore, far from its Texan roots. New high-frequency services linking Florida points replaced a similar network previously flown by Piedmont but later neglected by USAir.

Southwest's 737-500s eventually replaced the oldest of the airline's 737-200s, although over thirty 'Advanced' JT8D-powered Series 200s still remained in the fleet. However, it was with the 737-300 that Southwest based their prosperity, with nearly 200 of the variant in the all-737 fleet of over 300 operational aircraft by the year 2000.

Fellow low-cost operator, America West Airlines, also expanded well outside its geographical origins. Despite operating a fleet relying less on the 737, with 757s and Airbus types taking on an increasing percentage of the workload, America West was still flying over sixty 737-200s and -300s in 2000. Although still firmly rooted in the west, with major hubs at Phoenix and Las Vegas, America West also opened a base at Columbus, Ohio. The new hub was opened to serve routes further east, as well as southwards to Florida, and also linked up with the more western-based services. A code-share agreement with Continental Airlines also gave America West access to more Texan markets, via Continental's Houston hub.

Western Pacific and the 'LogoJets'

Undoubtedly one of the most colourful Southwest imitators first made its presence well and truly known when it burst on to the US airline scene in 1995. Western Pacific Airlines was originally formed to exploit the under-used Colorado Springs Airport. Denver's new airport is sited nearly forty miles from the city centre, to the north. Residents south of Denver found it much more convenient to use Colorado Spring's closer facility. As Denver fares were traditionally high, not helped by a local surcharge imposed on every ticket to help pay for the new airport, Colorado Springs was a low-cost airline hub waiting to happen.

Western Pacific's founder, Edward R. Beauvais, had a long history of association with regional carriers in the western half of the USA. Originally an employee of Bonanza Airlines, one of the original Air West components, Beauvais later went on to run his own consultancy company and became involved in a proposed Continental–Western merger. Beauvais was a leading member of the group that founded America West Airlines as the Phoenix-based airline's chairman until 1992.

One innovation that caught the travelling public's attention from the start was Western Pacific's 'LogoJet' programme. Although the idea of using an airliner for advertising purposes was not a new one – there had been several sports team-based and regional promotional liveries in the preceding years – actually selling the airliner as a flying billboard was a new twist on the theme. First customer to sign up for the revenue-boosting measure was the Broadmoor, a five-star Colorado Springs resort hotel owned by Edward L. Gaylord, a major investor in Western Pacific Airlines. The Broadmoor was soon followed by Colorado Tech, a technical college. Even the city of Colorado Springs itself promoted itself using one of the airline's aircraft. Most dramatic was the sale to Fox

(*Top*) **Fox Television rented space on Western Pacific's 737-300s.** Aviation Hobby Shop

(*Above*) **Western Pacific adopted a more sober livery once the logojet programme was cancelled.** Aviation Hobby Shop

Television of the space on ex-USAir 737-300, N949WP. Fox had Western Pacific paint the aircraft with its popular television cartoon characters 'The Simpsons'.

From 28 April 1995, Western Pacific's fleet of 737-300s linked Colorado Springs with Kansas City, Las Vegas, Los Angeles, Oklahoma City and Phoenix. San Francisco joined the network in May, and Chicago/Midway, Dallas/Fort Worth, Houston, Indianapolis, New York/Newark, San Diego, Seattle, Tulsa, Washington-Dulles and Wichita were all added by the end of the year as more aircraft became available.

The LogoJet programme was expanded with the swiftly growing, all 737-300 equipped fleet. Several Colorado ski resorts, Las Vegas casinos, car-hire companies and insurance firms all willingly laid out large fees for the privilege of having their name on the side of a Western Pacific airliner. There were a handful of aircraft operated in a 'standard' Western Pacific livery, as well as on mostly natural metal 737 that proclaimed the airline's aim to help its customers 'Beat the System'.

At its peak Western Pacific was operating no less than eighteen Boeing 737-300s. As well as providing a much-needed increase in passenger figures for Colorado Springs in its own right, Western Pacific's success attracted other airlines back to the airport, anxious to claim their share of the available traffic.

End of the Dream

However, although its high-profile and unique style of service was attracting passengers, Western Pacific Airlines was far from profitable. Eventually the main investors grew impatient for profits and, at the end of 1996, installed a new management team. Beauvais remained chairman, but with little or no authority and no influence over the new managers. The new team was headed by Robert Peiser, who promptly scrapped the LogoJet programme, in an attempt to attract a more business-oriented, higher-revenue, customer to the airline. Employee morale and service standards plummeted as debts built up. In a last

The attractive tail designs of Frontier's 737s are unique to each individual aircraft, depicting flora, fauna and the geography of the American West. Steve Bunting

desperate move, Peiser moved the operation to Denver's new International Airport, which put it in direct competition with several industry giants. Western Pacific did not stand a chance. After an abortive merger attempt with another carrier, Western Pacific Airlines was closed down on 4 February 1998.

A New Frontier

In July 1994, a new Frontier Airlines had started scheduled operations from Denver. Founded to take advantage of Continental Airline's drastic downsizing of its once substantial Denver presence, Frontier operated an initial fleet of Boeing 737-200s, later joined by -300s. As well as reviving the name of the region's still well-respected pioneer local carrier, Frontier made a name for itself in its own right with its eye-catching livery. Although the fuselage remained plain white, with only the airline's title and its motto, 'The Spirit of the West', it was raised from the mundane by the tail design. Each aircraft's tail surface was painted with a different graphic design featuring the natural wildlife or scenery of America's West.

Despite growing pains, Frontier Airlines survived, carrying 2.56 million passengers in only its third year. The route network soon encompassed both coasts, from San Diego to Boston, all points served via the Denver hub. It was Frontier that had considered merging with troubled Western Pacific, but wisely backed out of the deal. The owners of another low-cost scheduled 737-200 operator, Vanguard Airlines, took out a minority shareholding in Frontier. Vanguard operate a similar network, albeit on a smaller scale,

Alaska Airlines had spread its influence over routes far removed from its northern origins. A large fleet of 737-400s was acquired, with MD-80s, to service the expanded networks. Steve Bunting

145

MarkAir failed in its attempt to rival the giant Alaska Airlines. Steve Bunting

from Kansas City, but any full merger plans between the two were later abandoned. Vanguard's own re-equipment plans took the form of leasing in MD-80s to replace their much older Boeing 737-200 aircraft.

Although very satisfied with its all-Boeing 737 fleet, with seven -200s and seventeen -300s in service in 2001, Frontier Airlines chose not to order new versions to replace them. Instead, in October 1999, it announced an order for two Airbus types, the 114-passenger A318 and 132-passenger A319. Forty-six orders and options were taken out on the two types, with planned delivery for late 2001.

More 49th State 737s

Alaska Airlines had operated a handful of 737-200s alongside its Boeing 727s for several years. However, with the tri-jet becoming more of an economic liability, the 737 began to feature more in the airline's future plans. The carrier had started to expand well outside its traditional Seattle and Alaska-oriented markets since acquiring California-based Jet America Airlines in 1987. The takeover of the Los Angeles-based airline gave Alaska access to a much more southern-based market. This formed the basis of a route expansion programme that now saw the airline operating as far south as Mexico, as well as routes from California to the mid-west. Jet America had been in existence since 1981 and operated eight MD-80s. More of the McDonnell Douglas twin-jets were acquired by Alaska Airlines following the takeover. As well as the MD-80s though, Alaska eventually acquired no less than forty of the larger Boeing 737-400s, to replace the last 727-200s.

Despite the bankruptcy of Wien Air Alaska, another operator stepped in to replace them in the busier domestic Alaskan markets. MarkAir had originally been founded as a specialist cargo operator, Interior Airways. Later renamed Alaska International Air, the airline became famous for its worldwide *ad hoc* charter services with its fleet of Lockheed Hercules freighters. Five convertible 737-200s initially opened scheduled passenger services from Anchorage to several points in Alaska. The first 737s were later joined by another Series 200C, two 737-300s and three 737-400s. The route network was extended south to include Chicago, Las Vegas, Los Angeles, New York, Portland, San Diego, San Francisco and Seattle. Unfortunately, the company was soon losing money on the new services and finally ceased operations in 1992.

More Worldwide Presence

The CFM56-powered 737 versions were as popular worldwide as their JT8-D predecessors. In South America, the large 737-200 fleets of Cruziero and VARIG were amalgamated when the two airlines were merged under the VARIG name in 1993. Over thirty 737-300s eventually joined the fleet, operating over the vast regional and domestic Brazilian network. VARIG subsidiary, Rio Sul took delivery of a fleet of 737-500s, as well as a single Series 300. Rival Brazilian carrier, VASP, also supplemented its Series 200s with 737-300s. Sao Paulo-based independent, Transbrasil began replacing their Boeing 727-100s with 737-300s from 1986.

In Africa, Kenya Airways supplemented its small fleet of 737-200s with four Series 300s. Neighbouring Air Malawi and Air Tanzania both operated a single 737-300 and Air Afrique and Cameroon Airlines both fly small fleets of Series 300 on their scheduled services. Further north, Egyptair replaced their Series 200s with Series 500s, as well as introducing Airbus A320s and

The 737 and the Southwest 'Wannabes'

The spread of the low-cost carrier, worldwide as well as in the USA, has formed a major part of the story of the 737 in the last years of the twentieth century and beginning of the next. The continued success of Southwest Airlines, America West, and others, did not go unnoticed. There were many willing to sink their reputations and money into the new style of air travel. However, as always in the tough commercial world, there were as many, if not more, failures as successes.

Of the enthusiastic exploiters of deregulation, the previously mentioned Air Florida, Midway Airlines, Presidential Airways, Sunworld International Airways and Western Pacific were only some of the unlucky hopefuls that fell by the wayside. The likes of AirCal, Morris Air, New York Air and PeoplExpress were at least taken over as going concerns, with most of their employees having some sort of future to look forward to. Other enthusiastic workforces were less fortunate.

Eastwind Airlines, based at Greensboro, North Carolina and Trenton, New Jersey began operations in 1995. The second-hand Boeing 737-200s were later joined by brand new later versions on a network that covered routes from Florida to New England. Owned by UM Holdings, Eastwind initially enjoyed local success, especially at Trenton, with many of its passengers switching from nearby, but overcrowded, Newark and Philadelphia Airports. Unfortunately, the early traffic growth could not be maintained and, after UM Holdings supported the airline while an unsuccessful bid was made to find a buyer, the airline operation was closed down in 1999.

Another 1995 start-up was Air South, that began operations with leased Boeing 737-200s, operating a low-cost network from Columbia, South Carolina. Initially flying southwards to Florida cities via points in Georgia, Air South eventually turned its eyes north as well and its route network soon stretched as far north as New York. Despite attracting a loyal following, the airline ceased operations in 1997, following heavy losses.

Pro-Air was established with a head office in Seattle in 1995. However, it was to be much further east that the new airline made a name for itself, when commercial operations finally began in July 1997. Pro-Air set up its main hub at Detroit's old downtown airport, putting two new 737-400s into service on a low-fare network that eventually included Atlanta, Baltimore, Chicago, Indianapolis, New York, Orlando, Philadelphia and Seattle. An extra 737-400 and two smaller 737-300s also joined the original aircraft pair as service was expanded. However, in 2000, Pro Air had its certificate removed by the federal authorities, citing operational and maintenance discrepancies, and all operations were brought to a halt.

Even shorter-lived was Los Angeles/Long Beach-based Winair Airlines. Founded by Richard I. Winwood, Winair was originally based at Salt Lake City as a charter service. When 'scheduled' services began from Long Beach in 1998, they were still officially designated as 'direct-sales charters'. The fleet of 737-200s, later joined by leased Series 300s and 400s, operated from Long Beach to Las Vegas, Oakland, Sacramento and Salt Lake City. However, after only eight months of 'scheduled' operation, the airline ceased operations in July 1999, citing lack of investment as the cause of its financial difficulties.

Air South's short-lived operation utilized 737-200s on a busy schedule up the US east coast. Malcolm L. Hill

A321s. North African national carriers Air Algérie, Royal Air Maroc and Tunis Air all supplemented or replaced their earlier 737s with CFM56-powered versions.

Pakistan International Airlines introduced a fleet of Boeing 737-300s on domestic and regional flights, filling a niche between the wide-bodied international fleet of Airbus and Boeing types, and the turbo-prop Fokker F.27s and Twin Otters flown on local services. The Indian Airlines Corporation had chosen to replace their 737-200s with Airbus A320s and passed many of the surplus Boeings on to a new subsidiary, Alliance Air, which operates the aircraft on low-cost domestic services.

Malaysia Airlines had remained faithful to the 737, introducing a large fleet of Series 300s, along with several Series 400s and a trio of smaller Series 500s. New Malaysian independent airline, Transmile Air Service also operate several older 737-200s. Although Singapore Airlines itself no longer operated the Boeing 737, its subsidiary Tradewinds operated five 737-300s from 1990. Tradewinds' name was changed to Silkair in 1992 and the Boeings were

Behind the 'Bamboo Curtain'

Although remaining firmly under Communist control, mainland China began a major programme of regionalization of its airline operations in the mid-1980s. Until then, the Civil Aviation Administration of China (CAAC) had been solely responsible for the operation of China's vast domestic and international network. CAAC had operated a large fleet comprising a mixture of both Western-designed and Russian-produced airliners. Many of its more important domestic schedules were flown by a fleet of Hawker Siddeley Trident jet airliners, bought from the United Kingdom in the early 1970s.

CAAC's first Boeings had comprised an order for ten Boeing 707s, for use on the international network, placed after the USA and the People's Republic of China signed trade agreements for the first time since the Chinese Communists had come to power. Boeing 737-200s had entered service in 1983, originally imported to begin the replacement of some of the remaining Russian types such as the IL-18 turbo-prop and Tu-154 jet.

CAAC also acquired a number of McDonnell Douglas MD-80s, including some actually built under licence in China. McDonnell Douglas had originally hoped to establish a production line for the MD-80 series in China and provided parts for several aircraft after an agreement was reached with local manufacturers. However, in the event, only a handful were completed before the project was abandoned. Boeing, though, signed contracts with Chinese companies for the construction of aircraft components. Factories in Chengdu, Chongqing, Shanghai, Shenyang and Xian are now major subcontractors for Boeing.

The dissolution of CAAC into smaller carriers was preceded by the creation of a new independent carrier, Shanghai Airlines, originally founded by the local municipal government. However, all the other 'new' Chinese domestic airlines were created from the old regional divisions of CAAC. A 'Big Three' group of Chinese airlines soon emerged, with Air China, the old CAAC international division based at Beijing, China Eastern based at Shanghai and China Southern based at Guangzhou, easily becoming the biggest and most important carriers. Nonetheless, the smaller divisions were soon rapidly expanding under their new freedoms, promoting their own regional identities. Under the new liberalized system, even more independents were founded to take advantage of the increasing traffic.

The first new independent to appear was Xiamen airlines, soon followed by the likes of Shenzen Airlines, Hainan Airlines, Wuhan Airlines, China Great Wall Corporation and many others. As well as the reassigned CAAC fleet, more aircraft were imported to equip the new carriers, including 737s of varying models, many on leasing contracts as well as outright purchase. American types did not enjoy a monopoly though, as several Chinese airlines opted for Airbus aircraft, and even a handful of the more modern Russian types, such as the IL-86 and Yak-42, made an appearance.

As in any rapidly expanding, competitive, commercial situation, both winners and losers would soon appear. By the turn of the century the differing fortunes of the new airlines were becoming apparent. Both 'associate agreements' and mergers, of varying degree, soon started appearing between the airlines in an effort to minimize duplication and maximize efficiency. Outright takeovers and even more mergers were soon being mooted to bring the number of airlines down to a more manageable state.

(*Top*) CAAC's 737-200s initially passed to the new Air China. MAP

(*Above*) China Southern was one of the numerous airlines that appeared throughout China following the dissolution of CAAC. Steve Bunting

Brazil's major domestic operators, VASP and VARIG were long-established operators of the 737 on their regional services. Both pictures courtesy of Steve Bunting

(*Below*) Pakistan International introduced a fleet of 737-300s on to both its domestic and international routes from Karachi. PIA, via author

THE LAST OF THE OLD GENERATION

Hungary's **MALEV** pioneered the introduction of the 737 in service with airlines of the former communist nations of Eastern Europe. MAP

Croatia Airlines began operations with Boeing 737-200s from the former Yugoslav republic. Malcolm L. Hill

replaced by Airbus and Fokker narrow-bodied types from 1998.

East European Revolution

With the fall of the East European Communist regimes in the early 1990s, a huge market opened up for the Western aircraft manufacturers. Ever since the end of the Second World War, most of the airlines of the 'Iron Curtain' countries had relied on Russia to provide their aircraft needs. The factories of Antonov, Ilyushin, Tupolev and others, had produced several creditable aircraft over the years, at reasonable cost to the Warsaw Pact nations.

Western aircraft had made some inroads into the Warsaw Pact countries, although these were few and rarely sustained. More liberal Yugoslavia had operated a Western-built fleet, starting with Convair prop-liners in the 1950s. Poland's national airline, LOT had bought Vickers Viscount turbo-props and Romania's TAROM operated a large fleet of BAC One-Eleven jets, as well as Boeing 707s on long-range flights. Hungary's MALEV was one of the first to import the 737, when Series 200s were leased in as early as 1988, to begin the replacement of Tupolev Tu-134s and other Russian types. Series 300, -400 and -500 737s followed the initial leased fleet into MALEV service.

The later, CFM56-powered, 737s also found favour with the reorganized national airlines of Bulgaria, the Czech Republic, Poland, Romania and the Slovak Republic. The Series 500, especially, seemed to fill a niche on their thinner routes, with the larger models also making an appearance on busier sectors. In the Czech Republic the economy thrived enough to see the establishment of new charter airlines. Two of the new Czech airlines, Fischer and Travel Service Airlines, selected Boeing products, with the larger CFM56 737s their model of choice.

After breaking up into new republics and federations, the former Yugoslav nations also set about forming their own carriers. JAT began rebuilding itself as the flag carrier for Serbia, bringing its 737-300s back into service once international sanctions were lifted. Croatia and Macedonia also placed 737s into service, although Croatia Airlines later replaced their leased 737-200s with Airbus types.

Break-Up of Aeroflot

In the former USSR, the airline scene was changed out of all recognition. Newly formed republics were swift to establish their own national carriers and new independent airlines also sprang up to provide competition. For the most part, the established local directorate of the once giant Aeroflot simply broke away from the old regime and was renamed, usually with the old Russian-built fleet. Most outstanding exceptions were Russia itself, the Ukraine, and the Baltic States of Estonia, Latvia and Lithuania.

Ukraine International Airlines began operations with 737-200s leased in from Guinness Peat, that had a shareholding in the new airline, in 1992. In direct competition with the ex-Aeroflot directorate, now operating as Air Ukraine, UIA has gone on to operate 737-300s alongside the original -200s. Also in the Ukraine, AeroSvit flies regional and international services with a fleet of 737-200s.

All the Baltic States spawned 737 operators. Estonia Air began operations as a new flag carrier in 1992, eventually flying three 737-500s, alongside a fleet of Fokker 50 turbo-props. Riga Airlines of Latvia was also founded in 1992, to operate three 737-200s on international and regional flights. The airline's name was changed to Riair in 1995, but the carrier ceased operations in 2000. Lithuania's new carrier, Lithuanian Airlines was organized out of the old Aeroflot regional directorate, taking on its new identity just days before Lithuania regained independence. Eventually, Series 200, -300 and -500s all joined the Lithuanian fleet.

Russian Revivals

Transaero, a new Moscow-based independent, not associated with the old Aeroflot, was founded in 1993. Initially operating ex-British Airways Boeing 737-200s to Tel Aviv, Transaero swiftly expanded to include

The 737 also formed the initial fleet of Ukraine International Airlines when the new independent was formed to rival the local ex-Aeroflot Directorate, Air Ukraine. Steve Bunting

(*Above*) **Aeroflot Russian Airlines heralded in a new era with the Boeing 737-400.** Aeroflot

The 737-400 brought new standards of comfort to Aeroflot's passengers and crews used to the more 'basic' amenities of Russian-built types. Aeroflot

Boeing 757s in its fleet. Unfortunately, Transaero came close to becoming a victim of its own success, as route expansion and other costs soon started outstripping its revenue. Painful downsizing and reorganization followed a near-bankruptcy; however, by 2000, the revitalized carrier had recovered enough to be serving more than thirty domestic and international points with a fleet of 737-200s.

The airline operations that remained under the Aeroflot-Soviet Airlines name were reorganized as Aeroflot-Russian International Airlines, a new joint-stock company in 1992. The Russian government still held 51.17 per cent of the stock, the rest of the shareholding being held by Aeroflot's employees. The old Moscow-based Aeroflot international scheduled operations were taken under the new carrier's remit, as were routes throughout Russian territory and to other former members of the USSR, now the Commonwealth of Independent States (CIS). The name was further modified to Aeroflot-Russian Airlines in June 2000, to emphasize the airline's commitment to developing its domestic and CIS services, as well as its continued international presence.

Aeroflot became a 737 operator in 1998, leasing in the first of an initial fleet of ten Bermudan-registered Boeing 737-400s. The 737s were introduced onto the European network, as well as the more important domestic and regional services throughout the CIS. Over 130 destinations in seventy countries are served. In 2001, as well as the ten 737-400s, Aeroflot operates a modern fleet that includes two Boeing 777s, four Boeing 767s, eleven Airbus A310s and a single DC-10, as well as over seventy Russian airliners.

To the Future

The decision to offer the CFM56-powered versions of the 737 had proved a great success, as well as giving the whole programme a much-needed new lease of life. However, the competition, especially from Airbus Industrie, was still increasingly eating into Boeing's sales figures. Yet more improvements were needed to get Boeing back on top. It was time to move on again to the next step, to the next generation.

CHAPTER TEN

The Next Generation

Higher, Faster – and Cheaper!

By the 1990s, the increasing threat to Boeing's market-base by the European Airbus consortium was causing a great deal of concern in Seattle. The A320 model in particular, Airbus's nearest rival model to the 737, was selling in great numbers to airlines that had traditionally considered Boeing first. Not surprisingly, the European carriers began to favour the Airbuses. Air France, British Airways, Lufthansa and Sabena were among the once loyal 737 customers that chose to replace their older models with Airbus products.

Export sales, valuable as they were, were one thing, but even in the USA itself large fleets of Airbus A320s were being flown on domestic routes. America West Airlines, Northwest Airlines, United Airlines and US Airways operated the largest numbers. America West, United and US Airways operated their Airbus fleets alongside established Boeing 737s. All three airlines had also placed orders for the slightly smaller A318.

The Airbus threat to Boeing had grown from a mild annoyance, in the early days, to a major worry. Over the years, Boeing had suffered its share of industrial problems, development and production delays that had also contributed to some loss of customer confidence. Another serious rival was the last thing Boeing needed.

Although the CFM56-powered 737 models had certainly gone some way to offer some competition to Airbus, it was recognized that there was still room for further improvement to give Boeing back its lead. In particular, the 737 needed to fly higher, faster and even more economically if it was to continue to offer any competition to Airbus.

Looking to Boeing's Laurels

Other Boeing airliner programmes provided the 737 team with a host of improvements that could be incorporated into the basic aircraft to create yet further developed 737s. No less than five different major redesigns for a new aircraft were considered by Boeing. Eventually, however, the decision was made to proceed with the simpler proposal that comprised a 737 with a new, more efficient wing. The high degree of commonality with the current 737 models also meant that Boeing was able to avoid the expensive recertification costs of a type that was entirely new. The new version was initially designated the '737-X'.

An advisory airline group was set up, with contributions from customer airlines. One of the more surprising outcomes was the rejection by the group of the adoption of 'Fly-By-Wire' technology on the new

US Airways, as the rebranded USAir had become, was still a major user of the Boeing 737 in America. However, the airline had also introduced Airbus A318s, and A320s to replace the Boeings. Malcolm L. Hill

THE NEXT GENERATION

737. This had been a major new-technology feature used by Airbus in selling the A320. FBW had been successfully designed into Boeing's new long-range, wide-body type, the 777, and Boeing had seriously considered installing it on the 737-X. Instead, the advisory group members, in particular Southwest Airlines, were more in favour of retaining the 737's basic simplicity as well as commonality with previous models.

The major new feature, a larger, 'high-speed', wing had a 25 per cent increase in area, with a span increased to 112ft 7in (34.3m). The tip cord of the old wing was extended and a whole new wingbox was designed. More room for fuel was provided by moving the rear spar aft. No less than 30 per cent more fuel could now be carried, allowing a range of 3,200 nautical miles in the first 'Next Generation' models. To compensate for the larger wing, the dorsal fin and vertical stabilizer were lengthened and the span of the horizontal stabilizer was extended. These measures were also required to allow the use of higher-powered CFMB56-7B engines. The new version of the CFM56 engine was designed with 15 per cent lower maintenance costs and 8 per cent lower fuel burn. CFM International went to great lengths, offering to become a risk-sharing partner in the project, in return for the exclusive right to provide engines for the new type.

Launch Orders

The first of the 'Next Generation' 737s was to be the 737-700. Southwest placed the launch order in late 1993. In very basic terms the Series 700 was the Boeing 737-300, which it replaced on the production line, with the new features. The first -700 was rolled out in December 1996.

Six months later, the first Series 800, which replaced the -400, followed in June 1997. The -800 was first ordered by German charter airline Hapag Lloyd. Unlike the -700, the Series 800 does incorporate a further stretch over the Series 400. This allows an IT charter configuration of 189 passengers. To permit the higher capacity, the over-wing emergency exits were totally redesigned to be upward hinging units on all the new 737 versions, in place of the original inward-opening type.

Next to be launched, albeit somewhat out of numerical sequence, was the Series 600, a 'Next Generation' version of the

(*Above*) The Boeing 737-700 was difficult to distinguish purely by sight from the 737-300. Southwest painted the -700's flap hinge fairings bright orange to help ground crews tell the two apart. MAP

(*Below*) Hapag Lloyd ordered -800s for its extensive programme of IT charters from Germany. Steve Bunting

154

short-body Series 500, rolled out in December 1997. Launch customer for the -600 was Scandinavian Airlines System, which seemed to have got over its apparent reluctance to operate 737s after acquiring the ex-Linjeflyg -500 aircraft, most of which had been promptly leased out. SAS ordered no less than thirty-eight Series 600s, in addition to placing orders for fifteen Series 800s and a pair of -700s. Options were held on no less than sixty-eight other 737s. The airline planned to eventually replace its DC-9/MD-80/90 fleet with 'Next Generation' Boeing 737s. Boeing did not have it all their own way with SAS though, as orders were also placed for Airbus A321s, the European rival to the 757, and wide-body A330s and A340s were also ordered to replace Boeing 767s on SAS's long-haul flights.

The first -700 flew on 9 February 1997. By the time the first aircraft were entering Southwest Airlines service in early 1998, the order book for the 'Next Generation' 737s had reached a staggering 900 aircraft.

To EFIS Or Not EFIS?

Another innovation Boeing wanted to include in the 'Next Generation' 737s was new avionics and flight-deck displays, first developed for other aircraft in the Boeing airliner range. Not all the potential customers wanted the new-style technology though. Southwest, especially, wanted to remain with EFIS (electronic flight instrument system), as fitted to all its new 737s since all but the very first -300s onwards.

Mid-Atlantic 737s

Two island nations whose once strategically advantageous position in the mid-Atlantic had led to their becoming well-equipped for supporting air services were to become home to resident fleets of 737s. Both Iceland and the Azores archipelago had originally been developed as important refuelling stops for trans-Atlantic traffic linking the old world with the new, but were later overflown as technology improved. Meanwhile, their local populations had come to recognize the advantage of air travel, both locally and as a means to remain connected with the outside world.

In the north, Icelandair had been providing scheduled services to the island's scattered communities, and linking it to both Europe and the North American continent for several decades. However, the main scheduled carrier was not to be the first Icelandic operator of the 737. Staff of a failed charter carrier, Air Viking, formed a new charter airline, Eagle Air (Arnaflug), in 1976. Initially operating Air Viking's pair of second-hand Boeing 720Bs, Eagle Air flew IT and *ad hoc* charters from Iceland, mainly to Spanish resorts and to Germany. Eagle Air also became involved in leasing work with its 720Bs, sending them off on short-term contracts to other carriers in their own slow season.

Icelandair bought a majority shareholding in Eagle Air in 1979. Under the national airline's control, scheduled services were opened from Keflavik to Amsterdam, Dusseldorf and Zurich, using a 737-200 that replaced the 720Bs in 1981. The 737 was also used for the established charter network and leasing services. Unfortunately financial problems started to beset the small airline and it was closed down by Icelandair in 1990.

Icelandair itself, known locally as Flugfelag, preferred to utilize the Boeing 727 on its scheduled and charter flights, with both the -100 and -200 versions being acquired over the years. DC-8s played a brief part in the airline's operations following the merger of Icelandair and Loftleider, a leading independent low-fare Icelandic airline. Eventually, however, more modern 757s and 737s took over from the older tri-jets, including some 737 all-cargo operations.

Another leasing specialist was established in Iceland in 1986. Air Atlanta Icelandic's large fleet eventually included several 737s that were operated on both leasing contracts and IT charters in their own right. In 1991, Islandsflug, operator of a flight school and a handling and maintenance facility, opened scheduled services to sixteen destinations around Iceland using a Dornier turbo-prop. In 1998, a single 737 was used to open IT flights from Keflavik to Eindhoven, Manchester and Rimini. By 2001, the -200 had been joined by two -300s and leasing services were also operated under the name of Icebird Airlines.

Further south, the Azores archipelago had been served by the scheduled operations of SATA Air Acores, its own airline since 1947. SATA concentrated on providing vital links between the Portuguese island group with a fleet eventually comprising BAe and Dornier turbo-props. A new wholly owned subsidiary, SATA International, was formed when the assets of a failed local carrier, OceanAir, were taken over. In 1998, SATA International was awarded scheduled routes to mainland Portugal. Using a fleet of Boeing 737-300s and Airbus A310s, SATA International also undertook charter services from both the Azores and Portuguese resort areas to the UK and Europe.

Islandsflug operates its own IT programme from Iceland, as well as offering leasing services with its 737s. Aviation Hobby Shop

The continued use of the EFIS format would provide commonality, and allow Southwest greater flexibility in crew assignments and simplify conversion training. Nonetheless, the newer system, PFD/ND (primary flight display/navigation display), originally developed for the Boeing 777, was wanted by other operators. Many of these customers already operated similar equipment on other aircraft in their fleets.

In response to the differing requirements, Boeing solved the dilemma by developing a new CDS (common display system). The use of six Honeywell multifunction liquid crystal displays allowed the primary flight display and navigation data to be tailored to the airline's needs, in either format, as required.

The Douglas Factor

In 1997, the unthinkable happened in that Boeing's greatest competitor, ever since the days of the 247/DC-2 rivalry in the 1930s, vanished overnight. Even more unthinkable was that the company, the McDonnell Douglas Corporation, was actually bought out by Boeing.

Douglas had soundly beaten Boeing in the pre-war competition for the world's airliner market. Its main rival through the 1940s and 50s had been California neighbour, Lockheed. They had matched each other model for model through the Douglas DC-4/6/7 and elegant Lockheed Constellation series. As the jet age approached, Lockheed had placed all its airliner eggs in the turbo-prop basket, and been disappointed

Douglas and Lockheed worked tirelessly to outdo each other and design the ultimate piston-engined airliner. The results were the robust DC-7 (*top*) and aesthetic Super Constellation series (*above*). American Airlines C.R. Smith Museum/Aer Lingus

156

with the sales figures for its L-188 Electra. As a result, Lockheed had actually bowed out of the airliner market altogether, concentrating mostly on military projects until it produced the L-1011 Tristar wide-body. Although the aircraft was an operational success, with many examples built and enjoying long careers with a number of carriers, the L-1011 was also a financial failure, unable to follow up on its early promise.

Instead of Lockheed, Douglas had found itself up against a rejuvenated Boeing and an enterprising Convair in the competition for the US jetliner market. Convair was eventually to admit defeat up against the two giants and the Douglas DC-8 had come a very poor second to the Boeing 707. The expense of its jet airliner programmes was a major factor in Douglas's merger with McDonnell, to produce MDC. The Long Beach, California-based manufacturer had been increasingly struggling to survive as Boeing and, eventually, Airbus sales had encroached on its traditional markets and customers.

The wide-body DC-10 airliner had enjoyed an early success, but sales suffered after a number of accidents blighted the type's reputation. The long-established DC-9 short-haul jet had sold very well, but later, stretched, MD-80 versions suffered by comparison with the 737-300/400/500 series and new Airbus narrow-bodied types. Re-engined and updated MD-80s were being produced, as the MD-90 series, but were struggling to reach viable sales targets.

As with Boeing, MDC was not only involved in commercial airliner production, although, also like Boeing, it was probably its most public activity. Involvement in aerospace projects in the fields of missile technology, satellite, military and space-flight programmes, amongst others, also occupied the company, but none of them were making it much money either. As MDC's financial problems piled up, the situation worsened dramatically and there was a genuine possibility that the much revered company would collapse completely. Eventually, Boeing stepped in with the proverbial offer that could not be refused, and absorbed MDC.

MD-95 to Boeing 717

At the time of the takeover, MDC was producing the MD-11, an enlarged and longer-ranged version of the DC-10, and the stretched MD-90 series of twin-jets. Although acknowledged as one of the world's quietest jets in service, and into its third year of production, the MD-90 was a direct competitor to the 'Next Generation' 737s. So it came as no great surprise when the eventual closure of the MD-90 production line was announced by Boeing. However, curiously, in 1998, Boeing did decide to continue development of one of the newer MD-90 derivatives, the MD-95.

Much smaller than the MD-90s in service, the MD-95 was closer to the size of the older DC-9 series and intended to offer the advantages of the new technologies on less dense routes. Boeing redesignated the design as the Boeing 717-200 and continued with its development work. Only one operator, low-cost scheduled airline Valujet, had placed a definite order. Even this order was in the balance, as Valujet was busy reinventing itself following its grounding by federal authorities after the fatal crash in Florida by one of its DC-9-30s. Atlanta-based Valujet had recently merged with another low-fare airline, AirTran, that flew several Boeing 737-200s from Orlando.

The resulting 'new' AirTran confirmed the order for fifty of the new twin-jet, intending to standardize on the type. Boeing was eventually rewarded with more orders and options from TWA and other carriers worldwide.

717 and the 737-600

The decision to proceed with the MD-95/717 was even more of a surprise as the 100–120-passenger aircraft was close to the capacity and performance of the -600 version of the 'Next Generation' 737s. The 717 was seen by Boeing as more of a rival to the new 'regional jets' that had been making their appearance on local routes. Passenger capacities on the Bombardier/Canadair from Canada, Embraer's Brazilian-built local jets, developed from

The Boeing 717 still bore a striking resemblance to the DC-9 line from which it was directly descended. Only the much larger engines make identification easier. Aviation Hobby Shop

THE NEXT GENERATION

the turbo-prop Brasilia, Dornier's jets, also developed from a turbo-prop design, were all increasing. Passenger loads of 70–80 were now possible on the larger versions of what had originally been perceived just as stretched business jets, and it was this market that the 717 was aimed at.

The 717-200 first flew on 2 September 1998. Four aircraft were eventually used in the test and development programme and certification was granted just under a year later on 1 September 1999. A proposed 717-100 version, reduced in size to carry eight-five passengers in a mixed-class layout, was being considered to offer further competition to the 'regional jet' types.

The 'Next Generation' Goes into Service

Southwest Airline's, and the world's, first Boeing 737-700 'Next Generation' commercial flight took place on 18 January 1998. N700GS operated Flight 11 from Dallas/Love Field to Houston/Hobby and on to Harlingen, all within Southwest's home state of Texas. The first Hapag Lloyd 737-800 entered service from Germany in time for the 1998 summer season of IT charters. SAS placed the -600 into scheduled service in the autumn of 1998, on routes from Scandinavia to Paris. The first production -900 was delivered to Alaska Airlines in 2001, for entry into service that summer on the Seattle-based airlines' US regional and Alaskan network.

The large order book for the 'Next Generation' versions of the 737 meant that the new types were soon spreading their wings on air routes all over the world. Both scheduled and charter, established and new Boeing 737 operators were soon taking delivery of the -700s and -800s. Pioneer 737 airline, Braathens was an early -700 operator, placing the first of an order for fifteen in service on its Norwegian and European network in early 1998. Germania replaced its -300s with -700 'Next Generation' versions, operating on behalf of

(*Above*) BWIA of the Caribbean became a new 737 operator with the -800. Aviation Hobby Shop.

(*Below*) Futura introduced a new livery with the arrival of their 'Next Generation' 737-800s. MAP/Aviation Hobby Shop

158

The high capacity -800 found itself popular with many charter carriers. Novair operate them from Sweden to sunnier climes in southern Europe. Aviation Hobby Shop

Deutsche BA and fellow charter carrier LTU, as well as its own services. Dutch carriers KLM Royal Dutch Airlines and Transavia, the latter now a subsidiary of the former, took delivery of 737-800s for use on their European networks, supplementing earlier versions. The 737-800 made its first appearance in the Caribbean with the delivery of the first of a sextet of aircraft to BWIA West Indies to supplement and eventually replace their fleet of DC-9 and MD80 types.

Spanish leaders in the IT charter market, Air Europa, as well as operating a regional and long-haul scheduled network in its own right, took delivery of -800s to supplement the smaller -300s and -400s in the fleet. A new subsidiary, Air Europa Canarias, was established in 1999 to operate two of the parent company's 737-300s from Gran Canaria. Moves were actually made to merge Air Europa into Iberia, itself flying three -400s in its huge, varied, fleet, but the merger was finally called off in early 2001. Futura International also took delivery of the -800 for Spanish-based IT work. Five were in use for the 2001 summer season, operating with the earlier -400 series.

Denmark's IT Saga

As well as the multinational SAS and Norway's Braathens, other Scandinavian airlines soon placed the 'Next Generation' 737s into service. Denmark's Sterling European Airways had been born from the ashes of a long-established carrier, Sterling Airways, that had ceased operations in September 1993. Originally founded in 1962 by Tjaerborg Reiser, a large Danish travel company, Sterling had gained an enviable reputation as a quality charter carrier and was operating charter services from most Scandinavian countries, as well as serving its home market. Its original DC-6Bs had eventually been replaced by a large fleet of Caravelles and in turn these were replaced by Boeing 727-200s and 757s. Sterling's fortunes began to wane in the early 1990s and a takeover bid by France's Europe Aero Service failed in 1993, eventually leading to Sterling Airway's bankruptcy.

The 'new' Sterling European Airways began commercial operations in May 1994, with a fleet of six Boeing 727-200s. Although on a much smaller scale, the operations were similar to the original airline's, flying IT charters from Copenhagen to Mediterranean resorts. A Norwegian company, Fred Olsen, took a 95 per cent share in Sterling European in 1995, immediately implementing a modernization programme. Two 737-300s were acquired, followed in 1998 by the first of an order for five -800s. The 727s were converted to freighter configuration and operated on contract charters for the TNT organization.

Not connected in any way to the defunct UK 737 operator of the same name, Novair started charter operations from Stockholm in 1997. Owned by Swedish tour operator Apollo Resor, Novair initially flew a single Lockheed Tristar and one Airbus A320 on both long and medium IT charter flights. Four new 'Next Generation' 737-800s eventually took over the A320 services as Novair's operations expanded.

The 'Next Generation' and the Major US Carriers

A major coup for Boeing was an order for no less than 100 Series 800s from American Airlines. Since disposing of the ex-AirCal -200s and -300s in the late 1980s, American had relied on its large numbers of MD-82s and Fokker 100s to supplement Boeing 727-200s in its narrow-bodied fleet. The 737-800s entered service from American's Dallas and Chicago hubs during 1999, as replacements for the ageing 727s.

The American Airlines 737-800s carry twenty first-class passengers, with 126 in economy class. Both cabins feature new seating units, designed to offer more lumbar support and legroom, and adjustable headrests, as well as telephone and power ports at every seat and overhead aisle video monitors throughout the aircraft.

The delivery of the fiftieth Boeing 737-800, N951AN, to American was marked by the aircraft being painted in the airline's 1960s 'Astrojet' livery. A Boeing 757 had

Experience The New American Airlines
On Board Our All-New 737s.

As part of the most extensive aircraft acquisition, refurbishment and product enhancement program in our history, American Airlines is adding 100 "Next Generation" 737s to our domestic fleet.

Our new 737s, being delivered now through 2001, are equipped with a totally redesigned interior and more comfortable, state-of-the-art seats in First Class and Main Cabin.

These new 737s are just one more way we're taking American Airlines to the next level for the next millennium.

New First Class Comfort.

The new seats aboard our new 737s offer you the best in comfort and convenience, with a host of features to make your travel more enjoyable.

Our new, fully contoured First Class seats feature a thinner profile, leather and fabric appointments, a six-way adjustable leather headrest, generous legroom and recline.

Additional special accouterments include a telephone and power port in every seat and overhead aisle video monitors throughout the aircraft.

Our First Class seats offer new design and comfort

Our passengers can also enjoy CBS Eye On American programming with The Late Show with David Letterman, 60 Minutes, 48 Hours, CBS Sports and CBS sitcoms, plus movies and 12 channels of audio programming. Passengers will also be able to send/receive data and power laptop computers while in flight.

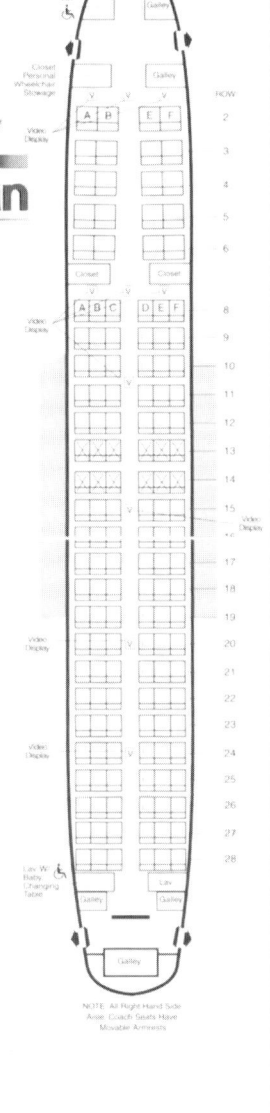

Main Cabin – A New Standard.

The Main Cabin of our new 737s features high-tech, slim-line seats with newly stylized upholstery, a six-way adjustable leather headrest, and a roomy 32" pitch.

The 126 Main Cabin passengers can also enjoy telephone communications at each seat row. There's ample Main Cabin storage space for carry-on baggage. And this aircraft is also equipped with special features for disabled passengers.

New Main Cabin features make flying American even more enjoyable.

(*Opposite*) **American airlines introduced many upgraded passenger features with their 737-800s.** American Airlines C.R. Smith Museum

(*Below*) **N951AN turned heads wherever it appeared on American's network in its smart 1960s 'Astrojet' livery.** American airlines C.R. Smith Museum

Continental placed its 737-800s on transcontinental service from its Houston and Newark hubs, as well as shorter, high-density routes. Aviation Hobby Shop

been painted in late 1950s style in 1999, to celebrate the fortieth anniversary of American's jet service, and had proved very popular. The 737 'Astrojet' attracted similar attention and, on 17 December 2000, only two days after entering revenue service, N951AN was chartered to carry the new President-elect George W. Bush and his entourage from Austin, Texas, to Washington DC, following the delayed announcement of his election victory.

Continental Airlines placed large orders for the 'Next Generation' 737 models as part of a massive re-equipment and modernization plan. Finally managing to throw off its post-merger reputation for mediocre and disorganized operations, Continental was soon winning award after award for its renewed style of service. The last remaining ex-Lufthansa/PeoplExpress Series 100s and all the -200s, as well as many old model

DC-9s and all the 727s in the fleet, were eventually replaced by the 'Next Generation' 737s. In addition, over sixty 737-300s remained, alongside the nearly seventy 737-500s, over thirty 737-700s and over fifty 737-800s in service, with nearly forty other 737s of various versions on order.

The improved performance of the 737-700 prompted Continental to study placing the version on trans-Atlantic service, on the New York/Newark–Shannon route. However, increased traffic demands saw larger 757s being utilized by Continental instead. Nonetheless, Aloha Airlines placed its 737-700s on new Hawaii–mainland routes to Oakland and Las Vegas, an unprecedented distance for the aircraft originally envisaged as a short-range, purely inter-city airliner.

Delta placed the 737-800 in service alongside its fleet of eighty 737-200s and -300s. The larger -800s were ordered to replace the airline's last 727-200s. As well as mainline services, the 737-800s also replaced the older Boeing tri-jets on the no-reservations 'Delta Shuttle' between New York, Boston and Washington, which Delta had originally purchased from Pan American.

Midway Revival

Yet another 'revived' regional airline in the USA was Midway, which restarted operations from Chicago in 1993 with a fleet of Fokker 100s. The Chicago network failed to make money, not least of all because Southwest had taken the opportunity of the original Midway Airlines' absence to develop a highly effective new hub at Midway Airport. Instead, the new Midway Airlines upped sticks in 1995 and moved its headquarters to Raleigh/Durham International Airport, in North Carolina. Raleigh/Durham had been developed as a new East Coast hub by American Airlines, but the large airline found its efforts from there to be unsuccessful and withdrew most of its services. Identifying an under-utilized niche catchment area, Midway set about establishing a new network far from its Midwest roots.

Initial results were promising and the Fokkers were joined by Airbus A320s on busier routes. Unfortunately, once again Midway was threatened with serious financial problems, after overstretching itself. The Airbuses were returned and a new start made with the Fokkers. In 2000, new Boeing 737-700s arrived along with new Bombardier/Canadair Regional Jets, destined to replace the long-serving Fokkers. Nine 737s and no less than twenty-four Canadairs were in use in 2001, along with six remaining Fokkers. As well as locally originating traffic, Raleigh/Durham acted as a hub for a network stretching throughout the eastern half of the USA.

The Delta Shuttle replaced its long-serving 727-200s with 737-800s on the high frequency, no-reservations service between New York, Boston and Washington.
Aviation Hobby Shop

The undoubted success of Southwest Airlines' low-fare services did not go unnoticed in the hallowed boardrooms of America's major airlines. They were losing traffic to Southwest and its copiers on most fronts and badly needed to regain the lost passenger revenue. One solution that was adopted by some was an 'If you can't beat 'em, join 'em' attitude.

In 1994, United transferred a number of its 737-300s to a new low-fare subsidiary, Shuttle By United, which took over a number of West Coast routes. Operating a low-cost philosophy, with only basic on-board facilities, Shuttle By United was later renamed United Shuttle and expanded with more 737s being moved into the fleet as a large order for Airbus A318s and A320s was delivered to the parent airline.

Delta set up Delta Express, again a wholly owned subsidiary, in 1996, specifically to combat Southwest's entry into the Florida vacation markets. This time 737-200s were used to equip the new division.

USAir had become US Airways in 1998, in a major rebranding exercise. The same year, it set up its own low-cost operation, MetroJet, based at Baltimore. Also established to directly combat Southwest Airline's expansion into its traditional markets, MetroJet was equipped with 737-200s, again transferred from the parent company.

During 2000, United made an offer to buy out US Airways that had continued to make losses despite improving its service reputation after the name change. Although at an advanced stage in negotiations, United called off the merger in mid-2001.

In the UK, British Airways was facing the loss of domestic and European traffic to new low-cost operators, Ryanair and easyJet. In response, a new London/Stansted-based subsidiary was established with leased 737-300s. Named Go Fly, the new carrier began scheduled flights from Stansted to European and domestic points in 1998. Sixteen destinations were served by 2001, and Go opened a new base at Bristol, in the west of England, later that year. However, also in 2001, British Airways decided that Go's operation was not compatible with its own image as a quality service provider and put the airline up for sale. After considering several offers, British Airways sold Go to the low cost carrier's own management.

KLM UK, previously Air UK and renamed after the Dutch airline had bought a majority shareholding, was suffering from the competition with its Stansted-based scheduled services after Ryanair and Go Fly moved in. In retaliation, in January 2000, KLM UK transferred eight BAe 146s to a new low-fare subsidiary, named Buzz. A total of fourteen routes from Stansted were in operation by 2001 and the BAe 146s were joined by a pair of Boeing 737-300s on the busier services.

On the other side of the world, Freedom Air International began operations from Auckland in 1995. Wholly owned by Air New Zealand, low-fare schedules operate alongside charters, not only within New Zealand, but also across the Tasman Sea to Australia. Despite serving a relatively sparsely populated region, Freedom Air's pair of 737-300s found themselves in demand, not least when Qantas New Zealand suddenly ceased operations in 2001. Freedom Air's aircraft, alongside Air New Zealand's own 737s, operated extra services to substitute for the defunct carrier.

The Big Boys Fight Back

(*Top*) US Airways transferred several 737-200s to its new low-cost Metrojet operation. MAP

(*Middle*) Although Go Fly's operation from Stansted was a success, British Airways decided to sell off the low-cost subsidiary. Aviation Hobby Shop

(*Bottom*) The bright yellow 737-300s of Buzz supplemented a larger fleet of BAe 146s. Aviation Hobby Shop

Boeing 737-700s were acquired by Midway Airlines to increase capacity on their Raleigh/Durham-based services. MAP

All Change in Canada

In Canada, the long-established, major, 737 operator Canadian Airlines International, was to lose its identity in a takeover battle that it lost with arch rival Air Canada. Through 2000 the CAI fleet of 737-200s was repainted in basic Air Canada livery, although still with Canadian titles and logo on the fuselage. In 2001, the merger took even more effect as the first totally repainted 737s started appearing, with the CAI identity finally disappearing. Both Air Canada and CAI had begun the process of replacing their older short/medium-haul fleets with Airbus types, a process likely to continue in the years following the merger with the new enlarged carrier.

An exception to the merger process was CAI's subsidiary, Canadian North. Providing vital social services in the arctic regions of Canada with two convertible 737-200Cs, Canadian North was sold off in September 1998, before the merger, to Norterra Inc, a holding company 100 per cent owned by native Canadian communities.

The Air Canada/Canadian Airlines International merger was pounced on by Canada's own growing band of low-fare operators as a chance to expand their influence. Citing the size of the newly enlarged Air Canada as a monopolistic threat, CanJet, Royal Airlines and West-Jet Airlines were 737 operators among the independent airlines all claiming their 'rightful share' of new route authorities. WestJet had been established in Calgary in 1995, and was flying twenty-two 737-200s on low-fare scheduled services in the region by 2001. Five 'Next Generation' Series 600s were on order, as were no less than thirty-one 737-700s.

Royal Airlines originally began operations with two Boeing 727-200s, as a charter airline in Montreal in 1992. Scheduled services were opened, with six 737-200s operating alongside the airline's Airbus A310 wide-bodies and Boeing 757s. In 2001 Royal was acquired by rival charter and scheduled carrier Canada 3000, that nursed ambitions to become the new 'second force' once CAI disappears. CanJet opened its scheduled network, from Toronto to Halifax, Ottawa and Windsor in September 2000, with a pair of 737-200s. Seven -200s were in use with CanJet by mid-2001.

Meanwhile, South of the Border

Liberalization saw the growth of new operators in both Central and South America, as well as the consolidation of old ones. Aerolineas Argentinas came up against a new low-cost rival when a previously small commuter airline, LAPA (Lineas Aereas Privadas Argentinas), sold off its fleet of turbo-props and placed its first second-hand Boeing 737-200 into service in 1993. LAPA experienced rapid growth, offering low-fare services throughout Argentina in direct competition with Aerolineas. More 737-200s were gathered from various sources, later joined by new Boeing 737-700s.

In both Central and South America, a number of carriers formed new alliances to combat the growing influence of mainline US carriers in the region. TACA International Airlines, the national carrier for El Salvador and Honduras, had operated 737s for many years. In the late 1990s, the neighbouring operations of Aviateca (Guatemala), LACSA (Costa Rica) and NICA (Nicaragua) were brought under the TACA influence, to co-ordinate their operations in the region and on routes to the USA. The combined fleets comprised a mixture of both Boeing and Airbus types. A new associate airline, TACA Peru, was set up to operate two 737-200s from Lima.

Also in Peru, Aero Continente began operations in 1992, initially focused on charter work in support of oil exploration in the northeast of the country. In July 1993, two 727-200s and a 727-100 opened scheduled

Aviateca joined forces with three other Central American airlines under the Grupo TACA banner, while Aero Continente of Peru also established a local subsidiary in Chile. Both pictures courtesy of Aviation Hobby Shop

services that eventually included an international network that stretched as far as Miami, in addition to domestic services. Aero Continente soon became Peru's major airline operator and in 2001 was flying five 737-200s, a single -100, three 727-100s and even a wide-body 767, as well as two Fokker F.28s and a small fleet of turbo-props. In 1999, a new associate airline was established in Chile in partnership with a Chilean investment group. Aero Continente Chile operates eight 737-200s on its domestic and regional services from Santiago.

A 49 per cent shareholding in Copa Airlines, of Panama, also a long-standing 737 operator, was bought by Continental in May 1999. Copa began the replacement of their fleet of 737-200s with 'Next Generation' -700s, with twelve on order. Another Continental/Copa alliance was formed with a new Chilean airline, Avant Airlines. Originally operating as Aero Chile, formed in 1996, the company was later renamed Lineas Aereas Chileanas, and renamed again in 1997. Domestic scheduled services were operated the length of Chile with a fleet of 737-200s until operations ceased in 2001.

Further East

The Series 800 found a new home with Mandarin Airlines of Taiwan. Mandarin had originally been formed as a subsidiary of China Airlines to take over schedules to Australia and Canada. However, a change in policy saw Mandarin switching its attention to domestic and regional flights after the operations of Formosa Airlines were taken over in 1999. A 737-400 was joined by five -800s on the busier flights, with Fokker F.100 jets and Fokker F.50 and Dornier 228 turbo-props operating lower-capacity services. China Airlines itself also took delivery of Series 800s, with thirteen ordered for its short and medium-range services.

Korean Air introduced fifteen 737-800s, to begin the replacement of older Fokker and McDonnell Douglas types. Otherwise, Korean Air operated an all-wide-bodied fleet of Airbus A300s, Boeing 747 and 777s.

Low Cost Goes Global

When the rest of the world followed the USA's deregulation lead, many new airlines sprang up to take advantage of the new order. Even where wide-reaching deregulation in the American style was resisted, there was usually enough liberalization to allow the limited entry of new blood into the local airline industry. The well-proven, widely and cheaply available Boeing 737 was often the choice of equipment for the new operators.

In the Far East, initial growth in an economic boom had been swiftly followed by recession. In the Philippines, a number of new independent carriers had been established and grew quickly. Of the numerous new independents, Air Philippines and Grand International Airways both built up large fleets of 737s only to have their new markets vanish overnight. Even the giant Philippine Air Lines itself was forced to cease operations temporarily. Eventually, the economic climate improved in the region, but often too late for the once hopeful new carriers, many of which had been forced to severely cut back their operations.

Mixed fortunes also met new independent airlines on the Indian subcontinent. Competition for the Indian Airlines Corporation was actively encouraged by the government in the early 1990s and a number of new operators rose to the challenge. IAC had already transferred most of its 737-200s to a new subsidiary, Alliance Air, based at New Delhi. East West Airlines began Boeing 737-200 and Fokker F.27 scheduled operations from Bombay in 1992, with scheduled flights to Mangalore and Cochin, later adding Goa, Jaipur and Trivandrum. Lufthansa provided backing for another of the first new Indian carriers, Modiluft, which began scheduled domestic operations with ex-Lufthansa 737-200s in 1994. Unfortunately, East West and Modiluft suffered numerous operational difficulties and ceased flying in 1997.

Much more successful were the 737 operations of Jet Airways and Sahara Airlines. Both new carriers began scheduled services in 1993, competing with Indian Airlines on domestic services throughout India. By 2001 both were operating large fleets of 737s, Jet Airways flying ten 737-400s, seven 737-700s and nine 737-800s, with nine more -800s on order. Sahara operated an all-737 fleet of three -400s, two -800s and single examples of the -200 and -700 versions.

New 737s in the Eastern Mediterranean

Liberalization also allowed growth in charter markets, as well as the scheduled service sector. A boom in holiday resort development saw Turkey, especially, spawn a number of new IT charter carriers, dedicated to

Despite strong backing from Lufthansa, which provided it with 737s, ModiLuft failed to survive. Aviation Hobby Shop

British 737 Disappointments and Revival

The growth of the Airbus threat was pressed home to Boeing with the decision of British Airways not to order the 'Next Generation' 737s for its European routes. Instead, a mixed order was placed for Airbus A318s, 319s and 320s, to eventually replace the earlier 737 models. British Airways' franchise associate, GB Airways, also placed its first Airbus A320s and A321s in service in 2001, planning to replace its seven 737s with an identical number of Airbus aircraft.

Still expanding its European and UK domestic scheduled network, British Midland Airways declined Boeing's offer of 'Next Generation' 737s, choosing instead the Airbus A320 and A321. The British Midland Boeing 737-300s and -400s were to be disposed of, although the 737-500s would remain in the fleet for the time being. The airline's name was modified, and a new livery and image unveiled, as 'british midland bmi', in preparation for trans-Atlantic Airbus services in 2001.

However, one prodigal return to the 737 fold was Britannia Airways. Britannia had replaced their last 737-200 in 1994, with the much larger Boeing 757 taking over as the airline's narrow-body aircraft. Although the 757s offered the flexibility of being capable of operating both long and short-haul charters, like the wide-bodied Boeing 767s

(*Below*) **British Airways Boeing 737s are eventually to be replaced by new Airbus types.** Via author

(*Bottom*) **Airbus A320s displaced 737-300s and -400s with the rebranded 'british midland bmi'.** Aviation Hobby Shop

British 737 Disappointments and Revival *continued*

(*Above*) The 737-800 made its first appearance in Britannia Airways' colours with the Scandinavian subsidiary, Britannia AB. Aviation Hobby Shop

(*Below*) Sabre Airways was renamed Excel Airways in 2001. Aviation Hobby Shop

also in the Britannia Airways fleet, the airline soon found it required a lower-capacity aircraft for less well-travelled routes and to help develop new markets not able to support the larger aircraft.

Three 180-passenger Airbus A320s were leased from Irish charter carrier TransAer to serve on thinner IT routes, in the late 1990s. However, any hopes that Airbus might have cherished that this would lead to a direct order from Britannia were soon to be dashed. In 1998, Britannia's owner, Thomson International, took control of Swedish tour operator Fritdsresor and its own charter airline Blue Scandinavia. The Swedish IT charter carrier was rebranded as Britannia Airways AB and took on the British airline's full identity.

In 1998, a single 737-800 was leased by the Swedish operation, from Danish IT carrier Sterling European, and operated alongside its three Boeing 757s. The same year, Britannia in Luton announced a $270 million order for five more 737-800s, to be operated by both 'Britannias'. In 2001 three were in use with Britannia AB and the other two entered service with the UK-based operation.

The 737-800 also found favour with another UK IT carrier, Sabre Airways. Originally formed in December 1994, Sabre had opened operations with a pair of 737-200s, later joined by two 727-200s. The airline had been established to take over IT charters previously contracted to Newcastle-based Ambassador Airways, which had ceased flying that November. Ambassador had flown Boeing 757s, 737s and A320s, but the bankruptcy of its travel company owners had led to its downfall. Sabre took over the 737s and the Gatwick and Manchester-based contracts that Ambassador had flown for other tour operators.

The 737-200s were leased out in 1997 to Peach Air, a subsidiary of Caledonian Airways. Peach Air initially flew the Sabre 737-200s and a Lockheed L-1011 Tristar leased from Air Atlanta Icelandic. The Peach Air operations came to an end in November 1998 and Sabre disposed of the -200s at the end of the lease contract. However, Sabre had continued to expand its own charter operations and the 727-200s were being replaced by new 737-800s, the first of which had entered service earlier in 1998. Two of the Boeing 737-800s were leased out to Miami Air, of Florida, during the winter of 2000/2001. In 2001, following its acquisition by Libra Holidays, Sabre was renamed Excel Airways, beginning operations under the new title in May, operating a fleet of six 737-800s.

THE NEXT GENERATION

Sahara Airlines enjoyed greater success than some new Indian carriers, eventually operating several versions of the 737. MAP

Both national carrier THY-Turkish airlines and leading independent Istanbul Airlines took delivery of 'Next Generation' 737-800s. Both pictures courtesy of Steve Bunting

serving the new resort areas. In addition, new legislation allowed the growth of independent scheduled airlines to compete against Turkish Airlines. Both the long-established state carrier and the new arrivals made good use of available 737s, both new and from the second-hand and leasing markets.

lines, originally established by Aer Lingus, and SunExpress that is backed by Lufthansa and Turkish Airlines. In addition, KTHY, the Turkish Cypriot airline, began 737 operations in its own right in 2001, after leasing in Turkish Airlines' aircraft of various types for many years. As well as flights from Turkish-held northern Cyprus, a number of IT

1990s. Those that chose the 737 as their main equipment include Axon Airlines (two 737-700s), Cronos Airlines (four 737-300s and two 737-400s, Galaxy Airways (one 737-400 and one 737-500) and Macedonian Airlines (Greece) (one 737-400). Olympic Airways continued to be a loyal 737 operator, flying the original

New Cypriot independent, Helios, began flying IT charters with a single 737-400. Aviation Hobby Shop

A leading light among the new independents was Istanbul Airlines, which commenced operations with Caravelles in 1986. Initially concentrating on charters to Europe, Istanbul later established a scheduled domestic network, introducing the first of a number of 737s in 1988. By 2000 the fleet consisted of nine 737s, of the -300, -400 and -800 series and a single 727-200. Unfortunately, the Turkish authorities withdrew Istanbul's operating certificate on 28 August 2000, following mounting financial problems, and the airline ceased flying.

Other private Turkish airlines followed Istanbul's pioneering lead, many of them utilizing 737s. Bosphorus Air, Holiday Airlines, Sultan Air and VIP Air all introduced 737s before succumbing to financial difficulties. More successful have been the Boeing 737 operations of Air Rose, Pegasus Air-

charters operate from mainland Turkish resorts to Western European points.

Independent southern Cyprus also eventually allowed an expansion of private competition with the established national carrier, Cyprus Airways. As was becoming usual, tour companies were the majority shareholders in the new enterprises, using the capacity to feed the expanding holiday resorts on the island. The dormant TEA (Cyprus) was revived in 1998 and renamed Helios Airways. A single 737-400 opened charter flights to Europe from Larnaca, with 737-800s set to be delivered shortly afterwards. A year later, the Louis Tourism Organisation established Capital L Airlines, flying leased 737-700s from both Larnaca and Paphos.

Greece experienced a positive explosion in independent airlines in the late

eleven 737-200s as well as one 737-300 and twelve 737-400s. The national airline's subsidiary, Olympic Aviation, became an early customer for the Boeing 717-200.

One More Step

The widespread acceptance and commercial success of the 'Next Generation' 737s had gone a long way to re-establish Boeing and help it fight off the growing European competition. Long passing the milestone of the most produced jet airliner of all time, Boeing was still looking at ways of improving the popular aircraft and keeping it in its well-earned number one position. Even more surprises were in store.

CHAPTER ELEVEN

The BBJ and Beyond

Ex-airline 737s sometimes found new lives as executive aircraft. N147AW was originally Aloha Airlines N729A 'King Kahekill'. Unusually, it later returned to airline work with America West. Jenny Gradidge

The BBJ

The use of Boeing 737s as corporate transports, either as 'Flying Boardrooms' or for more utilitarian private use, has been a long-standing practice. The 737 was far from the only large transport aircraft to be used this way. A number of ex-airline BAC One-Elevens were converted in the early 1970s, as were Boeing 727s and even longer-range 707/720 and DC-8s at the end of their airline careers. The majority of the 'private' 737s had also once been airliners, although a handful were delivered to private or corporate customers straight off the production line.

In July 1996, Boeing took the decision to market a designated executive version of the 'Next Generation' 737, the Boeing Business Jet, or BBJ. Developed from the 700 series, the BBJ was to combine the 737-700 forward and rear fuselage with the centre section, wing and landing gear of the larger -800. Up to nine extra fuel tanks can be fitted into the cargo hold space, rarely needed on executive missions, bringing fuel capacity up to a maximum 8,905 gallons. Interior arrangements offered range from first-class sleeper seat arrangements, to ultra-luxurious combinations of lounges, conference areas, bedrooms, shower rooms, and so on, to suit the customer's requirements. The BBJ is developed and marketed by a separate division within Boeing, in recognition of the very different market as opposed to the established airline customer.

As well as private and corporate-based work, BBJs operated by Swiss carrier, Privatair, are also used on VIP quality tour and charter work in all-first-class configuration. Occasional worldwide tours operate over several weeks, with accommodation being provided in top hotels with VIP service standards on board the aircraft. This is in addition to Privatair's established business as an executive operator, providing *ad hoc* and contracted corporate transport with a Boeing 737-300, three BBJs and a single 757.

The first BBJ, N737BZ, was rolled out at Renton in July 1998 and first flew on 4 September. The first orders were placed by General Electric, for two aircraft. By October 2000, over seventy BBJs had been ordered by private individuals, corporations, government agencies and military authorities around the world. The BBJ2, based on the Boeing 737-800 airframe, first flew in 2001, offering even more range and capacity.

The BBJ soon found a ready market. N737MC is operated for General Electric by Atlas Air Inc. Jenny Gradidge

'Next Generation' in the Military

A single 737-700C, the first convertible version of the 'Next Generation' series, was delivered to the US Navy in 2000. Designated the C-40A in Navy service, the aircraft is expected to be just the first of many to eventually replace the large fleet of C-9Bs with the USN. The C-9Bs, a convertible military transport version of the DC-9, have been in service since the 1970s. Continuing the 737's long-established role as a preferred VIP aircraft, one -800 is operated in this role by the Taiwan Air Force.

Australia committed itself to an order for seven 737 Airborne Early Warning and Control (AEW & C) aircraft. Fitted with a modern multirole radar array giving 360 degree coverage, the new military aircraft would be based around the BBJ airframe. A dispute between the US authorities and Boeing over release of confidential and sensitive technology has stalled the programme, but interest has also been shown in the new aircraft by the governments of Turkey and South Korea.

The Low-Fare Vision in Western Europe

Aer Lingus found itself challenged in Irish markets by one particular new 'upstart', Ryanair. Beginning scheduled operations in 1985, with a single, 18-passenger, Embraer Bandierante, over a route from Waterford in western Eire to London/Luton, Ryanair skilfully exploited the emerging low-fare market and grew rapidly. Originally concentrating on services from regional Irish points to Luton, Ryanair introduced larger BAe 748 turbo-props and, later, One-Eleven jets. A Dublin–Luton route was opened in 1986 and Ryanair increasingly turned its attention to new low-fare services from Dublin to regional UK and European points, often in competition with Aer Lingus. Operating fourteen aircraft of four different types, Ryanair managed to lose £20 million in two years.

A new management team completely overhauled the airline in 1990–91, relaunching the airline as the first of a new breed of European 'no frills' airlines, along the Southwest Airlines model. Just five of the nineteen routes then in operation were retained and all turbo-prop aircraft were disposed of. With an all-jet fleet of six One-Elevens, Ryanair managed to make its first-ever profit.

The first 737s, second-hand Series 200s, were leased in by Ryanair from 1994 and the fleet increased steadily, replacing the last One-Elevens. Eventually, a second base was set up at London/Stansted and low-fare routes were opened from there to both domestic and European points. These mostly served under-used airports such as Prestwick for Glasgow, Charleroi for Brussels, and Beauvais for Paris. By 2001, thirty-six 737s, including fifteen 'New Generation' 737-800s, were in use by Ryanair. In 2001, Charleroi was designated as Ryanair's next regional base, with plans to base two aircraft at the airport, south of Brussels.

Ryanair can also be credited with bringing the concept of the LogoJet to Europe. As Western Pacific Airlines, in the USA, had done before it, Ryanair offered its aircraft on the open market as 'Flying Billboards'. British car manufacturer, Jaguar, was one of the first customers, producing a very pleasing result. Other early customers to take advantage of the publicity opportunities included *The Sun* and *News of the World* newspapers, Kilkenny Beer and Hertz.

easyJet at Luton

The Luton-based easyJet airline was founded by businessman Stelios Haji-Ioannou, in 1995. Two Boeing 737-200s were used to open low-fare Luton–Glasgow and Luton–Edinburgh schedules in November that year. More routes were opened, with international services being introduced and expanded as the initial -200 aircraft were replaced by larger Series 300s. In 1998 a 40 per cent shareholding was bought in TEA Switzerland, the ex-Trans European subsidiary. Since the demise of the Belgian parent company, TEA Switzerland had continued to operate as an independent IT

THE BBJ AND BEYOND

Ryanair's 737-200s replaced the BAC One-Eleven, the Boeing fleet quickly expanding as new routes were opened. Steve Bunting

Hertz Rent-a-Car was one of many companies willing to pay to use one of Ryanair's 737s as a flying billboard. Aviation Hobby Shop

Initially, like the British-based aircraft, easyJet Switzerland's 737s wore the company's UK reservations telephone number. As technology progressed and the internet became a major source of direct bookings, the airline's web address was substituted, fleetwide. The first of easyJet's 'Next Generation' 737-700s were delivered in early 2001. MAP/Aviation Hobby Shop

charter carrier from Basle with a fleet of 737-300s. When easyJet took control of the company, the name was changed to easyJet Switzerland and operations moved to Geneva. Scheduled low-fare flights opened from Geneva to the UK.

A new UK easyJet base was developed at Liverpool, in the northwest of England, opening up a continental network that had not been available from the city in many years. Between them, easyJet and easyJet Switzerland were operating over twenty 737s in 2001, operating twenty-eight routes between eighteen destinations. The first of a substantial order for over thirty 'New Generation' 737-700s had recently been delivered to begin the gradual replacement of the -300s. In 2001, another European easyJet operational base was established at Amsterdam.

Enter Virgin

Trans European's replacement in the Belgian charter market, EuroBelgian Airlines, eventually entered the scheduled market, serving leisure-orientated destinations. In April 1986, the Virgin Group acquired a controlling interest and the company name was changed to Virgin Express. Operating a European network complementary to Virgin Atlantic's London-based long-haul services, Virgin Express operates to eight scheduled destinations from Brussels. Virgin Express was also contracted to take over the operation of a number of Brussels–UK schedules for Sabena. Operating a fleet of seven 737-300s and four 737-400s, charter services also continue with *ad hoc* flights throughout Europe and to Africa.

A French operator, Air Provence Charter, was taken over in 1998 and rebranded as Virgin Express France. A handful of scheduled European services were opened but the French carrier soon reverted to an all-IT charter operation. Even more unfortunate was Virgin Express (Ireland), which started scheduled Shannon–London services, using Stansted, in December 1998. The Stansted route was later extended to Berlin and Shannon–Brussels and Shannon–London/Gatwick flights also opened. Virgin Express (Ireland) actually beat off early competition on the London routes from AB Airlines, a UK operator eventually flying One-Elevens and 737-300s on a low-fare network from Gatwick. However, the Irish operation remained unprofitable and was put up for sale. Five 737-300s and two 737-400s were in service when the airline was closed down in 2001 after failing to find a buyer.

AB Airlines had started operations in the early 1990s, as Air Bristol, flying a corporate shuttle on behalf of British Aerospace from its Filton facility, near Bristol, to Toulouse in connection with Airbus contracts. Air Bristol set up a Shannon-based subsidiary, AB Shannon, with one One-Eleven and, after losing the BAe contract, concentrated on developing a scheduled network from London/Gatwick, Stansted and Shannon under a new name, AB Airlines. The limited scheduled network was to take in flights to Berlin, Lisbon and Nice, as well as the Shannon flights to London and Birmingham, but was not strong enough to sustain the carrier. Despite switching to more economic Boeing 737-300s, to supplement the ageing One-Elevens, AB airlines ceased operations in September 1999.

Shortly before closing down, AB airlines signed an agreement with Luton-based Debonair, for code-sharing on certain key routes. Debonair flew BAe 146s on its network from Luton, but one of the AB Airlines 737-300s took on Debonair titles for the joint operations. Debonair also ceased operations at about the same time as AB Airlines.

Virgin Express's various divisions met with mixed fortunes, with the French and Irish operations being forced to retrench or close down altogether. Via author

THE BBJ AND BEYOND

The small route network of AB Airlines was unable to support the 737-300s. G-OABL previously served with VASP, in Brazil, and Jet Airways, in India. Aviation Hobby Shop

Following the current fashion, Virgin Blue's aircraft display the reservations website address. MAP

Virgin Down-Under

Much further afield, Virgin turned its sights on Australia, itself indulging in an airline deregulation and liberalization programme. Earlier attempts at introducing low-fare operators in Australia in the early 1990s had swiftly failed. Compass Airlines commenced scheduled low-fare services linking the major cities on both the east and west coasts of Australia from the end of 1990. Airbus A300s were leased from Monarch Airlines of the UK, but heavy losses forced the airline to cease operations a year later. Compass was revived in September 1992, with a small fleet of MD-80s, but lasted only until the following March, when the airline was finally closed down for good.

commercial operations until August, following delays in receiving its Air Operator's Certificate. Brisbane–Sydney services opened first, on 31 August, followed by Brisbane–Melbourne on 7 September. Brisbane–Adelaide flights were opened on 7 December, some six weeks earlier than originally planned.

CityBird

After the sale of EuroBelgian to the Virgin Group, the Belgian airline's original owner, Victor Hassen of City Hotels, set up a new carrier, CityBird. At first City-Bird opened scheduled low-cost, long-range services to the USA, Caribbean and

The 900

Not content with the extra stretch of the -800 over the -400, Boeing elected to offer an even larger 737, in the form of the Series 900. The largest 737 version to date, the Series 900 received its FAA certification on 17 April 2001. The 138ft 2in (42m) long -900 is an impressive nearly 40ft (12.2m) longer than the -200 and has more than a thousand miles (1,609km) longer range. The formal certification had been delayed by six weeks by refinements to its flight controls and an improved flap seal system. Unexpected vibration had been discovered in the elevator, requiring a redesign of the elevator hinge and strengthening of the tab. Two aircraft took

CityBird's 737-400s arrived as the airline shifted its operational focus away from long-haul schedules to European IT charters. MAP

No other candidates came forward to exploit the Australian low-fare market for several years, with Ansett and Qantas remaining the main domestic scheduled service providers. However, in June 2000, a new operator, Virgin Blue Airlines, of Brisbane, took delivery of the first of five Boeing 737-400s. Nine 'Next Generation' 737-700s are on order to replace the initial aircraft. Established by the UK-based Virgin Group, owners of Virgin Atlantic Airways and the European Virgin Express airlines, Virgin Blue was unable to start

Africa with a fleet of wide-bodied MD-11s and 767s. Many routes were later flown in association with Sabena, often in the larger airline's full colours.

However, a change in direction saw most of the scheduled services being dropped on economic grounds, although long-range charters were still operated. Instead, a fleet of 737-300s and -400s were acquired and more emphasis was placed on European IT charters to Mediterranean and North African resorts. Three -800s were on order for 2001 delivery.

part in the certification programme, between them logging 649 flight hours in 296 flights and 156 hours of ground tests.

An even further stretched 737-900, the -900X, was being studied and being offered to the -900's current customers, Alaska Airlines, Continental Airlines, KLM and Korean Air. Curiously, the -900, although longer, was not certified to carry more than the passenger capacity of the -800. Loads would be restricted until improved emergency evacuation systems and procedures could ensure the off-loading of the higher

THE BBJ AND BEYOND

737-900 customers, KLM and Alaska Airlines already operated large fleets of 'Next Generation' 737s, KLM -800s, and Alaska -700s and -800s. Aviation Hobby Shop

capacity available in the same time as smaller passenger loads.

The Losses

Considering the proliferation of the 737 throughout the world, its service has been remarkably trouble-free. Pure statistical probability dictates that there would be incidents, but most were minor. Among the best-known exceptions are the Air Florida and British Midland accidents outlined earlier, one due to adverse weather and a pressured crew and the other possibly down to unfamiliarity with new technology. Both were also possibly attributable, at least in part, to shortcomings in crew training procedures then in use, since much improved as a result of the tragedies. Of course, accidents did happen. As with most aviation tragedies, human factors and errors of judgement played their part in a high proportion of the incidents. Hijackings and sabotage also featured in 737 hull losses and accidents. Actual structural or control problems more directly concerned with the aircraft itself are rarer, but there have been incidents.

178

In 1981, a Far East Air Transport 737 was lost due to structural failure in flight, its break-up blamed on corrosion in the lower fuselage. All 110 occupants perished on a domestic scheduled flight from Taipei to Kaohsiung. The aircraft had disintegrated at 22,000ft (6,700m) and the wreckage was scattered over an area of 5mi (8km). In 1988, an Aloha Airlines 737 lost most of its forward cabin roof in-flight, at 24,000ft (7,315m). The high-time aircraft had spent most of its career island hopping from Honolulu with Aloha; the frequent and higher than average number of cycles and the Pacific atmosphere eventually weakened the fuselage structure. Most of the forward cabin walls and roof, from the floor level upwards, peeled away following the failure of the cracked structure. One cabin crew member was lost, but everyone else on board survived, mostly thanks to prompt action and superb airmanship by the pilots. The fact that the rest of the aircraft held together, under power and at altitude with most of the forward cabin walls missing, still says something for the basic soundness of its structure. Following the incident, Aloha withdrew its other highest-time 737s from service.

One Morning at Manchester

The 737's JT8D engines gave little cause for concern over the years, with few catastrophic failures. The Pratt & Whitney engine was also used on several other aircraft types, very successfully. On one occasion though, the failure of a combustion chamber outer casing blotted the engine's otherwise enviable record. Only three other cases of combustion chamber rupture had previously been recorded in over 300 million hours of operation.

On the fateful day, 22 August 1985, British Airtours 737-200, G-BGJL, 'River Orrin' was assigned to an IT holiday charter from Manchester to Corfu. A full load of 130 passengers, plus two infants, two pilots and four cabin crew were on board as 'JL began its take-off run shortly after 7am. As the aircraft reached 140mph, the outer casing of the compression chamber on the number one engine split and 'petalled' apart. The outer casing had ruptured along a crack caused by thermal fatigue. A fuel tank access panel on the left wing was punctured by debris and escaping fuel was ignited by the now burning engine.

On hearing the thump of the engine failure, the crew considered they were dealing with a tyre failure and abandoned the take-off, turning onto a taxi-way. Unfortunately, as well as delaying the evacuation, the turn off the runway also placed the aircraft fuselage downwind of the rapidly increasing fire on the wing. Smoke was immediately blown into the packed cabin, contributing to the passengers' panic. The fire entered the rear cabin in twenty seconds, the tail section burning off and falling to the ground within a minute.

Despite one of the forward doors jamming momentarily, the cabin crew in the forward cabin did a magnificent job of evacuating the frantic survivors, assisted by the flight-deck crew. In the rear section, the cabin staff managed to open the doors, but, courageously ignoring their own chance to escape, remained on board to try and begin an evacuation. Unfortunately both were overcome by the smoke and flames and perished along with fifty-three of their passengers.

The tragic consequences of the Manchester accident brought a number of problems to light. Earlier cracks on the same unit had been repaired and other JT8Ds on other British-registered aircraft were found to have similar cracks, leading to some aircraft being grounded until full inspections and repairs could be initiated. The composition of passenger cabin furnishings was examined and regulations tightened, poisonous fumes from burning upholstery having contributed to many of the deaths. Seating was also rearranged to give better access to emergency exists, and floor-level lighting, to guide anyone caught in a smoke-filled cabin, became compulsory. A debate concerning supplying smoke-hoods to passengers continues to rage, although they are now fitted for cabin-crew use to assist in evacuation.

Rudder Investigations

Two other accidents focused attention on the 737's rudder control system. In 1991, a United 737-200 plunged into the ground on a flight to Colorado Springs, killing everyone on board. In 1994, a USAir 737-300 on approach to Pittsburgh, rolled over without warning and dove straight to the ground, again instantly killing all the occupants. In both incidents, the aircraft hit the ground so hard that the wreckage was buried several feet into the earth. Both accidents had investigators stumped for several years. There were as many differences as similarities between the two. Sabotage theories abounded, especially when an unconfirmed rumour spread that FBI agents and an important trial witness were on board the USAir flight.

Although the accidents were still not officially blamed on the aircraft, Boeing issued several precautionary bulletins, recommending various modifications to the rudder control system, to prevent any possible reoccurrence. In new aircraft the system was redesigned. Interestingly, following the, as yet, unexplained loss of an Egyptair 767 over the North Atlantic in similar circumstances, the Egyptian authorities asked that the 767's pitch control system be examined with the same 'level of examination and analysis' that had been applied to the 737 rudder control system.

Into the Future on Winglets

Never let it be said that, at least in aviation, there is any such thing as a new idea. High-flying birds know full well that if they can turn up their wing-tip feathers, they soar better. Mankind, of course, insists on inventors, patents and the like, so it was not until the closing years of the twentieth century that the effect was finally applied to mechanical flight.

The constantly rising price of oil was the main prod for aerodynamicists to finally take advantage of the bird's long-known 'secret'. In the USA, in the 1970s, research was started under the direction of NASA's Dr Richard Whitcomb, focusing on applying the principle to reduce fuel consumption. In September Boeing's military division at Wichita was awarded the contract to design, produce and test a set of winglets based on Dr Whitcomb's research.

A KC-135 was fitted with the winglets in May 1979 and first flew with them in July. Over fifty flights were completed by the end of the programme that validated the theory of a performance gain using the aerodynamic extensions. A 6.5 per cent saving on fuel was shown using the winglets, but the military authorities still failed to embrace the research and no further action was taken.

However, the fuel savings could not be ignored and winglets finally started to appear on smaller aircraft, especially executive jet designs. The Boeing 747-400 was the first large aircraft design to incorporate significant winglets. The 6ft (1.8m) tall extensions added aerodynamic efficiency,

'Winglets' began appearing on BBJs, later becoming an option on airline aircraft. Jenny Gradidge

effectively increasing the wing area although only adding a minimum extra to the actual wingspan. Airbus had adopted small winglets for the A310 and A320/321/318/319, but also fitted larger versions to its later wide-body designs. McDonnell Douglas fitted winglets to its MD-11 and Globemaster transports and even in Russia, the IL96-300 wide-body took up the idea.

The BBJ version of the 'Next Generation' 737 was offered with the option of new design 'blended' winglets and a 737-800 made the first flight with them fitted on 29 May 1998. The fuel savings were just as great on the 737 and many BBJ had them fitted, some on the production line, some retroactively. With the success of the winglet-equipped BBJs, Boeing proceeded to offer the option on airline 737-800s. The first customer to take this up is South African Airways, with their first 'Wingleted' aircraft due to fly at the time of writing. American Transair, Hapag Lloyd and Air Berlin have also ordered the modified 737-800s and a 'retrofit' programme is being offered to previous customers.

End of an Era – 1

The very last of the 'Classic' 737s was handed over to CSA Czech Airlines in January 2000. OK-FGS was the last Series 400, of 486 of the variant. The last of 389 -500s built had been delivered to ANK-Air Nippon in July 1999 and the last of the most popular of the second-generation 737s, the 1,112th -300 was handed over to Air New Zealand in December that year. From then on, all 737s produced would be of the 'Next Generation' versions, the -600/700/800/900 or 'BBJ' designs.

OK-FGS was the last -400 Series and last 'Classic' 737 built, delivered in early 2000. MAP

'Spirit One' displays Southwest's new livery, a radical departure from the established scheme.
Aviation Hobby Shop

End of an Era – 2

In 2001, Southwest, as part of its 30th anniversary celebration, unveiled its first major livery change since operations had begun. Other than a relatively minor change in the positioning of the airline's titles, undertaken quite early in the airline's history, the Southwest 737s had continued to carry their orange, red and 'Desert Gold' colours throughout the years. The obvious exceptions to the rule were a long line of special 'promotional' schemes. Beginning with aircraft painted to represent Seaworld's famous killer whale 'Shamu', various other designs were taken up by individual aircraft, usually promoting the different US states served by Southwest as its network grew. America West also adopted similar schemes with their aircraft promoting the airline's routes and even local sports teams that chartered the aircraft for tours.

However, Southwest's advertising agency, GSD&M, of Austin, came up with a new design for the whole fleet, in honour of the anniversary. Still based on the original design, the most dramatic change was the main fuselage colour. 'Canyon Blue' replaced the 'Desert Gold', over a slightly modified red and gold lower fuselage. The overall effect is meant to reflect a desert sunrise or sunset. The aircraft interiors also received a make-over, with orange and blue leather seating installed. Repainting and refitting of the entire 340 aircraft in the fleet is expected to take ten years, but three aircraft will remain in the traditional livery to reflect the original three Texan cities served, Dallas, Houston and San Antonio. The first aircraft to wear the new colours were two 'Next Generation' 737-700s, N793SA, 'Spirit One' and N794SA, 'Spirit Two'.

Possibly even more dramatic was the announcement of the impending retirement of Southwest Airline's long-serving Chairman and mentor, Herbert D. Kelleher. Kelleher had been the guiding hand behind Southwest – and its not insignificant input into the development of most versions of the Boeing 737 since the 737-200 'Advanced' series. One of the last great airline 'Showmen', Kelleher was not averse to appearing in Southwest advertisements in an Elvis Presley costume. Even when the airline had left the bright orange hot pants era behind it, in favour of a more businesslike image, Kelleher managed to introduce a certain amount of his own outgoing personality into the airline. Ever since, in fact, he had said to fellow Southwest Airlines' founder, Rollin W. King, 'Rollin, you're crazy. Let's do it!'.

End of an Era – 3

Also in 2001, Boeing announced that it would be moving its corporate headquarters out of Seattle. Although the factories in the Seattle area would continue to provide most of the company's aviation output, along with the ex-MDC facilities in California, Seattle would no longer be the head office. This was decided in order to make the company's projects in other areas more accessible to the senior management teams. Eventually, after much debate, Chicago was chosen over other candidates as diverse as St Louis and even Wichita.

OUR QUICKET® MACHINES ARE MORE RELIABLE THAN OUR CHAIRMAN.

No offense, Mr. Kelleher.

But Southwest Airlines' Quicket® automatic ticket machines dispense thousands of tickets every day without a hitch.

You simply slide in your major credit card, punch in your destination, select Executive or Pleasure class, one-way or roundtrip, and out pops your ticket in just seconds!

In fact, about the only thing that can go wrong is *human* error. Like letting your credit card expire.

Right, Herb?

FLY SOUTHWEST
We're keeping fares low and spirits high!

Reprinted courtesy of *Southwest Airlines*.

(*Opposite*) Herb Kelleher was never averse to helping out Southwest's advertising department. Here, in one of his more subdued appearances, he promotes Southwest's then revolutionary 'Quicket' machines. Southwest via Tim Kincaid

(*Below*) For over thirty years, countless airline passengers around the world have enjoyed safe, comfortable air transport on the Boeing 737. Lufthansa

(*Bottom*) In a dawn scene repeated at different airports, with different airlines worldwide, United Shuttle and Southwest 737s are prepared for another day's work, in this case at San Diego, California. Malcolm L. Hill

Thirty Years and Climbing

The 35th anniversary of the Boeing 737's first flight is not far off. Boeing originally envisaged a probable market for a few hundred units. To date, over 5,000 have been ordered and the 737 can confidently claim its place as one of the world's most successful commercial aircraft. It survived being a late-comer on to the scene, it survived moves to sell it off to Japan when sales figures dipped, it survived fuel crises and industrial unrest, as well as commercial and political manoeuvrings.

The worldwide proliferation of the Boeing 737 means that there can be few airports of any size that do not enjoy a regular visit by the type most days of the week. Even the older models, many of which are still in frequent use, belie their age with their modern lines and comfortable accommodation. Thirty years after they introduced the type to the travelling public, the likes of Braathens, Lufthansa and United still feature the aircraft in their fleets, albeit the later versions.

Nearly 400 different operators, from airlines, private and corporate owners, military and government authorities, fly Boeing 737s. Even a brief outline of all the aircraft's past and present operators would be impossible without producing several volumes. Those covered in this book can only give a flavour of the 737's versatility and its effect on day-to-day air transport services throughout the world. Whether on prestige international scheduled service, or bulk travel holiday charters and low-fare inter-city shuttles, from single aircraft set-ups to fleet numbers well into three figures, the 737 fulfils all their very different needs.

Any decision as to whether the 'Next Generation' will be the 'Last Generation' lies in the future. Whatever other modifications or developments are incorporated in any new versions to come, the 737 will certainly be here for a few more decades.

It will be doing what it was designed to do – working hard day after day, safely and reliably earning its keep.

APPENDIX I

Early 737s – Comparisons with their Contemporaries

BOEING 737-100	
Length	93ft 9in (28.6m)
Wingspan	87ft (26.5m)
Engines	2 × P&W JT8D-7
Typical range	1,150mi (1,850km)
Seating	99–107

Jenny Gradidge

BOEING 737-200	
Length	100ft 2in (30.5m)
Wingspan	93ft (28.3m)
Engines	2 × P&W JT8D-9A
Typical range	2,136mi (3,437km)
Seating	115–130

Via author

AÉROSPATIALE SE-210 CARAVELLE 12	
Length	118ft 6in (36.1m)
Wingspan	112ft 6in (34.3m)
Engines	2 × P&W JT8D-9
Typical range	1,580mi (2,542km)
Seating	104–139

Via author

BAC
ONE-ELEVEN 500

Length	107ft (32.6m)
Wingspan	93ft 6in (28.5m)
Engines	2 × RR Spey 512
Typical range	1,420mi (2,285km)
Seating	99–119

MAP

BOEING 727-100

Length	133ft 2in (40.6m)
Wingspan	108ft 7in (33.1m)
Engines	2 × P&W JT8D-1
Typical range	1,380mi (2,220km)
Seating	90–130

Via author

DASSAULT MERCURE

Length	114ft 3½in (34.8m)
Wingspan	100ft 3in (30.6m)
Engines	2 × P&W JT8D-15
Typical range	575mi (925km)
Seating	120–155

Via author

185

FOKKER F.28-4000

Length	97ft 1¾in (29.6m)
Wingspan	82ft 3in (25.1m)
Engines	2 × RR Spey 555
Typical range	1,162mi (1,870km)
Seating	75–85

Via author

HS 121 TRIDENT 2

Length	114ft 9in (35m)
Wingspan	98ft (29.9m)
Engines	2 × RR Spey 512
Typical range	3,155mi (5,075km)
Seating	70–100

Hawker Siddeley, via author

MDC DC-9-30

Length	119ft 3½in (36.4m)
Wingspan	93ft 5in (28.5m)
Engines	2 × P&W JT8D-7
Typical range	1,725mi (2,775km)
Seating	99–115

Via author

EARLY 737s – COMPARISONS WITH THEIR CONTEMPORARIES

TUPOLEV Tu-104B

Length	131ft 5in (40m)
Wingspan	113ft 4in (34.5m)
Engines	2 × AM-3M-500
Typical range	1,305mi (2,100km)
Seating	70–104

Aviation Hobby Shop

TUPOLEV Tu-124V

Length	110ft 4in (33.6m)
Wingspan	83ft 9½in (25.5m)
Engines	2 × D-20P
Typical range	760mi (1,225km)
Seating	56

Aviation Hobby Shop

TUPOLEV Tu-134A

Length	122ft (37.2m)
Wingspan	95ft 2in (29m)
Engines	2 × D-30-2
Typical range	1,243mi (2,000km)
Seating	70–80

Via author

APPENDIX II

The 737, 100–900

737-100

Length	93ft 9in (28.6m)
Height	37ft 1in (11.3m)
Wingspan	87ft (26.5m)
Gross Weight	111,000lb (50,350kg)
Range	1,150mi (1,850km)
Seating	99–107

Lufthansa

737-200

Length	100ft 2in (30.5m)
Height	37ft 1in (11.3m)
Wingspan	93ft (28.3m)
Gross Weight	128,000lb (58,060kg)
Range	2,136mi (3,437km)
Seating	115–130

Jenny Gradidge

737-300

Length	109ft 7in (33.4m)
Height	36ft 6in (11.1m)
Wingspan	94ft 9in (28.9m)
Gross Weight	139,000lb (63,050kg)
Range	1,860mi (2,993km)
Seating	128–149

Steve Bunting

737-400

Length	119ft 7in (36.4m)
Height	36ft 6in (11.1m)
Wingspan	94ft 9in (28.9m)
Gross Weight	150,500lb (68,270kg)
Range	2,487mi (4,002km)
Seating	146–170

Malcolm L. Hill

737-500

Length	101ft 9in (31m)
Height	36ft 6in (11.1m)
Wingspan	94ft 9in (28.9m)
Gross Weight	125,200lb (56,790kg)
Range	1,800mi (2,896km)
Seating	110–132

Aviation Hobby Shop

737-600

Length	102ft 6in (31.2m)
Height	41ft 3in (12.6m)
Wingspan	112ft 7in (34.3m)
Gross Weight	143,000lb (64,865kg)
Range	3,509mi (5,646km)
Seating	110–132

Steve Bunting

737-700

Length	110ft 4in (33.6m)
Height	41ft 2in (12.5m)
Wingspan	112ft 7in (34.3m)
Gross Weight	154,500lb (70,080kg)
Range	3,751mi (6,035km)
Seating	126–149

Aviation Hobby Shop

737-800

Length	129ft 7in (39.5m)
Height	41ft 2in (12.5m)
Wingspan	112ft 7in (34.3m)
Gross Weight	174,200lb (79,020kg)
Range	3,383mi (5,443km)
Seating	162–189

Aviation Hobby Shop

737-900

Length	138ft 2in (42.1m)
Height	41ft 2in (12.5m)
Wingspan	112ft 7in (34.3m)
Gross Weight	174,200lb (79,020kg)
Range	3,158mi (5,081km)
Seating	177–189

Aviation Hobby Shop

Index

AB Airlines 175–6
AB Shannon 175
Abelag Airways 97
Aer Lingus 23, 44, 49–50, 62–3, 68, 70–1, 97, 108, 122, 138, 140, 170, 172
Aeris 141
Aerlinte Eireann 49, 156
Aero Chileanas 165
Aero Continente 164–5
Aero Continente Chile 165
Aeroflot 7, 151–2, 187
Aerolineas Argentinas 79, 164
Aeromaritime 140–1
Aerospace Industries Association 24
Aerospatiale 124
AeroSvit 151
Aerotour 109
Air 2000 126, 138–9
Air Algérie 70, 80–1, 114–15, 146
Air Anglia 186
Air Atlanta Icelandic 155, 168
Air Atlantis 114
Air Belgium 97, 122
Air Berlin 132, 180
Air Bristol 175
Air California 55–6, 72, 109, 116
Air Canada 164
Air Charter 141
Air China 148
Air Espania 122
Air Europa 121–2, 125, 159
Air Europe 105–6, 108–9, 116, 120–5, 128, 188
Air Europe Express 122–5
Air Europe (Scandinavia) 22
Air Florida 87–90, 96, 108–9, 147, 178
Air France 13, 15, 49, 86, 97, 100, 124, 132, 140–1, 153
Air Gabon 80
Air Holland 131
Air Inter 86–7, 141, 185
Air Madagascar 80
Air Mail Act 11
Air Malawi 146
Air Malta 114–15
Air Nauru 80–1, 134
Air New Zealand 61, 132, 162, 180
Air Norway 122
Air Outre Mer 141
Air Pacific 134
Air Philippines 166
Air Provence Charter 175
Air Rose 170
Air Sinai 97, 99
Air Southwest 71–3
Air Spain 48
Air Sunshine 88
Air Tanzania 80, 146
Air Toulouse International 141
Air Tran 157
Air Transport Association of America 24
Air Transport World 118
Air UK 125, 162
Air UK Leisure 125–6
Air Ukraine 151
Air Vanuatu 134
Air Viking 155
Air West 28, 41
Air Zaire 80
Airbus Industrie 124
  A300 85, 93, 124–5, 166, 177
  A310 124, 133, 152, 155, 164, 180
  A318 146, 153, 162, 167, 180
  A319 140, 146, 167, 180
  A320 119, 124–7, 130, 132, 138, 140–2, 146–7, 153–4, 159, 162, 167–8, 180
  A321 126, 140, 142, 146, 167, 180
  A330 155
  A340 155
AirCal 109, 116–21, 147, 159
AirCal Investments 116
Airline Deregulation Act 87–8
Airline Pilots' Association (ALPA) 23–4
Airtours 125
Airways International Cymru 112–14, 116, 124
Alaska Airlines 34, 94–5, 146, 158, 177–8
Alaska International Air 146
Alitalia 15, 47
All Nippon Airways 50, 64–5, 134
Allegheny Airlines 27, 104–5
Alliance Air 147, 166
Allison 501 engine 27, 66
Allstate Insurance 72
Aloha Airlines 65, 79, 162, 171, 179
Ambassador Airways 168
Amberair 125
America West Airlines 98, 112, 142–3, 147, 153, 171, 181
American Airlines 6, 11, 17, 19, 23, 72, 87, 117–21, 124, 156, 159–61
American Airways 10–11
American Finance Group 109
American Overseas Airlines 132
American Trans Air 180
ANK Air Nippon 134, 180
Ansett Airlines 132–3, 177
Ansett-ANA 61
Ansett New Zealand 132
Ansett Worldwide 109
Antonov AN-24 97
AOM French Airlines 141
Apollo Resor 159
Arizona Airlines 65–6
Arkia 114–15
Arnaflug 155
Asiana Airlines 132
Aspro Holidays 125
Atlas Air 172
ATR 42 126
Australian Airlines 132
Avant Airlines 165
Aviaco 47
Aviaction 63
Avianca 23, 34, 78–9
Aviateca 164–5
Aviation Traders' Carvair 49, 127
Aviogenex 111–12
Axon Airlines 170

BAC One-Eleven 7, 18–19, 24–5, 33, 39, 44, 46, 50, 61–2, 65, 71, 79–80, 83, 86, 103–5, 107–8, 112, 119, 127–9, 131–2, 138, 151, 171–2, 175, 185
Bavaria Fluggesellschaft 108–9
BEA Airtours 103
Beauvais, Edward R. 143
Berlin European UK 132
Bethune, Gordon 142
Birmingham European Airways 138
BKS Air Transport 57
Blue Scandinavia 167
Boeing Air Transport 8–9, 11
Boeing Airplane Company 7, 8, 9, 11
  40A 8
  80A 9
  247 9–11, 35, 156
  307 11
  314 11–12
  377 12, 16
  7-7 102
  707 8, 12–13, 15–17, 19–20, 29, 32, 45–6, 49–50, 71, 79, 82, 84–5, 87–8, 97, 101, 103–4, 114, 138, 148, 151, 157, 171
  717 157, 170
  720/720B 16–18, 20–1, 28, 33–4, 49–50, 71, 85, 94, 107–8, 112, 114, 155, 171
  727 16, 20–1, 23, 25, 27, 28, 31, 34–5, 39, 41, 53, 59, 61, 65–8, 79, 82, 84, 86, 88, 91, 93–7, 99, 101, 104–5, 107, 112, 114, 117–20, 129, 131–2, 142, 146, 159, 162, 164–5, 168, 171, 185
  747 32, 35, 80, 82, 91–2, 93, 97–8, 122, 140, 166, 179
  757 88, 101–3, 109, 112, 122, 125, 127, 130, 138, 142, 152, 162, 164, 167–8, 171
  767 101–2, 125–7, 152, 155, 165, 167, 179
  777 152, 154, 166
  7J7 102–4
  7N7 101
B-1 8, 32
B-17 11
B-29 22, 32
B-47 22
B-52 14
B&W Model 1 8
C-40A 172
C-97/KC-97 12, 32
  KC-135 8, 13–14, 32, 101, 104, 179
  Model 2 8
  Model 3 8
  Model 4 8
  T-43A 110
Boeing Business Jet 171–2, 180
Boeing, William E. 8, 11
Bombardier Regional Jet 162
Bonanza Airlines 25, 28
Bosphorus Air 170
Braathens 23, 41–2, 62–3, 68–71, 80, 136, 158–9, 183
Braniff Airways 17, 25, 50, 68, 72–3, 75, 87–8, 91, 119–21
Branson, Richard 129
Bristol 175 Britannia 12, 42–3, 45–6, 48, 57–8, 68, 108
Britannia Airways 23, 41–7, 57–8, 68–9, 83–5, 101, 107–8, 112–13, 116, 125, 130, 167–8
British Aerospace BAe 146 98, 104, 119, 124, 126, 128–9, 132, 162–3
  Jetstream 98
British Air Ferries 127
British Airtours 103, 116, 127, 129–30, 179
British Airways 103, 127–30, 132, 137–8, 151, 153, 162–3, 185, 189
British Caledonian Airways 127, 130
British Caledonian Charter 127
British Eagle International Airlines 44–5
British European Airways 15, 44–5, 103, 130, 132, 186
British Midland Airways 106, 112, 138–9, 167, 178
British Overseas Airways Corporation 11–12, 15–17, 36, 42, 44–5, 57, 103
British United Airways 44
British World Airlines 127
Brown, Walter 11
Brymon Airways 138
Brymon European Airways 138
Burke, E. Paul 67
Burr, Don 89, 92–3
Buzz 162–3
BWIA West Indies 158–9

Cal Air International 127
Caledonian Airways 46, 127, 129–30, 179
California Central Airlines 39–40
California Public Utilities Commission 39, 55
49–50, 71, 85, 94, 107–8, 112, 114, 155, 171
727 16, 20–1, 23, 25, 27, 28, 31, 34–5, 39, 41, 53, 59, 61, 65–8, 79, 82, 84, 86, 88, 91, 93–7, 99, 101, 104–5, 107, 112, 114, 117–20, 129, 131–2, 142, 146, 159, 162, 164–5, 168, 171, 185
747 32, 35, 80, 82, 91–2, 93, 97–8, 122, 140, 166, 179
757 88, 101–3, 109, 112, 122, 125, 127, 130, 138, 142, 152, 162, 164, 167–8, 171
767 101–2, 125–7, 152, 155, 165, 167, 179
777 152, 154, 166
7J7 102–4
7N7 101
B-1 8, 32
B-17 11
B-29 22, 32
B-47 22
B-52 14
B&W Model 1 8
C-40A 172
C-97/KC-97 12, 32
KC-135 8, 13–14, 32, 101, 104, 179
Model 2 8
Model 3 8
Model 4 8
T-43A 110
Boeing Business Jet 171–2, 180
Boeing, William E. 8, 11
Bombardier Regional Jet 162
Bonanza Airlines 25, 28
Bosphorus Air 170
Braathens 23, 41–2, 62–3, 68–71, 80, 136, 158–9, 183
Braniff Airways 17, 25, 50, 68, 72–3, 75, 87–8, 91, 119–21
Branson, Richard 129
Bristol 175 Britannia 12, 42–3, 45–6, 48, 57–8, 68, 108
Britannia Airways 23, 41–7, 57–8, 68–9, 83–5, 101, 107–8, 112–13, 116, 125, 130, 167–8
British Aerospace BAe 146 98, 104, 119, 124, 126, 128–9, 132, 162–3
Jetstream 98
British Air Ferries 127
British Airtours 103, 116, 127, 129–30, 179
British Airways 103, 127–30, 132, 137–8, 151, 153, 162–3, 185, 189
British Caledonian Airways 127, 130
British Caledonian Charter 127
British Eagle International Airlines 44–5
British European Airways 15, 44–5, 103, 130, 132, 186
British Midland Airways 106, 112, 138–9, 167, 178
British Overseas Airways Corporation 11–12, 15–17, 36, 42, 44–5, 57, 103
British United Airways 44
British World Airlines 127
Brown, Walter 11
Brymon Airways 138
Brymon European Airways 138
Burke, E. Paul 67
Burr, Don 89, 92–3
Buzz 162–3
BWIA West Indies 158–9

Cameroon Airlines 80, 112
Canada 3000 164
Canadair Four 42
Canadian Airlines International 94–5, 112, 164
Canadian North 164
Canadian Pacific Air Lines (CP Air) 50, 56–7, 94
CanJet 164
Capital L Airlines 170
Carter, Ron 59
CASA 124
Central Airlines 67
Central British Columbia Airways 49
CFM International 101, 154
  CFM56 101–2, 136, 142, 146–7, 151–4
Challenger Airlines 65–6
Chance Vought Corporation 8
Channel Airways 44
China Airlines 80, 166
China Eastern 148
China Great Wall Corporation 148
China Southern 148
CityBird 177
City Hotels 177
CityFlyer Express 125
Civil Aeronautics Board 34, 39, 66–7, 72, 87
Civil Aviation Administration of China 148
Civil Aviation Authority 108
Clarkson Holidays 83, 106
Compass Airways 177
Condor Flugdienst 71, 84, 131
Connectair 122
Continental Airlines 17, 72, 75, 87, 92–3, 96, 112, 142–3, 145, 161–2, 165, 177
Convair CV-340 16, 21, 66
  CV-440 20, 88
  CV-580 25–7, 66–7, 92–3
  CV-600 67
  CV-640 49
  CV-880 17, 83, 94
  CV-990 15, 17, 94, 122
COPA Airlines 165
Corsair 141
Cosmos Holidays 108, 112
Cossey, Errol 105–6, 122
Court Line Aviation 83
Crandall, Robert J. 118
Croatia Airlines 150–1
Cronos Airlines 170
Cruziero 146
CSA Czech Airlines 180, 187
Cunard Eagle Airways 45–6
Curtis C-46 49
Cyprus Airways 170

Dan-Air Services 44, 105, 107, 112, 128–9
Dassault Mercure 86–7, 103, 124, 185
Dawsey, Melrose 91
De Havilland Canada DHC6 Twin Otter 68, 147
De Havilland DH106 Comet 12–13, 15, 35, 44–5, 79, 97, 107
  DH114 Heron 45
Debonair 175
Delta Air 132
Delta Air Lines 83, 87, 97, 117–18, 143, 162
DETA 80
Deutsche Aerospace 124
Deutsche BA 132, 158
Deutsche Luft Hansa 21
Deutscher Aero Lloyd 21
Dome Petroleum 110
Douglas Aircraft Company 7, 10, 17–18, 156–7

C-9B 172
DC-1 10–11
DC-2 11, 21, 156
DC-3 11, 21, 25–7, 34, 36, 38–40, 49, 57, 61–2, 65–6, 73, 88
DC-4 156
DC-6 16, 18, 33, 41–2, 47, 49, 53, 57, 62, 84, 94, 132, 156, 159
DC-7 16–18, 48–9, 156
DC-8 16–17, 28, 57, 61, 86, 136, 155, 157, 171
DC-9 7, 18, 20, 24–5, 33, 39, 47, 50, 53, 55, 61, 65, 75, 86, 88, 93, 96, 103–5, 112, 118–19, 124, 130, 136, 138, 142, 157, 159, 162, 172, 186
DC-10 88, 93, 117, 127, 152, 157
Dragonair 133
Dymond, Lewis W. 66–7

Eagle Air 108, 155
Eagle Airways 45
Eastern Air Lines 11, 17, 20, 23, 28, 85, 87, 89, 93, 124
Eastern Air Transport 11
Eastern Provincial Airlines 71, 94–5
East West Airlines 166
Eastwind Airlines 147
easyJet 162, 172, 174–5
E.G. & G. 110
Egyptair 97, 146, 179
El Al 114
Eldorado Oil 110
Emerald Airlines 119
Empire Airlines 118
Essex International 110
Estonia Air 151
Euralair 136, 140
Euravia (London) 42
EuroBelgian Airlines 130, 175, 177
EuroBerlin France 132
EuroGatwick 129
Europe Air Service 140–1, 159
Euroworld 125
Excalibur Airways 130
Excel Airways 168

Fairchild F-27 28, 34, 38, 40
FH-227 59, 68
Falcon Air 137
Far Eastern Air Transport 80, 91, 178–9
Federal Aviation Administration (FAA) 24, 29, 31–3, 57, 86–7, 108, 177
Federal Express 97, 99
Finnair 15, 103
First Choice 126
Fischer 151
Flight Engineers International Association (FEIA) 23–4
Florida Express Airlines 119
Flugfelag 155
Flying Tiger Line 46
Focke-Wulf Fw 200 Condor 21
Fokker 10, 124
  F.27 36, 38, 42, 49, 61, 63, 79, 107, 132, 138, 147, 166
  F.28 61, 63, 80, 118, 124, 136, 165, 186
  F.50 126, 166
  F.100 122, 132, 136, 159, 162, 166
Ford Trimotor 10
Formosa Airlines 166
Freedom Air International 162
Friedkin, Kenneth 39, 41
Fritdresor 167
Frontier Airlines (1) 65–8, 92–3, 96
Frontier Airlines (2) 145–6
Frontier Holdings 92
Futura 122, 158–9

INDEX

Galaxy Airways 170, 190
Gates, Mark T. Jnr 54
GATX/Booth Aircraft Corporation 55–6, 109
GB Airways 130, 167
GB Leisure 130
General Dynamics 17
General Electric 101, 171–2
Germania 131–2, 158, 190
Gibraltar Airways 130
Gitner, Gerald 91
Go Fly 162–3
Goodman, Harry 105, 122
Grand International Airways 166
Grant, Joe 59
Guernsey Airlines 122
Guinness Peat Aviation 109, 122, 133, 151
Gulf Air 80, 97
Gutelman, G.P. 85

Hainan Airlines 148
Haji-Ioannou, Stelios 172
Hamilton Aero Manufacturing 8
Handley-Page HPR-7 Herald 45, 127, 138
Hapag Lloyd 131, 154, 158, 180
Harrison, Chris 106, 116
Hassen, Victor 177
Havelet Leasing 112
Hawaiian Airlines 65
Hawker Siddeley 124
 HS (BAe) 748 79, 129, 133, 172
 Trident 44–5, 103, 148, 186
Helios Airways 170
Henson Airlines 118
Hispania 122
Holiday Airlines 170
Holtje, Gerhard 22, 51
Horizon Travel 83, 106, 109, 125
Hubbard, Edward 32
Hughes, Howard 11
Hukk, J. Kenneth 55

Iberia 15, 47, 63, 122, 159
Icebird Airlines 155
Icelandair 155
Ilyushin Il-18 97
 Il-86 148
 Il-96-300 180
Indian Airlines Corporation 79, 82, 147, 166
Indonesian Air Force 110
Indonesian Government 110
Intasun Leisure Group 105, 109
Integrated Aircraft Corporation 109
Inter Cargo Service 141
Inter Ciel Service 141
Inter European Airways 125–6
Interflug 21, 187
Interior Airways 146
International Air Transport Association (IATA) 47, 49
International Lease Finance Corporation (ILFC) 109, 114, 116, 138
International Leisure Group 109, 122
Iran Air 80, 97
Iraqi Airways 80, 97
Islandsflug 155
Istanbul Airlines 169–70

Japan Air Lines 134
Japan TransOcean Air 134
Jet Airways 166, 176
Jet America Airlines 146
Jugoslovenski Aero Transport (JAT) 111–12, 151
Junkers JU-52 21
 JU-88 21
Junkers Luftverkehr 21

Kelleher, Herbert D. 71–2, 75, 104, 181–2
Kenya Airways 146
Kewison, Alan H. 54
King, Rollin 71–2, 181
KLM Royal Dutch Airlines 130, 159, 177, 186, 190
KLM UK 162
Korean Air 166, 177–8

Korean Air Lines 133
KTHY 170
Kuhl, Emil 51
Kuwait Airways 80

LACSA 164
L'Aeropostale 141
Lake Central Airlines 23, 25–7, 37
Laker Airways 44, 57, 127
LAPA 164
Leisure International Airways 126
Libra Holidays 168
Lineas Aereas Chilenas 165
Linjeflyg 136–8, 155
Lithuanian Airlines 151
Lockheed Aircraft Co. 156–7
 Constellation 18, 20–2, 33–4, 39, 42–3, 47, 49, 52, 156
 C130 Hercules 49, 146
 L-188 Electra 12, 17, 23–4, 33, 40–1, 53, 55, 61, 88, 116, 157
 L-1011 Tristar 83, 103–4, 130, 133, 136, 159, 168
Loftleider 155
Lorenzo, Frank 91–3, 142
LOT Polish Airlines 136, 151
Louis Tourism Organisation 170
LTU 63, 159
Luftag 21
Lufthansa 20–3, 30, 36, 51–2, 58, 60, 68, 71, 83, 90–1, 104, 112, 131–2, 135–6, 141–2, 153, 161, 166, 170, 183, 188
Luxair 97, 100

Macedonian Airlines (Greece) 170
Maersk Air 107, 109, 112, 125, 127, 136
Maersk Air (UK) 137–8
Malayan Airways 36
Malaysia-Singapore Airlines 24, 36, 64, 77, 184
Malaysian Airline System 78–9, 126, 147
Malaysian Airways 36
Malev Hungarian Airlines 150–1
Malmo Aviation 136
Mandarin Airlines 166
Maritime 110
MarkAir 146
Martin 202 28, 39
 404 28, 38, 59, 68, 118
McDonnell Douglas Aircraft Co. 156–7
 MD-11 122, 157, 177, 180
 MD-80 75, 92–3, 104, 116, 119, 124, 142, 146, 148, 157
 MD-90 157
Mellberg, Dave 52–3
Mellberg, William F. 52–3
Meridiana 122
Metrojet 162–3
Mexicana 23–4
Mey Air Transport 84
Miami Air 168
Midway Airlines (1) 96, 147
Midway Airlines (2) 162–4
Minerve 141
Ministry of Aviation 44
Modiluft 126, 166
Mohawk Airlines 39, 104–5
Monarch Airlines (UK) 107–8, 112
Monarch Airlines (US) 65–6
Morris Air 142–3, 147
Muse Air 75–6
Muse, Michael 75
Muse, M. Lamar 72–5
Myers, William 54

National Aeronautics & Space Administration (NASA) 35, 86, 179
National Air Transport 8, 11
National Airlines 23, 87, 96, 185
New York Air 93, 96, 112, 147
New Zealand National Airways Corporation (NZNAC) 50, 61–2, 132
Newmans Air 132
NICA 164
Nigeria Airways 80
Nihon Kinhori Airways (NKK) 134

Nihon (NAMC) YS-11 38, 59, 68, 118, 134
NOGA 110
Nord 262 25–7
Nordair 23, 33, 56–7, 61, 94
Norterra 164
Northern Consolidated Airlines 23–4, 34
Northwest Airlines 87, 124, 153
NortJet 122
Norway Airlines 122
Novair 159
Novair International Airways 127–8

Oceanair 155
Odyssey International 126
Olympic Airways 97, 170
Olympic Aviation 170
O'Regan, Martin 105–6, 122
Organization of Oil Producing and Exporting Countries (OPEC) 83–4, 101
Orion Airways 106, 108–9, 112, 114, 116, 122, 125
Overseas Aviation 42
Ozark Airlines 53

Pacific Aero Products Company 8
Pacific Air Lines 23, 27–8, 37, 40–1, 55
Pacific Air Transport 8–9, 11
Pacific Aviation Holding Company 109
Pacific Northern Airlines 33–4, 61, 94
Pacific Southwest Airlines 23, 28, 37, 39–41, 53–4, 72, 88, 104, 117, 143
Pacific Western Airlines 23, 33, 48–9, 56, 61, 94, 119
Pakistan International Airways 112, 147, 149
Pan American World Airways 11–12, 15, 34, 87, 96–7, 124, 132
Paramount Airways 125
Peach Air 168
Pegasus Airlines 170
Peiser, Robert 144–5
PeoplExpress Airlines 89–93, 98, 112, 142, 147, 161
Pereira, William L. Jnr 54
Petrolair 110
Pettit, Roger 89
Philippine Air Lines 166
Piedmont Airlines 23, 37–9, 53, 58–9, 68–9, 104, 112, 117–19, 143
Piedmont Commuter 118
PLUNA 108
Polaris Aircraft Leasing Corporation 119
Pratt & Whitney 8
 JT8D 19, 31, 59, 64, 86, 101–2, 135–6, 143, 179
 Wasp 10
Presidential Airways 98, 147
Presidential Express 98
Privatair 171
Pro-Air 147
Putnam, Howard D. 75

Qantas 55, 132, 134, 177
Qantas New Zealand 132, 162
Quebecair 94, 108

Rank Organization 127–8
Red Dragon Travel 112
Renick, Lud 54
Riair 151
Riga Airlines 151
Rio Sul 146
Rolls Royce Spey 63
 RJ500 101
Rotterdam Airlines 130–1
Royal Air Maroc 80, 146
Royal Airlines 164
Royal Brunei Airlines 80
Ryanair 162, 172–3

SAAB 340 132
Sabena 15, 49, 97, 99–100, 153, 175, 177

Sabre Airways 168
Sahara Airlines 166, 168
SAHSA 80
SAT 131
SATA Air Acores 155
SATA International 155
Saudia 80, 82, 97
Scandinavian Airlines System (SAS) 15, 41, 85, 136, 138, 155, 158–9, 189
Shanghai Airlines 148
Shenzen Airlines 148
Short Bros & Harland 63
 330 122
 360 122, 126
 Sandringham 12
Silkair 147
Singapore Airlines 77, 79, 88, 147
Skutnick, Lenny 89
Skyways 42
SNECMA 101
SNOMAC 86
SNPL 86
Sobelair 97, 100
Societa Aerea Mediterranea (SAM) 47
Solomons Airlines 134
South African Airways 23, 65, 79, 180
South East European Airways 126
Southwest Airlines (Japan) 134
Southwest Airlines (US) 7, 71–7, 88, 104, 112, 135–6, 142–3, 147, 154–6, 158, 162, 172, 181–3
Spantax 47, 122
Star Europe 141
Sterling Airways 159, 184
Sterling European Airways 159, 168
Stout Airlines 8
Sud-Est Aviation 18
 SE-210 Caravelle 7, 13–6, 18, 41, 49, 53, 74, 84–6, 97, 114, 131–2, 141, 159, 170, 184
Sudan Airways 80, 97
Sultan Air 170
SunExpress 170
Sunworld International Airlines 112, 114, 147
Supair 109
Swissair 15, 84–5

TAAG Angola Airlines 80
TACA International Airlines 164
TACA Peru 164
TAE 47
Taiwan Air Force 172
TAN Airlines 80
TAP Air Portugal 114
TAROM 151
Texas Aeronautics Commission 72
Texas Air Corporation 75, 91–3, 112
Texas International Airlines 73–5, 77, 89, 91, 93, 142
Thai Airways 80, 133
Thai Airways International 133–4
Thomas Cook Travel 107
Thomson Group 83, 125
Thomson International 167
THY Turkish Airlines 169–70
TIFA 85
Time Air Sweden 136
Titan Airways 126–7
Tjaerborg Reiser 159
Tradewinds 147
Trans Australia Airlines 61, 132
Trans Europa 47
Trans European Airways 84–6, 97, 114, 122, 130, 172–3
 Cyprus 130, 170
 France 130
 Italy 130
 Switzerland 130, 172
 UK 122, 130
Trans Texas Airways 72–3
Trans World Airlines (TWA) 23, 66, 83, 87, 157
TransAer 168
Transaero 151–2
Transair 61, 94
Transavia 84–5, 88, 103, 108, 114, 130–1, 159

Transbrasil 146
Transcontinental & Western Air 10–11
Transmile Air Service 147
Transport Aerien Transregional 141
TranStar Airlines 75–6
Transwede Airways 136
Transwede Leisure 136
Travel Service Airlines 151
Tunisair 85, 114, 147
Tupolev Tu-104 7, 187
 Tu-124 7, 187
 Tu-134 7, 112, 151, 187
 Tu-154 148
TUR 122, 130
Turbomeca Baston 27

Ukraine International Airlines 151
UM Holdings 147
Union Aeromaritime de Transport Aerienne (UAT) 13
Union de Transports Aériens 141
United Air Lines 9–11, 16–18, 20, 22–4, 29, 33, 39, 41, 52–3, 64, 68–9, 84–5, 87–88, 93, 96–7, 101, 104, 112, 142, 153, 162, 179, 183, 188
United Aircraft & Transport Corporation (UATC) 8–11
United Express 98
United States Air Force 14, 110
United States Navy 16, 172
Universair 122–3
Universal Sky Tours 42
US Airways 153, 162–3
USAir 104–5, 109, 112, 117–18, 134, 143, 153, 162, 179, 189

Vacationair 126
Valujet 157
Vanguard Airlines 145–6, 184
VARIG 146, 149
Varney Airlines 8, 11
VASP 79, 82, 146, 149, 176
Vickers Armstrong Vanguard 12, 45, 141
VC-10 44, 52–53
Viking 42
Viscount 12–13, 16, 18, 20, 36, 45, 49–50, 61–2, 65, 71, 79, 106, 127, 138, 151
Viking International 125
VIP Air 170
Virgin Group 129, 175
 Atlantic Airways 126, 175, 177
 Blue 176, 177
 Express 175, 177
 Express (France) 175
 Express (Ireland) 175
Viva 122

Wallick, S.L. 'Lew' Jnr 28
West Coast Airlines 28
West German Air Force 79
Western Air Lines 23–4, 31, 33–4, 39, 41, 53–4, 56, 60, 86–7, 94, 104, 112, 117–19, 143
Western Pacific Airlines 143–5, 147, 172
Westervelt, Cdr G. Conrad 8
Westgate-California Corporation 116
WestJet Airlines 164
Wheaton, Capt Larry 89
Whitcomb, Dr Richard 179
Wien Air Alaska 79, 94, 114, 146
Wien Alaska Airways 23–4, 34
Wien Consolidated Airlines 23, 33, 53, 55, 58, 60, 79
Williams, J.E.D. 44–7
Winair Airlines 147
Winwood, Richard I. 147
Wolfe, Thomas 55
Wright 1820 10
Wuhan Airlines 148
Wygle, Brien 28–9

Xiamin Airlines 148

Yakalov YAK-42 148
Yemen Airways 80

Zambia Airways 80